Post-Execution Punishment: Attitudes, Legislative Initiatives and Policies

Post-Execution Punishment: Attitudes, Legislative Initiatives and Policies

Jordan Jacobs

Willford Press
www.willfordpress.com

Published by Willford Press,
118-35 Queens Blvd., Suite 400,
Forest Hills, NY 11375, USA

ISBN: 978-1-64728-493-0

Cataloging-in-Publication Data

Post-execution punishment : attitudes, legislative initiatives and policies / Jordan Jacobs.
p. cm.
Includes bibliographical references and index.
ISBN 978-1-64728-493-0
1. Punishment. 2. Human dissection. 3. Hanging. 4. Dead.
5. Capital punishment. 6. Executions and executioners.
I. Jacobs, Jordan.
HV8551 .P67 2023
364.660 92--dc23

For information on all Willford Press publications visit our website at www.willfordpress.com

WILLFORD PRESS

Contents

Preface

This book was inspired by the evolution of our times; to answer the curiosity of inquisitive minds. Many developments have occurred across the globe in the recent past which has transformed the progress in the field.

The mutilation of an already dead body as a form of punishment is known as post-execution punishment. The extensive application of the death penalty and post-execution punishments along with the fact that vast numbers of criminals were hanged on the gallows have long been described by historians as a crucial component of social interactions throughout the eighteenth and early-nineteenth centuries. This was the pinnacle of a terror-based criminal justice system. After late eighteenth century, the potential of expanding the usage of post-execution punishments and notably public dissection was still being advocated widely. However, in the late eighteenth century, critics of the death penalty have emphasized on the requirement of substituting it with non-capital alternatives such as transportation, solitary confinement, or life imprisonment with hard labor. This book is compiled in such a manner, that it will provide in-depth knowledge about the attitudes, legislative initiatives and policies with respect to post-execution punishment. It will provide comprehensive knowledge to the readers.

This book was developed from a mere concept to drafts to chapters and finally compiled together as a complete text to benefit the readers across all nations. To ensure the quality of the content we instilled two significant steps in our procedure. The first was to appoint an editorial team that would verify the data and statistics provided in the book and also select the most appropriate and valuable contributions from the plentiful contributions we received from authors worldwide. The next step was to appoint an expert of the topic as the Editor-in-Chief, who would head the project and finally make the necessary amendments and modifications to make the text reader-friendly. I was then commissioned to examine all the material to present the topics in the most comprehensible and productive format.

I would like to take this opportunity to thank all the contributing authors who were supportive enough to contribute their time and knowledge to this project. I also wish to convey my regards to my family who have been extremely supportive during the entire project.

Jordan Jacobs

1

Post-Execution Punishment: An Overview

1 Core Aims

By analysing the development of attitudes, legislative initiatives and actual policies in relation to post-execution punishment and other aggravated execution practices, this volume aims to establish the important role the criminal corpse played within penal policy in the eighteenth and early-nineteenth centuries. A variety of execution procedures, involving either a more painful death or further punishment of the criminal's corpse after death (or both), were extensively discussed in this period. Many of these were never actually used in England and Wales but a limited range of post-execution punishments—most notably dissection and hanging in chains—were widely utilized by the courts and the criminal justice authorities in various contexts between 1700 and the 1830s. Using newly collected data on court sentences involving post-execution punishments covering every county in England and Wales, this volume presents the first systematic analysis of the ways the use of the criminal corpse added a new depth to the capital sanctions imposed on the bodies of offenders in this vital period.

This research forms part of a much broader project funded by the Wellcome Trust entitled 'Harnessing the Power of the Criminal Corpse', which focused mainly on the period from the late-seventeenth to the nineteenth century and explored the social, medicinal, symbolic and curative power of the criminal corpse, as well as its use for judicial/penal purposes. In particular the arguments presented here intersect with those put forward in two detailed studies by other members of the Wellcome project team—Elizabeth Hurren's volume on 'Dissecting the Criminal Corpse' and Sarah Tarlow's work on hanging in chains, both of which cover much the same sub-period as this volume—the eighteenth and early-nineteenth centuries.[1] These two volumes focus on the journey of the criminal corpse after the formal legal process was completed, uncovering, for example, the remarkably varied and sometimes central role that penal surgeons played in the execution process, and the long-term impact of hanging offenders' corpses in chains at prominent points in the landscape. Readers who want to trace the journey, and frequently the diaspora, of the corpses of executed criminals after the criminal justice system had made the decision to subject them to post-execution punishments should refer to Hurren and Tarlow's work as well as to the broader comparative volume *A Global History of Execution and the Criminal Corpse* edited by Richard Ward and the monograph produced by two other scholars who are also Wellcome project members, Owen Davies and Francesca Matteoni, entitled *Executing Magic: The Power of Criminal Bodies.*[2] This volume, by contrast, centres on the criminal justice dimension of post-execution punishment and of its less frequently used partner: rituals involving aggravated pre-execution practices. It looks at both penal debate and penal practices, at the reasons why these punishments were, or were not, adopted by the legislature and at the changing sentencing policies that resulted from those laws that were eventually passed. Although it also refers to the later stages of the criminal corpse's journey, and occasionally offers insights into the discretionary decisions made by those responsible for carrying out post-execution punishments (such as the surgeons' decisions about when to use the ultimate punishment of dissection followed by skeletal reconstruction and public display) the main aim is to provide, for the first time, a detailed history of aggravated and post-execution punishment in an era when the latter played an important role in penal policy.

The resulting analysis, it will be argued, not only adds a vital new dimension to the history of capital punishment in the eighteenth and nineteenth centuries, but also forces us to reassess some of our broader models of penal change and of the logic and chronology of the process by which capital punishment was reformed. As we will explore further in Sect. 3 of this chapter and the conclusion to the whole volume, historians relative neglect of the history of post-execution punishment has led some to embrace too simple a model of the transition from a terror-based public 'early modern' phase to a more private and humane 'modern' one.[3]

Moreover a lack of information and analysis about the timing of the collapse of the use of certain post-execution punishments has meant that other historians have put too much emphasis on the 1830s as the key moment in the decline of capital punishment.[4] Equally the growing use of post-execution punishment in later eighteenth-century Britain challenges various models of penal change that are based on underlying assumptions about long-term unidirectional changes—either in sensibilities towards violent punishments, or in the development of new technologies of power and social control that focused on the mind rather than the body.[5]

2 Historiographical Context

The widespread use of the death penalty and the fact that large numbers of offenders were executed on the gallows has long been seen by historians as an important (and some would say central) aspect of social relations in the eighteenth and early-nineteenth centuries.[6] 'The rulers of eighteenth-century England', Douglas Hay argued in his seminal article, Property, Authority and the Criminal Law 'cherished the death sentence .... This was the climactic moment in a system of criminal law based on terror'.[7] The large ambivalent crowds that gathered at executions, the problems the authorities had in directing them, the painful process of the execution itself and the changing attitudes of various social groups to capital punishment have also been subjected to detailed analysis, most notably in Vic Gatrell's much acclaimed book, *The Hanging Tree*.[8] The 'Bloody Code', which by the mid-eighteenth century had made a huge variety of offences into capital crimes, and the subsequent campaign for its reform, have also received much attention from historians.[9] So has the pardoning process which, by enabling many capital convicts to avoid the gallows, helped to create one of the main paradoxes of the eighteenth-century criminal justice system—that while the number of capital offences steadily increased, the number of people actually hanged did not.[10] However, historians of crime and justice have almost exclusively focused on the *breadth* of the capital punishment system—on the number of offenders who were executed and on the wide range of offences for which it was possible to receive the death penalty. By contrast they have largely neglected another important dimension—the *depth* of the capital punishment process—that is, the degree to which it was not simply about hanging but also about other execution practices that either exacted further punishment on the corpse of the offender after their death on the gallows, or added aggravation to the sentence by inflicting various forms of pain (such as breaking on the wheel) on the convict before his or her life had ended. One of the main aims of this volume is to redress this balance.

Some particular aspects of the history of post-execution punishment in this period have already been discussed by historians of the eighteenth century. The tiny number of murderers and other capital offenders who were subjected to burning at the stake have, for example, recently received some attention[11] and the much more widely used post-execution punishments of dissection or gibbeting have been discussed in passing.[12] However, no coherent analysis of this aspect of the capital punishment system has yet been written. Although, as we will see in Chap. 2, Randall McGowen has recently begun to explore the ways this issue was discussed in the first half of the eighteenth century,[13] the vast majority of the pre-1750 writings that advocated the introduction of more aggravated forms of execution have been almost completely neglected by historians[14] and the few contemporary writers that have been quoted have often been written off as 'foredoomed to failure' without being systematically studied.[15] Moreover, the growing depth of capital punishment in the main era during which post-execution punishment was a legislatively required and frequently used part of penal policy, the period between 1752 and the early 1830s, has also been largely neglected. The two most important legislative moments—the 1752 Murder Act which made the dissection or gibbeting of murderers' corpses compulsory and the Anatomy Act of 1832 which put an end to the former practice—have received some attention.[16] However, no serious discussion has yet been offered of the century-long debate on aggravated execution punishments; of the long-term origins of the Murder Act and its relationship to the problems created by the growth of the Bloody Code; of the many other post-1752 legislative initiatives that attempted to introduce (or modify) the use of post-execution punishments[17]; of the reasons why the post-execution punishment regime codified in the Murder Act lasted for so long, or of the number and types of offenders that were subjected to such punishments between 1752 and 1832. Whilst the extent of capital punishment has been studied in detail, the various ways in which greater depth was added to 'the spectacle of the gallows' in England has not received anything like the same attention.

This is surprising for two reasons. First, there was clearly extensive contemporary debate about the need to introduce post-execution or aggravated execution practices. A very considerable number of early-eighteenth-century publications on penal policy argued in favour of (and helped to instigate legislative initiatives designed to introduce) both post-execution punishments and other aggravated forms of the death penalty such as breaking on the wheel, which were still widely practiced on the continent[18] but which were not part of customary penal practice in England. The much quoted 1701 pamphlet *Hanging Not Punishment Enough*,[19] which advocated not only breaking on the wheel but also starving to death and hanging in chains, has usually been treated by historians as highly exceptional. However, (as Chap. 2 will indicate) a closer inspection of the pamphlet, periodical and newspaper sources suggests that this anonymous pamphlet was part of a much larger and longer-running discourse.[20] Although many of these late-seventeenth and early-eighteenth-century writers discussed the possibility of replacing hanging with other non-capital forms of punishment, the starting point for most of these works was the writer's severe doubts about the effectiveness of *just hanging* the offender. 'Hanging is nothing at all' a pamphlet recommending 'sharper deaths' complained in 1695. 'Much gentler and less painful than bed-death', mere hanging involved 'so little terror … in itself' that it seemed to the condemned to be 'a most easy death.'[21] Four decades later this issue was still being widely discussed. The 'quick dispatch' of hanging, one writer noted was 'so slight and unterrifying' that 'an execution that is attended with more lasting torment' was surely necessary.[22] 'Even the gallows cannot terrify' the *Gentleman's Magazine* observed in 1738, 'death without pain can be terrible to none',[23] and this theme that 'hanging only signifies nothing' was echoed in several London and provincial newspaper articles that, having first pointed out that 'the gallows will not deter' went on to argue that 'these shocking barbarities undoubtedly deserve a severer death than bare hanging.'[24]

Although these writings almost certainly helped to prepare the ground for the Murder Act of 1752, the doubts they expressed about the efficacy of the gallows were not raised in relation to murderers alone. The 'shocking barbarities' referred to in the later 1730s were committed by highwaymen, and the full title of the 1701 Pamphlet—'Hanging Not Punishment Enough for Murtherers, High-way Men, and House-Breakers Offered to the Consideration of the Two Houses of Parliament'—makes it clear that aggravated forms of capital punishment and/or post-execution punishment were also thought by some to be necessary for many offences that did not involve the taking of life. Nor did this issue disappear after the 1752 Murder Act. The context began to change after mid-century. Continental punishments such as breaking on the wheel, which were designed to ensure that the convicts 'felt their death', were much less likely to be seriously advocated after that point, but the possibility of further extending the use of post-execution punishments—and particularly of public dissection—was still being widely advocated in the late-eighteenth century and beyond. In 1786 the Prime Minister himself supported a bill introduced by William Wilberforce designed to extend the post-execution punishment of dissection from murder to several other offences including burglary and highway robbery, and similar (if less well-supported) attempts were made in 1796 and in 1830.[25] Although from the mid-eighteenth century onwards critics of capital punishment increasingly emphasized the need to replace it with non-capital options, such as transportation, life imprisonment with hard labour or solitary confinement,[26] one of the core themes of many early-eighteenth-century critiques—that hanging was not punishment enough and needed additional post-execution punishments to be attached to it—clearly continued to have resonance, and to gain considerable support within governing circles, not only in the 1780s and 1790s but also well into the nineteenth century (Chap. 4).

The second reason why it is so surprising that this subject has been neglected by historians is that the period from the mid-eighteenth century to the 1830s witnessed the high point of post-execution punishment in Britain. Following the Murder Act of 1752,[27] all convicted murderers were either dissected or gibbeted, while the latter punishment continued to be used on a discretionary basis against considerable numbers of major property offenders, as it had been since at least the beginning of the century. This meant that large numbers of offenders underwent these punishments. In England and Wales more than 1000 offenders were dissected or gibbeted under the Murder Act, and between 1740 and 1800 another hundred or so were gibbeted for other offences.[28] In most parts of England and especially around London, which was the epicenter of the Bloody Code,[29] the public would have been all too aware of these punishments. The regular use for at least 80 years of formal sentences of public dissection, and the widespread eighteenth-century practice of hanging the corpses of the condemned on gibbets placed in prominent places, meant that post-execution punishment had both a highly visible and, in the case of gibbeting, a very long-lasting impact on public life. Approaching eighteenth-century London by either road or water usually involved passing at least one gibbet (and sometimes several) and the capital's reputation as 'the city of the gallows'[30] suggests that post-execution punishment was much more important in helping to shape public consciousness than its relatively brief treatment in existing historical work would imply.

In order to redress this imbalance this volume looks in detail both at changing attitudes to aggravated and post-execution punishments and at the ways those punishments were used by the courts and shaped by the judicial authorities. It surveys the different types of post-execution punishments and other aggravated execution practices that were suggested by contemporaries, the reasons why they were advocated, the debates in Parliament about the introduction of such policies, the origins of the 1752 Murder Act, and the ways that this major legislative initiative was actually put into practice. It also analyses the changing use of different post-execution punishments over time and the reasons for their final abandonment between 1832 and 1834, before then attempting to identify the main underlying ideas/presuppositions that led contemporaries first to advocate these punishments and then to turn decisively away from their use. The English state made a unique attempt to harness the power of the criminal corpse in the eighteenth and early-nineteenth centuries and the aim of this volume is not only to explore and explain that phenomenon for the first time, but also to try to understand the important, but largely unexplored, role the Murder Act played within the broader capital punishment system well into the nineteenth century. In the process this analysis will also suggest that the history of post-execution punishment raises a number of important questions about many of the broader models of penal change often used by criminal justice historians.

3 The Broader Questions Raised by the Study of Post-execution Punishment

The fact that the origins, nature and role of the Murder Act have been relatively neglected by historians partly reflects their deep ambivalence towards it, and the awkward questions it frequency raises about the frameworks of explanation they have used to account for penal change in the eighteenth and early-nineteenth centuries. Neither of the two models historians have most frequently used to explain the changing nature of capital punishment in the eighteenth and early-nineteenth centuries fits comfortably with the increased use of post-execution punishment that occurred between 1752 and the early 1830s as a result of the Murder Act.

The first of these models is based on the work of Norbert Elias, which stressed the important role that cultural values and sensibilities played in shaping changes in attitudes to violence.[31] Although this model, and in particular Pieter Spierenburg's detailed application of it to the history of penal policy, has been subjected to considerable criticism by some historians who prefer to stress the role of specific economic, political or governmental factors, it has rightly maintained considerable purchase amongst those working on the history of capital punishment. Spierenburg, has argued that 'an original positive attitude towards the sufferings of convicts slowly gave way to a rising sensitivity, until a critical threshold of sensibility was reached in the nineteenth century—the growth of that sensibility being the main reason why aggravated execution rituals and the display of criminal corpses were gradually abolished.[32] Similarly, Paul Friedland in his chapter on 'Executions in the Age of Sensibilite'—part of a broader study entitled *Seeing Justice Done; The Age of Spectacular Capital Punishment in France*—has recently pointed out that 'in the first half of the eighteenth century … the seventeenth-century ideal of sensibilite, which had originally been conceived of as a unique gift of the privileged few, was increasingly being understood as a kind of automatic predisposition to compassion, a natural human reflex that made it impossible for one human being to witness the suffering of another without suffering themselves.'[33] This idea —that the eighteenth century witnessed a growth in sensibility towards other's pain and an increasing desire to put restraints on all forms of violence, including those inflicted by the criminal justice system—is, however, of very limited use in explaining the Murder Act. If, as John Beattie has argued, the more severe and public forms of post-execution punishment introduced by the Act were designed, 'to reassert the centrality of hanging and deterrence by terror at the heart of the English penal system,'[34] how does this fit with the notion that the eighteenth century witnessed a growing sensibility towards violence—a 'mental sea change', which condemned cruelty in punishment as fundamentally 'unacceptable in a civilized society'?[35] This idea, which as James Cockburn has pointed out, was widely discussed by Enlightenment commentators attempting 'to distance their own era from the violence and insensitivity of earlier ages'[36] is extremely hard to reconcile with the 80 years of public post-execution punishments that followed the 1752 Murder Act.

The increased use of gibbeting and dissection against murderers and property offenders in the period 1752–1832 was, Ruth Richardson has recently argued, not only designed to overtly flout the customary concern to honour the bodies of the dead, which manifested itself in contemporary funereal rituals, but was also intended, implicitly at least, to deny the soul a resting place by refusing to allow the intact burial of the corpse.[37] These post-execution punishments were essentially acts of violence. This was, to quote Richardson, 'public corpse abuse under the protection and patronage of the state,' which exposed the dead to public indignity, maltreatment and dismemberment.[38] The increased use of highly public dissections and of gibbeting in the second half of the eighteenth century, and the continued use of penal dissection throughout the first third of the nineteenth century, raises questions about the ways Spierenburg and others have applied Elias's model to penal policy in England. As Richard Ward has pointed out in his recent work on the origins of the Murder Act, 'by imposing a more severe and exemplary form of punishment on convicted murderers, the Act in some ways cuts across the growing humanitarianism, civility and urbanity which several historians have posited as defining features of penal reform in the eighteenth and nineteenth centuries.'[39]

The other major model of penal change that is widely used by historians of this period—Michel Foucault's notion that elaborate and violent forms of public execution were increasingly regarded as both unnecessary and dysfunctional as forms of governance after the mid eighteenth century—also offers little help in explaining either the passing of the Murder Act or the growing use of public post-execution punishments in the 80 years that followed it.[40] Foucault's model of a transition from punishments centred on the body to those designed to discipline and reshape the mind has much to offer, but the transition was not as smooth or as unproblematic as he implies. His failure to address the questions raised by the passing of the Murder Act has made his work less applicable to the English case. His portrayal of the transition in penal policy from 'an art of unbearable sensations' to 'an economy of suspended rights' may or may not fit the evidence in France, but the work presented here suggests that when applied to England his ideas fit poorly with the chronology of change and have an air of inexorability that does not fit well with the evidence.[41] After his famous opening description of the tortured public dismemberment of Damiens in 1757, Foucault argued that 'a few decades saw the disappearance of the tortured, dismembered, amputated body … exposed alive or dead to public view. The body as a major target of penal repression disappeared. By the end of the eighteenth and the beginning of the nineteenth century, the gloomy festival of punishment was dying out.'[42] Yet while, as we will see, this chronology has at least some resonance with the history of gibbeting in

England, it does not explain the continuance of highly public criminal corpse dissections throughout the first three decades of the nineteenth century. The history of capital punishment, and the role of post-execution punishment within it, are more complex and less unilinear than this model suggests, and for this reason the conclusion to this volume will also argue that David Garland's model of changing 'modes' of capital punishment (which borrows quite heavily from Foucault) may need to be rethought.[43]

In his seminal paper 'Modes of Capital Punishment; The Death Penalty in Historical Perspective' Garland's analysis of the period from the sixteenth to the nineteenth centuries distinguishes two specific, and 'sharply differentiated' modes of capital punishment–the 'early modern' and the 'modern'—each of these modes being associated not only with different periods but also with distinctive forms of social organization and state development.[44] The 'early modern' mode was, he argues, characterized by the depth and intensity of the capital punishment rituals used across Europe, seen in the horrifying and extended execution and post-execution practices and in the use of elaborate and varied public ceremonies designed to proclaim the power and sovereignty of the state during a period when it was often weak and vulnerable.[45] Needing to develop tactics that would strike fear into the hearts of their enemies, early modern states were endlessly inventive in their elaboration of these execution processes and in ensuring that the bodies of the most serious offenders continued to be punished even after they were dead.[46] This 'old … early modern style' of death penalty had disappeared, Garland argues, by the early-nineteenth century and was replaced by what he terms the 'modern' mode in which capital punishment was used less extensively and had much less depth as a process. As the death penalty changed from being a vital instrument of rule to becoming simply another potential sanction amongst a range of penal options, the use of capital punishment was largely confined to cases involving murder or treason. It also became increasingly private and humane as elements of aggravated or post-execution punishment were abandoned. In Garland's analysis this 'long-term movement toward a more restrained, refined and reduced death penalty' followed a definite 'developmental pattern' linked to state formation, rationalization, liberalization and democratization' as well as to the broader processes of 'civilization and humanization.'[47] However, this two-phase model pays little attention to the potentially unique nature of the long eighteenth century as a separate era in British penal history.

Detailed work by historians of the long eighteenth century has already established that the English criminal justice system developed a number of important new characteristics during that period. Execution rates, which had peaked at very high levels in the late-sixteenth and early-seventeenth centuries, had fallen to unprecedentedly low levels by the early-eighteenth century.[48] However, the same period witnessed the growth of the so-called 'Bloody Code' as a succession of parliamentary acts rapidly increased the number of relatively minor offences that could be punished by death.[49] The long eighteenth century also witnessed the creation of a much more finely differentiated punitive system. The penal regimes of the sixteenth and seventeenth centuries had relied mainly on physical punishments such as whipping, branding and hanging, but the introduction, and widespread use, of transportation and imprisonment in the eighteenth century added new flexibility to the sanctions available and encouraged the growing use of pardoning in capital cases.[50] Moreover, as will become clear as this study unfolds, the period from the late-seventeenth century to the early years of the nineteenth also witnessed a considerable expansion in the depth of capital punishment. Aggravated pre-execution techniques were much discussed and two forms of post-execution punishment were increasingly used as the century progressed, creating (for murder at least) a new level of differentiation within the capital punishment system that paralleled the similar change that took place amongst non-capital sanctions as the new intermediate sanctions of transportation and imprisonment came to dominate punishments for property crime.[51] When this new post-execution punishment-based perspective is added to the detailed work already done by a wide range of eighteenth-century criminal justice historians,[52] it becomes clear, I will argue, that we need to rethink Garland's two-stage model and to acknowledge that the period from the late-seventeenth century to the early nineteenth was a distinct phase in the history of capital punishment rather than just a time of gradual transition from an early modern to a modern mode.[53]

The study of post-execution punishment also raises important questions about the very different perspective offered by Gatrell in his influential book *The Hanging Tree*.[54] Gatrell's explanation of the transformation of capital punishment policies contrasts sharply with that put forward by Garland. The latter focused primarily on the long-term forces behind changing capital punishment practices. The transition from early modern to modern modes occurred, Garland argued, 'within a larger arc of development' and of state transformation, as 'the newly stabilized states of the late-seventeenth century gave way to the enlightened monarchies of the eighteenth century and eventually to the unified and bureaucratized nation states of nineteenth century Europe'.[55] Gatrell, by contrast argued for extreme discontinuity as the key to understanding penal change, at least in England. 'There has been no greater nor more sudden revolution in English penal history', he argued, 'than this retreat from hanging in the 1830s,' and that retreat was quite simply, in his view, a short-term reaction to the very high numbers of convicts being sentenced to death in the 1820s and the impossibility of hanging significant proportions of them without alienating public opinion.[56] For Gatrell this was a dramatic watershed and was very definitely not a product of the medium- to long-term factors foregrounded by Foucault, Elias, Spierenburg or Garland. The capital code 'did not collapse because of a revolution in sensibilities' he argued, but rather 'there was a revolution in sensibilities because the code was collapsing already.'[57] However, as Chap. 3 will make clear, fundamental changes in the use of post-execution punishments, in hanging policies and in the use of techniques such as scene-of-the-crime hangings had all occurred during the half-century before Gatrell's watershed. The analysis presented here, I will suggest in the final chapter, therefore gives considerable further weight to the recent critiques of Gatrell's work produced by Simon Devereaux and others.[58] Moreover, another weakness of Gatrell's watershed theory—his failure to address the fact that it lacks any real purchase as an explanation of the decline of capital punishment elsewhere in Europe—is also highlighted by another broad sub-theme that gradually emerges from this volume. Although significant differences between British and continental practice can clearly be identified, overall the detailed study of aggravated and post-execution policies presented here suggests that the English capital punishment reform process was much less dissimilar to that found on the continent than either contemporary commentators or many subsequent historians have assumed.

In exploring both the widespread advocacy of torment-based aggravated execution techniques in the first half of the eighteenth century, and the large-scale compulsory use of post-execution punishment in the 80 years after the Murder Act, this study is therefore focusing on aspects of punishment policy that offer a rare opportunity to test the applicability and explanatory capacity of the broader models of penal change on which historians of the period have mainly founded their ideas. In the process it will also offer new perspectives on the Murder Act itself, the passing (and timing) of which has proved difficult for historians to fully explain. In his article on 'Punishment and Brutalization in the English Enlightenment', for example, Cockburn concluded that 'no single episode better illustrates the inconsistencies and contradictions implicit in attempts to accommodate the "traditional" and "enlightened" strands of eighteenth-century penal thinking than the Murder Act'... The timing seems ... extraordinary'.[59] Philip Rawlings also found the Act problematic and contradictory. 'In spite of the Murder Act', he observed, 'there was generally a shift away from such calls for increased severity by mid-century'.[60] However, through an exploration of the Act's key role in creating a new scale of capital punishment penalties by introducing a significant differentiation between the forms of execution used on property offenders and those imposed on murderers, this volume will suggest that the Act was neither inconsistent nor contradictory. On closer study, it will be argued (Chap. 5), it is clear that the Murder Act was both a logical extension of the Bloody Code, and played an important role in legitimizing and maintaining that code.

4 Plan of the Book

Five major types of mainstream criminal prosecutions sometimes resulted in sentences involving aggravated or post-execution punishments during these years—trials for high treason; for petty treason; for piracy and other crimes on the high seas tried by the Admiralty Courts; for murder; and for capital property offences deemed heinous enough by the Assizes or Old Bailey judges to be worthy of gibbeting as well as hanging.[61] The final two categories in this list—murder and major capital crimes against property—attracted by far the most debate about the need for aggravated or post-execution punishments and accounted for the vast majority of the criminal corpses that were eventually subjected to those processes (as the statistics discussed in Chap. 3 will indicate). These two categories were also the primary targets of the most important legislative initiatives involving the extension of post-execution punishment that were discussed during this period—the Murder Act of 1752, which made dissection or hanging in chains compulsory for those found guilty of homicide, and the unsuccessful Dissection of Convicts Bill (passed by the House of Commons but not by the Lords in 1786) that attempted to extend the former punishment to the corpses of executed burglars, robbers and other offenders. The bulk of this book will therefore focus on these final two categories and to a lesser extent on the practice of burning offenders at the stake either for specific types of murder—the killing of a husband or master—or for property crimes related to coining. The relatively small number of cases involving aggravated execution and post-execution practices in relation to treason and to Admiralty Court offences will not receive the same level of attention here, but will be included in the statistical analysis (Chap. 3) and the discussion of penal change in order to offer a more fully rounded model of the rise and fall of pre- and post-execution punishment between 1700 and the 1830s.

After briefly reviewing the use of post-execution punishments before 1700 in the final section of this chapter, the study will then move on in Chaps. 2, 3 and 4 to look in detail at the period from 1700 until the final abandonment of the two main post-execution punishments—dissection and gibbeting—in the 1832 Anatomy Act and the 1834 Act for the Abolition 'Hanging the Bodies of Criminals in Chains'.[62] Drawing on all the available forms of contemporary discourse—pamphlets, works by legal commentators, articles in newspapers and periodicals, judge's comments, parliamentary debates and reports etc.—Chap. 2 will trace the chronological development of the debates about the introduction of either aggravated pre-execution policies or about the post-execution punishment of the criminal corpse, particular attention being paid to the key moments when legislative change was either achieved or seriously debated. It will focus on the period from the 1690s to the passing of the Murder Act of 1752, when a wide variety of aggravated and post-executions punishments were discussed, and will end with an analysis of the reasons for the passing of the 1752 Act, which made dissection and hanging in chains a formal part of sentencing policy for the first time. In Chap. 3 the analysis will shift temporarily from discursive formations and legislative initiatives to the actual decisions made by the courts. The primary focus will be the period from 1752 to the 1830s and the use that the courts made of sentences involving post-execution punishments in the key period between the Murder Act and its repeal. A previously neglected source—the Sheriff's cravings—will be used to create a detailed statistical analysis of two broad patterns: changes across time in the use of punishments such as gibbeting and dissection, and geographical variations in sentencing policies. Chapter 4 analyses the same period but moves from this quantitative focus on the patterns of court decision making back to a qualitative study of changing discourses and debates about policy. It focusses on the key developments of the period between the passing of the Murder Act and its repeal in 1832, particular attention being given to both the later eighteenth- and early-nineteenth-century debates about extending the post-execution punishments laid down in the Murder Act to include major property offences, and the growing doubts about gibbeting, and eventually about dissection, which culminated in the final abandonment of post-execution punishment in the early 1830s. The conclusion then highlights the various ways in which the study of the punishment of the criminal corpse and of aggravated execution policies challenges both the eighteenth-century reformers own key 'civilizing' narrative, and many of the models modern historians have developed about the chronology of penal change. It also explores the relationship between changes in the quantity of capital punishment (i.e. in the frequency of executions) and changing policies in relation to the quality of that punishment (i.e. in the level of post-execution punishments inflicted on the corpse of the condemned), and argues that, right up until the penal reforms of the 1830s, post-execution punishment was seen as an important part of the penal landscape and as a vital means of differentiating between the punishment of murder and that of other more minor capital crimes.

5 Post-execution Punishment Before the Early-Eighteenth Century

A variety of different forms of post-execution punishment and of aggravated execution practices that often involved further punishment of the convict's corpse after death were used in England in the period leading up to 1700. However, outside cases involving treason or petty treason, the repertoire of such punishments was much smaller than that found in most other European countries, and the options that were available in England were also used much less frequently with one notable exception—a brief period in the mid-sixteenth century when large numbers of British heretics were burnt at the stake (a punishment deemed particularly appropriate because it was also an effective post-execution punishment leaving no remains for burial).[63] The execution practices used in medieval England are difficult to analyse because they were poorly documented, often non-statutory and sometimes highly localized. It is unclear, for example, whether the practice of executing felons by drowning, found in fourteenth-century Kent, was also in use elsewhere.[64] Some long-established local practices such as the Halifax 'gibbet', a relatively humane mechanism very similar to a guillotine, continued to be used fairly extensively until the mid-seventeenth century.[65] Everywhere else in England and Wales beheading, which was regarded throughout Europe as involving less dishonour than hanging, was usually reserved for high status offenders.[66]

Pieter Spierenburg's suggestion that prolonged death on the gallows was 'practically unknown' in early modern England slightly exaggerates the differences between Britain and the continent.[67] The practice of boiling convicted poisoners to death, for example, was briefly given statutory backing in 1531 and several offenders, including a Norfolk maid-servant who had poisoned her mistress, suffered this punishment before the statute was repealed in 1547.[68] Later attempts to revive it were not, however, successful[69] and although examples of the hand of the condemned being cut off and nailed up in a public place can be found in sixteenth-century England, and as late as the mid-eighteenth century in Scotland, there can be no doubt that by the later seventeenth century aggravated forms of execution designed to torment the convict were very rare in England, unless the offender had committed a treasonable offence.[70] Historians working on early modern punishment in continental countries such as Germany, Holland and France—where breaking on the wheel, boiling and burning, not to mention burying alive, starving to death and drowning often remained in use well into the eighteenth century and beyond[71]—have therefore drawn a very different picture to those working on England and Wales. In the later sixteenth and seventeenth centuries the English gradually extended their use of two forms of aggravated execution—gibbeting and dissection—that were not based on increasing the torment experienced by the condemned, but were entirely post-execution punishments targeted at the criminal corpse. These punishments, far from fading away, were growing in importance by the early-eighteenth century. Although, as we will see, many early-eighteenth century English commentators argued vehemently for the introduction of continental torment-inducing execution practices, they were not successful. Post-execution dissection or hanging in chains remained the central forms of aggravated execution procedure acceptable to those who shaped English capital punishment procedures in relation to murderers and property offenders throughout the eighteenth century.

Both of these punishments had long histories by 1700. Gibbeting for both murderers and other heinous offenders such as violent robbers had been practiced since at least the thirteenth century.[72] The precise methods by which offenders were gibbeted (or hung in chains as the process was more commonly described) and the various policies that were developed in relation to location, construction and so forth will be not discussed in detail here because Sarah Tarlow's forthcoming book *Hung in Chains; The Golden and Ghoulish Age of the Gibbet in Britain* will deal with this subject in detail. However, the core characteristics of gibbeting—the secure and highly visible suspension of the corpse in a public location (and often for many years) in order to create a lasting warning and example, were well established by the seventeenth century.[73] In the later Middle Ages the gibbeting of the condemned while they were still alive was occasionally used to punish particularly heinous premeditated murders,[74] but there is no serious post-1600 evidence of this in England.[75] The English were not, however, averse to such practices when they dealt with colonial slaves. Following a slave rebellion in 1736 the authorities in Antigua burned fifty-eight rebels alive and broke five of them on the wheel, while a further six were reported to have been 'hung in chains upon gibbets and starved to death (of whom one lived nine nights and eight days without any sustenance)'. After death their corpses were subjected to further punishment as 'their heads were then cut off and fixed on poles, and their bodies burnt'.[76] Since convicted slaves were also starved to death on gibbets or had their heads displayed on poles in many other eighteenth-century British colonies, even though their offences were often more routine,[77] the boasts of many eighteenth-century English writers that, in contrast to 'the scenes of barbarity … so often exhibited' on the continent, 'such tormenting and lingering deaths cannot mix well with our constitution,' need careful evaluation. Englishmen may have been fond of highlighting 'the lenity of our laws, the boast and felicity of our constitution', but their unwillingness to embrace torment-based execution practices was highly dependent on context, even though they steadfastly refused to acknowledge this.[78] This said, however, in England and Wales at least the rhetoric was usually matched by the reality, and gibbeting remained very much a post-execution punishment until it was completely abolished in 1834.

Before the Murder Act of 1752 hanging in chains, as gibbeting was most commonly termed, even though it usually involved the use of a metal cage, was based on customary law and more specifically on the belief that the bodies of condemned men were at the King's disposal.[79] It was imposed by a form of executive order on the basis of customary procedure, rather than being laid down by statute as a formal punishment, and it is unclear whether it was always (or even usually) recorded in court when sentence of death was passed.[80] This doubt about the proportion of gibbetings that were announced by the judges and therefore formally recorded in the surviving assize records, makes it very difficult to gauge how frequent the practice was in the late-sixteenth and seventeenth centuries. On the basis of finding only one instance in the assizes records of the five Home circuit counties between 1559 and 1625, and just a single isolated example in the seventeenth-century Oxford Circuit records, Cockburn has argued that gibbeting was uncommon before the eighteenth century.[81] It is possible, however, that it was quite frequently not recorded by the courts' clerks and therefore largely invisible to the historian because other non-court sources, such as newspapers, which would later record such events quite extensively, were not in existence until the final years of the seventeenth century. Gregory Durston has argued, by contrast, that gibbeting was 'common practice in heinous cases' long before the eighteenth century, and although he only quotes a few examples, such as the gibbeted corpse described in Pepys's diary in 1661, Hartshorne's work on the period 1671–1690 which includes four well-evidenced cases of murderers being gibbeted in various parts of England, suggests that by the final third of the century this practice may well have been fairly widespread.[82] As we will see in Chap. 3, gibbeting was fairly common by the time fuller newspaper coverage developed in the early-eighteenth century and may well have reached an all-time peak in the 1740s. Moreover, as soon as newspapers and printed *Ordinary's Accounts* become available towards the end of the seventeenth century reports of the gibbeting of London thieves and murderers immediately began to appear. In 1691 the *Ordinary's Accounts* describes the gibbeting at Mile End of the murderer James Selby and five years later the same source, and a London Newspaper—the *Post Man*, reported the gibbeting of Thomas Randall for murder and highway robbery at Kingsland 'where he is to hang in irons till his body be consumed'.[83] The *Ordinary's Accounts* of the hanging in 1684 of a notorious London highwayman and murderer reported that after his execution his body was 'cut down and put into a frame of iron … and afterwards hung up again on the gibbet', giving further credence to the French visitor Henri Misson's observation in the late 1690s that 'robbers in the highway that have doubled their felony by the addition of murder to theft' usually had their bodies enclosed in 'several iron hoops' and exposed 'upon the gibbet'.[84]

The Admiralty Courts were also making quite widespread use of gibbeting by the beginning of the eighteenth century—a tradition that seems to have been a longstanding one and had originally included Admiralty courts outside London.[85] Two very different forms of post-execution gibbeting were used by the Admiralty courts when they punished offenders for capital crimes committed in a maritime context. First, the bodies of all those hanged by the court were secured and left well below the high tide mark for three consecutive tides. Then, if selected for further punishment, the corpse would be hung in chains at a more permanent site on land. In July 1700, for example, ten pirates were hanged at Execution Dock on two gibbets specially erected 'within flood-mark', two of whom were then 'carried down in a boat in order to be Hang'd in Chains; one of them at halfway Tree between this City and Graves-End, and the other at the Hope'.[86] In the same month the London newspapers also reported the gibbeting at Mile End of two offenders found guilty of murder by the Old Bailey judges,[87] and since we also have evidence of two further gibbetings in metropolis in 1700 and 1701—one being the hanging in chains of Captain Kidd at Tilbury[88]—gibbeting was clearly established as a fairly frequent metropolitan occurrence by the end of the seventeenth century, even though the precise numbers of involved, and how those numbers varied between that century and the eighteenth, remain very difficult to establish.

The post-execution dissection of the condemned person's body (the detailed history of which is the subject Elizabeth Hurren's recent volume)[89] also developed as a significant element of capital punishment procedures in the early modern period. Much of the original impetus for this development came from medical institutions. As medical training gradually became more sophisticated in the early modern period and as the study of anatomy rose in importance because of the growing belief that it was a vital part of a surgeon's training,[90] corpses came to be increasingly seen as valuable commodities and the bodies of executed criminals began to have a significant role in the mixed (and often makeshift) economy that developed to supply cadavers to those who needed them.[91] The custom of giving the corpses of executed criminals to selected members of the medical profession was well established by the late-seventeenth century.[92] As early as 1506 the Edinburgh Guild of Surgeons and Barbers was granted the body of at least one executed felon a year, and in 1540 the newly formed London Company of Barbers and Surgeons was given the annual right to four such corpses.[93] In the following decade a similar level of provision was made available to Caius College Cambridge and by the mid-1560s the Royal College of Physicians had also been granted the bodies of four of those 'condemned and put to death for Theft, Murder or any other Felony' in the City of London, Middlesex 'or anywhere else within 16 miles of the said City'. This was increased to six bodies in 1641, the entire county of Surrey being added to the catchment area.[94]

The transformation of the surgeons' involvement in the execution process—from the marginal, sporadic and scarcely visible role they played in the sixteenth century to the very different, official and highly visible role they regularly enacted after the Murder Act—was a lengthy and uneven process. The surgeons' need for cadavers drew them gradually, but inexorably, into a deeper involvement in the criminal justice process. In the sixteenth and early-seventeenth centuries the surgeons took such a small proportion of the very large number of bodies that died on the gallows that their profile remained extremely low and they experienced very little hostility.[95] However, as the number of felons being executed fell drastically in the mid- to late-seventeenth century,[96] and as the surgeons' increasing needs continued to stimulate the market in corpses, the activities of the surgeons and those they employed to collect the bodies of the condemned from the gallows became more conspicuous and began to draw the anger of the crowd. By the end of the seventeenth century, Jonathan Sawday has argued, a 'crisis in the provision of corpses for the various anatomy schools' was beginning to develop.[97] Though we know very little about the precise number of criminal corpses that were being used by the surgeons at this point, they were clearly not confining themselves to the quotas formally allowed them by the authorities. By the 1690s there is evidence that some of the condemned were selling their bodies to the surgeons before their executions,[98] and in 1700 a foreign observer noted that that if any bodies were left unclaimed by family or friends after an execution they were 'sold to the surgeons to be dissected'.[99] Their growing visibility in the early-eighteenth century, combined with that the fact that the surgeons increasingly paid their beadles and porters considerable sums to also collect the corpses of criminals who *did* have family and friends (who were themselves often deeply opposed to dissection), played a key role in creating the conflicts expressed in the Tyburn riots against the surgeons that Peter Linebaugh has shown were so frequent in the first half of the eighteenth century.[100]

However, the hostility of the crowd was not the only problem the surgeons faced in their attempts to obtain the corpses of criminals executed at Tyburn. They also competed between themselves. In 1710 the President of the London College of Physicians expressed anger at 'the connivance of the Sheriff's Officers' who allowed a body that was supposed to be given to the College 'to be violently taken away and carried to St. Thomas's

Hospital where it was privately dissected'.[101] By the 1720s the College of Physicians was so angry at the failure of the sheriff's officers to actively assist them in securing even the small number of criminal corpses they were legally entitled to, that they obtained specific orders from the City authorities in an attempt to ensure that they were given that assistance. The battles between the crowd and the surgeons, and between the rival groups among the anatomists themselves, continued despite the City's intervention and the notices they put into the papers threatening to prosecute under the Riot Act. However, the College of Physicians bitter complaints in 1720 that 'the Sheriff's Officers pretend that they are not obliged to secure and detain such bodies for the College',[102] suggest that the problem lay partly in the surgeon's ambivalent status within the criminal justice system in the years before the Murder Act.

Although Ruth Richardson has argued that the privileged access to criminal corpses given to the surgeons from the sixteenth century onwards meant that 'dissection became recognized in law as a punishment' and that 'dissection was added to the array of punishments available to the bench',[103] in practice the situation was much more fluid. As Sawday has pointed out, dissection had only a 'quasi-legal status' until the Murder Act and the terms 'penal dissection' or 'penal anatomy' can therefore only be properly applied to the situation after that act. Before 1752 dissection very rarely, if ever, appeared in the formal sentences recorded by the courts, but this did not mean that it had no impact on the experience of the condemned or on thinking about penal policy. The post-execution punishments of dissection and hanging in chains were well established by 1700 as the main forms of aggravated death penalty imposed on murderers and property offenders. However, their supremacy was not assured at this point. Several waves of pamphlets and articles explored various other options during the first half of the eighteenth century, many of which argued strongly for more continental (and from the point of view of the condemned more painful) solutions, and it is to these works that we now turn in Chap. 2.

Notes

1. E. Hurren, *Dissecting the Criminal Corpse: Staging Post-execution Punishment in Early Modern England* (London, 2016), S. Tarlow, *Hung in Chains; The Golden and Ghoulish Age of the Gibbet in Britain* (Forthcoming, Palgrave 2017).

2. Hurren, *Dissecting*; Tarlow, *Hung*; R. Ward (ed.), *A Global History of Execution and the Criminal Corpse* (Basingstoke, 2015); O. Davies and F. Matteoni *Executing Magic: The Power of Criminal Bodies* (London, Palgrave forthcoming).
3. D. Garland, 'Modes of Capital Punishment: The Death Penalty in Historical Perspective' in D. Garland, R. McGowen and M. Meranze (eds.), *America's Death Penalty; Between Past and Present* (New York, 2011), pp. 30–71; M. Foucault, *Discipline and Punish: The Birth of the Prison* (London, 1979).
4. V. Gatrell, *The Hanging Tree* (Oxford, 1994).
5. P. Spierenburg, *The Spectacle of Suffering* (Cambridge, 1984); Foucault, *Discipline and Punish*; D. Garland, *Punishment and Modern Society; A Study in Social Theory* (Oxford, 1990), pp. 131–176 and 213–248.
6. D. Hay, 'Property, Authority and the Criminal law' in D. Hay, P. Linebaugh, E.P. Thompson and C. Winslow (eds.), *Albion's Fatal Tree* (London, 1975); Gatrell, *The Hanging Tree*, p. 32.
7. Hay, 'Property', pp. 17–18.
8. Gatrell, *The Hanging Tree*. For an excellent review see R. McGowen, 'Revisiting the Hanging Tree; Gatrell on Emotion and History' *British Journal of Criminology*, 40 (2000), pp. 1–13; T. Laqueur, 'Crowds, Carnival and the State in English Executions 1604–1868' in A. Beier, D. Cannadine and J. Rosenheim (eds.), *The First Modern Society* (Cambridge, 1989), pp. 305–355.
9. L. Radzinowicz, *A History of English Criminal Law and its Administration from 1750,* (London, 5 Vols., 1948–1986) 1; R. McGowen, 'A Powerful Sympathy: Terror, the Prison and Humanitarian Reform in Early Nineteenth-Century Britain' *Journal of British Studies*, 25 (1986), pp. 312–334; R. McGowen, 'The Body and Punishment in Eighteenth-Century England' *Journal of Modern History*, 59 (1987). The role of religion in debates about the death penalty has also attracted considerable attention—R. Follett, *Evangelicalism, Penal Theory and the Politics of Criminal Law Reform in England, 1808–1830* (Basingstoke, 2001); H. Potter, *Hanging in Judgement: Religion and the Death Penalty in England* (London, 1993).
10. P. King, *Crime, Justice and Discretion in England 1740–1820* (Oxford, 2000); Hay, 'Property', p. 22; D. Hay, 'Writing about the Death Penalty' *Legal History*, 10 (2006), pp. 35–51; D. Hay, 'Hanging and the English Judges: The Judicial Politics of Retention and Abolition' in Garland, McGowen and Meranze (eds.), *America's Death Penalty*; D. Gray and P. King 'The Killing of Constable Linnell: The Impact of Xenophobia and of Elite Connections on Eighteenth-Century Justice' *Family and Community History*, 16 (2013).

11. S. Devereaux, 'The Abolition of the Burning of Women Reconsidered' *Crime, Histoire & Societes/Crime, History and Societies*, 9 (2005), pp. 1–22; R. Campbell, 'Sentence of Death by Burning for Women' *Journal of Legal History*, 5 (1984), p. 44–59.
12. Gatrell, *The Hanging Tree*, pp. 87–91, 255–257, 267–269; F. McLynn, *Crime and Punishment in Eighteenth-Century England* (London, 1989), pp. 272–274; Potter, *Hanging in Judgement*, p. 8; Radzinowicz, *A History*, 1, pp. 206–227; P. Rawlings, *Crime and Power: A History of Criminal Justice 1688–1998* (Harlow, 1999), p. 49.
13. R. McGowen, 'The Problem of Punishment in Eighteenth-Century England' in S. Devereaux and P. Griffiths (eds.), *Penal Practice and Culture 1500–1900; Punishing the English* (Basingstoke, 2004), pp. 210–231 and R. McGowen, 'Making Examples and the Crisis of Punishment in Mid-Eighteenth-Century England' in D. Lemmings (ed.), *The British and Their Laws in the Eighteenth Century* (Woodbridge, 2005), pp. 182–205.
14. J. Beattie, *Policing and Punishment in London 1660–1750; Urban Crime and the Limits of Terror*, (Oxford, 2001), p. 321 contains only passing reference to this subject. J. Beattie, *Crime and the Courts in England 1660–1800*, (Oxford, 1986), pp. 488–490 uses 3 main pamphlets. His later discussion of the Murder Act debates (pp. 525–530) draws on some further material. Two of the same pamphlets are quoted by D. Lemmings, *Law and Government during the Long Eighteenth Century* (Basingstoke, 2011), pp. 95–96; Radzinowicz, *A History*, 1, p. 38.
15. Radzinowicz, *A History*, 1, p. 238; J. Potter, *The Fatal Gallows Tree* (London, 1965), p. 71 describes these writers as 'fringe groups of blood-thirsty fanatics'.
16. Beattie, *Crime*, pp. 525–530; R. Ward, *Print Culture, Crime and Justice in Eighteenth-Century London* (London, 2014), pp. 157–203: R. Richardson, *Death, Dissection and the Destitute* (London, 1989).
17. One particular moment is, however, the subject of two interesting recent articles—R. Ward, 'The Criminal Corpse, Anatomists and the Criminal Law: Parliamentary Attempts to Extend the Dissection of Offenders in Late Eighteenth-Century England' *Journal of British Studies*, 54 (2015), pp. 63–87; S. Devereaux, 'Inexperienced Humanitarians? William Wilberforce, William Pitt, and the Execution Crisis of the 1780s' *Law and History Review, 33 (2015)*, pp. 839–885.
18. Spierenburg, *The Spectacle of Suffering*; R. Evans, *Rituals of Retribution: Capital Punishment in Germany 1600–1987* (Oxford, 1996); Foucault, *Discipline and Punish*; P. Friedland, *Seeing Justice Done: The Age of Spectacular Capital Punishment in France* (Oxford, 2012).
19. Anon, *Hanging Not Punishment Enough* (London, 1701).
20. Radzinowicz, *A History*, 1, pp. 231–238; Beattie, *Crime*, pp. 488–490.

21. Anon, *Solon Secundus: Some Defects in the English Laws* (London, 1695), p. 7. This pamphlet also considered other options such as life imprisonment and transportation.
22. G. Ollyffe, *An Essay Humbly Offer'd, for An Act of Parliament to Prevent Capital Crimes* (London, 1731), p. 7.
23. *Gentleman's Magazine*, 8 (1735), p. 286.
24. *Derby Mercury*, 3 May 1733, 17 April 1735, 4 Nov 1736—these were reproducing articles from a London publication—*Wye's Letter*—R. Wiles, *Freshest Advices* (Ohio, 1965), p. 200.
25. See Chap. 3 and Ward, 'The Criminal Corpse'; Devereaux, 'An Inexperienced Humanitarian?'
26. Beattie, *Crime*, pp. 538–618.
27. 25 Geo II, c.37.
28. See Chap. 3 for sources and analysis of the frequency of post-execution punishment.
29. P. King and R. Ward, 'Rethinking the Bloody Code in Eighteenth-Century Britain: Capital Punishment at the Centre and on the Periphery' *Past and Present* (2015) 228, pp. 159–205.
30. Gatrell, *The Hanging Tree*, pp. 267–269; D. Rumbelow, *The Triple Tree: Newgate, Tyburn and Old Bailey* (London, 1982), p. 158; Potter, *Hanging in Judgment*, p. 8.
31. N. Elias, *The Civilizing Process, I. The History of Manners* (Oxford 1978) and *II. State Formation and Civilization* (Oxford, 1978); Garland, *Punishment and Modern Society*, pp. 215–241 is the best review of Elias's influence on this field.
32. Spierenburg, *The Spectacle of Suffering*, p. x; Evans, *Rituals*, p. 15.
33. Friedland, *Seeing Justice Done*, p. 165.
34. Beattie, *Crime*, p. 530.
35. Ibid., p. 631.
36. J. Cockburn, 'Punishment and Brutalisation in the English Enlightenment' *Law and History Review* 12 (1994), p. 178.
37. R. Richardson, 'Popular Beliefs about the Dead Body' in C. Reeves (ed.), *A Cultural History of the Human Body. Volume 4. In the Age of the Enlightenment* (Oxford, 2010), pp. 99–100.
38. Ibid., p. 100.
39. Ward, *Print Culture*, p. 159.
40. Foucault, *Discipline and Punish*.
41. Ibid., p. 11.
42. Ibid., p. 8.
43. Garland, 'Modes'.
44. Ibid., p. 35.
45. Ibid., p. 30.

46. Ibid., pp. 36 and 41–42.
47. Ibid., p. 31.
48. P. Jenkins, 'From Gallows to Prison? The Execution Rate in Early Modern England' *Criminal Justice History*, 7 (1986), pp. 51–71; J. Sharpe, *Crime in Early Modern England 1550–1750* (Harlow, 1984), p. 65.
49. For a good recent summary see D. Grey, *Crime, Policing and Punishment in England 1660–1914.* (London, 2016), pp. 276–295.
50. Beattie, *Crime*, p. 620.
51. Beattie, *Policing*, p. 473.
52. Hay, 'Property' remains the seminal work. Key monographs include King, *Crime, Justice*; Beattie, *Crime*; Beattie, *Policing*; R. Shoemaker, *The London Mob: Violence and Disorder in Eighteenth-century England* (*London, 2004*) but much of the best work has been done in groups of articles most notably by Shoemaker, Hay, Devereaux and McGowen. Gray, *Crime* provides the most recent survey.
53. Garland, 'Modes', p. 30.
54. Gatrell, *The Hanging Tree.*
55. Garland, 'Modes', p. 49.
56. Gatrell, *The Hanging Tree*, p. 10; Gray, *Crime*, p. 284.
57. Gatrell, *The Hanging Tree*, pp. viii–ix.
58. S. Devereaux, 'England's "Bloody Code" in Crisis and Transition; Executions at the Old Bailey 1760–1837' *Journal of the Canadian Historical Society/Revue de la Societe Historique du Canada* 24, (2013), pp. 71–113.
59. Cockburn, 'Punishment', pp. 171–172.
60. Rawlings, *Crime and Power*, p. 49.
61. Military executions are excluded here. They require separate treatment and followed a different pattern. Executions in Hyde Park were quite frequently reported—*Old England or the National Gazette*, 1 February 1752. The punishment of suicides' corpses is also excluded see: Radzinowicz, *A History*, 1, pp. 195–200; R. Houston, *Punishing the Dead? Suicide, Lordship and Community in Britain 1500–1830* (Oxford, 2010).
62. 2 & 3 William IV, c.75, and 4 & 5 William IV, c.26.
63. G. Durston, *Crime and Justice in Early Modern England: 1500–1750* (Chichester, 2004), p. 677.
64. W. Andrews, *Bygone Punishments* (London, 1899), p. 96.
65. Radzinowicz, *A History*, 1, p. 183.
66. Ibid., 1, pp. 223–224.
67. P. Spierenburg, 'The Body and the State; Early Modern Europe' in N. Morris and D. Rothman (eds.), *The Oxford History of the Prison; The Practice of Punishment in Western Society* (Oxford, 1995), p. 54.

68. Andrews, *Bygone Punishments*, pp. 106–107; Radzinowicz, *A History*, 1, pp. 238–239.
69. Durston, *Crime*, p. 688.
70. Radzinowicz, *A History*, 1, pp. 213–214; *Anon, The History of the Lives and Extraordinary Adventures of the Most Famous Pyrates, Highwaymen, Murderers* (Portsmouth, 1772); J. Louthian, *The Form of Process before the Court of Justiciary in Scotland* (Edinburgh, 1732), p. 238; Rachel Bennett's Leicester Ph.D. 2015 'Capital Punishment and the Criminal Corpse in Scotland 1740–1834' discusses several eighteenth-century examples—see her forthcoming Palgrave volume.
71. Evans, *Rituals*, pp. 27–86, 193–234; Spierenburg, *The Spectacle*; Friedland, *Seeing*; J. Ruff, *Violence in Early Modern Europe 1500–1800* (Cambridge, 2001), pp. 98–102.
72. On thirteenth-century evidence—S. Pegge in *Gentlemen's Magazine* (1789), pp. 65, 207–208; Radzinowicz, *A History*, 1, p. 213; Five Derbyshire offenders were gibbeted in 1341 alone. Until the later sixteenth century those condemned for particularly heinous premeditated murders might still be gibbeted alive. Andrews, *Bygone Punishments*, pp. 41–42, 74–78.
73. For a contemporary definition, *Gentlemen's Magazine* (1789), 65, p. 208.
74. Ibid., p. 208; On gibbeting alive as long disused by 1700—*Old England or The National Gazette*, 1 February 1752.
75. Radzinowicz, *A History*, 1, p. 214.
76. *Gentleman's Magazine*, 7 (1737), p. 187; *Country Journal*, 26 March 1736–1737.
77. D. Paton, 'Punishment, Crime and the Bodies of Slaves in Eighteenth-Century Jamaica' *Journal of Social History*, 31 (2001), pp. 931–939. Burning alive and the display of the severed heads, hands and quarters of slaves in public places also occurred in the American Colonies—S. Banner, *The Death Penalty: An American History* (Harvard, 2002), pp. 70–76.
78. Publicus in *London Magazine*, December 1746, p. 638; Philandros in *British Journal*, 2 April 1726. For pre-colonial aggravated death penalty rituals in Africa see S. Hind, 'Dismembering and Remembering the Body: Execution and Post-execution Display in Africa 1870–2000.' in Ward (ed.), *A Global History*, pp. 222–228.
79. A. Hartshorne, *Hanging in Chains* (New York, 1893), p. 71; J. Beattie, *Crime*, pp. 528–529.
80. Hartshorne, *Hanging*, p. 71.
81. Cockburn, 'Punishment', p. 160.
82. Durston, *Crime*, pp. 669–670; Andrews, *Bygone Punishments*, pp. 43–44; Hartshorne, *Hanging*, pp. 53–54.

83. *Post Man and the Historical Account*, 28 January 1696.
84. H. Misson, *Memoirs and Observations in his Travels over England* (London, 1719) recording journeys in 1697–1698.
85. On the Humber Admiralty Court's fifteenth-century use of gibbeting; Andrews, *Bygone Punishments*, pp. 3–4.
86. *Flying Post*, 13 July 1700.
87. *London Post with Intelligence Foreign and Domestic*, 19 July 1700.
88. R. Cavendish, 'Execution of Captain Kidd' *History Today*, 51 (May 2001) p. 53; Hartishorne, *Hanging*, pp. 53–71.
89. Hurren, *Dissecting*.
90. Anatomic knowledge was increasingly seen as an important component in surgeons' training: R. Porter, *Disease, Medicine and Society in England 1550–1860* (Cambridge, 1993), pp. 28–29.
91. R. Richardson, *Death*, pp. 32–35.
92. On seventeenth-century practice K. Cregan, 'Early Modern Anatomy and the Queen's Body Natural: The Sovereign Subject' *Body and Society*, 13 (2007), pp. 51–53.
93. J. Sawday, *The Body Emblazoned: Dissection and the Human Body in Renaissance Culture* (London, 1995), pp. 56–57.
94. Ibid., p. 56; *A Bill for … Providing a Remedy for the … College of Physicians in London to have the Bodies of Persons Executed for Felony* (London, 1720), p. 5.
95. Sawday, *The Body*, pp. 56–57; Cockburn, 'Punishment', p. 170.
96. J. Sharpe, *Crime in Early Modern England 1550–1750*, (London, 1984) p. 85.
97. Sawday, *The Body*, p. 57.
98. J. Cockburn, 'Punishment'; J. Sharpe, 'Last Dying Speeches: Religion, Ideology and Public Execution in Seventeenth-Century England' *Past and Present*, 107 (1985), p. 149.
99. Durston, *Crime*, 668; Beattie, *Crime*, p. 527.
100. Cregan, 'Early Modern', p. 63 argues the surgeons were not vigorously opposed until after 1660; P. Linebaugh, 'The Tyburn Riots Against the Surgeons' in D. Hay et al. (eds.) *Albion's Fatal Tree*, pp. 65–118.
101. T. Forbes, 'A Note on the Procurement of Bodies for Dissection at the Royal College of Physicians of London in 1694 and 1710' *Journal of the History of Medicine*, 1974, p. 334; on bodies being fought for to sell them on—Beattie, *Crime*, p. 527.
102. *Monthly Chronicle*, December 1729; *London Gazette*, 15 March, 13 September and 8 November 1729; *A Bill for … Providing*, pp. 5–7; Linebaugh, 'The Tyburn', p. 74.
103. Richardson, *Death*, pp. 33–34.

2

Debate on Aggravated Execution and the Origin of Murder Act

1 Introduction and Historiography

The majority of the small group of historians who have written on the history of capital punishment in the early-eighteenth century has given relatively little attention to those contemporaries who advocated increasing the severity of capital punishment and/or adding post-execution punishments to it. Leon Radzinowicz, for example, only refers to two pamphlets, the anonymous *Hanging Not Punishment Enough* (1701) and George Ollyffe's *Essay ... to Prevent Capital Crimes* (1731), which both advocated extreme forms of execution that also had elements of post-execution punishment inscribed within them, such as breaking on the wheel or gibbeting and starving to death. He then writes these ideas off as completely irrelevant because 'the system they devised was utterly foreign to the spirit of the English people and so foredoomed to failure'.[1] While rightly rejecting Radzinowicz's teleological framework, John Beattie also confined his discussion of this issue to these two pamphlets and two or three other pieces—most notably Nourse's comments published in 1700—and therefore provides only a preliminary analysis of contemporary ideas about the possibility of increasing the use of aggravated execution practices and/or post-execution punishment.[2] Randall McGowen's important work on 'The Problem of Punishment in Eighteenth-Century England' offers a more detailed exploration of the fluid range of penal ideas and proposals that were circulating in the first half of the century.[3] The three most common themes in these writings, he suggests, were dismay at the failure of the gallows, belief in the potential of imprisonment with hard labour and criticism of the negative effects of prisons as they were currently managed, but he also discusses the role played by aggravated forms of capital punishment.[4] By drawing on a handful of newspapers and monthly periodicals, as well as the pamphlets already referred to, McGowen provides a much more nuanced analysis of contemporary penal discourse, but within this he also tends to marginalize, or at the very least downplay, the possibility that in the first half of the eighteenth century aggravated forms of capital punishment were still a viable option, a real (if eventually rejected) penal policy alternative. His discussion of 'Hanging not Punishment Enough' and Ollyffe's 1731 pamphlet stresses their modest and apologetic tone, and concludes that they were 'scarcely ringing endorsements of severity'.[5] Moreover he does not include aggravated execution practices as one of the three common themes that regularly appeared in writings about punishment, arguing instead that these 'extreme and unusual measures' played a significant role only occasionally at moments of crisis or of frustration at the failure of current policies.[6] Through a detailed survey of the debates about post-execution punishment and aggravated execution policies that arose in the period between the mid-1690s and the end of March 1752—when the Murder Act was passed by Parliament—the analysis presented here aims to reassess the views of these historians by recovering and analysing the chronological rhythm of the debate, the extent of its impact and the changing forms of aggravated punishment that were most frequently advocated at different points. It then concludes by suggesting a different way of thinking about why the Murder Act was passed, which integrates the Act more fully within the overall history of the Bloody Code.

2 The Structure and Depth of Contemporary Discourse

The first important finding that emerges from the research presented here is the sheer depth of material that a survey of contemporary discourse can uncover, now that a reasonable proportion of eighteenth-century newspapers, periodicals and pamphlets can be keyword searched—a facility unavailable to earlier historians. The sources remain extremely patchy for a number of reasons. Surviving runs of newspapers and periodicals have many gaps. Many of the provincial (and some of the London) newspapers are still not available for online keyword searching and even when searches are possible they do not, of course, pick up all the relevant references.[7] Finally, it appears that not all the relevant pamphlets have survived. For example, the 'Register of Books Published in April 1733' printed in the *Gentleman's Magazine* included reference to a work that does not appear to have survived entitled *Some Reasons, in a Letter to a Member of Parliament, setting forth the Defect of our laws in the Punishment of Execrable Murders, and for Changing that of Hanging into something more Severe.* We may never know, therefore, what specific punishment this author advocated. However, even though we do not have access to all the relevant material, it is clear that a wide range of writings that included discussions of, and recommendations about, the introduction of post-execution and aggravated execution options were published between 1700 and 1752.

A total of twenty-nine different and separate pieces of published writing specifically advocating one or more forms of post-execution or aggravated pre-execution punishment for non-treasonable offences can be found in the pamphlets, periodicals and newspapers we were able to gain access to.[8] A further two advocated castration as an aggravated punishment for robbery, theft and rape. 'Tis an operation not without a suitable degree of pain, sometimes danger' one wrote, 'and perhaps Newgate would tremble more at the approach of such an execution than at the parade at Tyburn'. Many offenders, he argued, 'were more anxious about the safety of their bodies' than about death itself, for 'their bodies are themselves. The body relishes pleasure and enjoyment and is the only object of their concern'.[9] The other, which was reprinted several times, argued that 'since the pleasures of love, and the hope of issue are almost universal, no punishment can be invented that will have a deeper impression on the mind'. It then went on to point out (in a line of argument that drew widespread support in the later nineteenth century) that since 'Rapine and Theft, like Madness, very often run in the blood and … become Hereditary … this Law … by disabling a set of vile people from leaving their pernicious breed behind them' would be of great advantage. The punishment of castration could only be applied to males, of course, but it was thought it would also affect 'the female felons' because for them it would 'be a severe mortification to think that their husbands, lovers and friends may come under this punishment'.[10] These pamphlets have, however, been excluded from the sample analysed in detail here (Table 1) because, in theory at least, the punishment advocated did not include the execution of the convict, although death would not infrequently have followed its infliction.

Table 1 Types of aggravated execution and post-execution punishment advocated for murderers and property offenders between 1694 and 1752

Type of aggravated execution/Post-execution punishment positively advocated by writer	*Number*	*%*
A. *Major overall categories*		
Dissection of corpse post-execution	8	20
Breaking on the wheel	7	17
Lex Talionis (execution mirrors violence victim suffered)	7	17
Burning at stake (Whether dead or still alive)	6	15
Gibbeting (Alive or dead—different types)	7	17
Other aggravated forms	6	15
Total	41	
B. *Detailed sub-categories*		
Dissection of corpse post-execution	8	
Breaking on the wheel	7	
Lex Talionis (execution mirrors violence victim suffered)	7	
Burning at the stake: alive	4	
Gibbeting: Post-execution only	3	
Burning at the stake: after strangling	2	
Gibbeting: alive and starving to death	2	
Fed to the lions/tigers in the tower	2	
Gibbeting: alive after cords wound around arms/legs	1	
Gibbeting: alive after limbs broken	1	
Death on rack under weights (as in *Peine Fort et Dure*)	1	
Whipping to death	1	
Execution as if treason (disembowelled, beheaded, etc.)	1	
Death by bite from Mad Dog	1	
Total	41	

Sources see Note 8

The vast majority of these twenty-nine writers targeted either murderers or highway robbers, and a considerable number were aimed at both categories or at the overlap between them, that is, at extremely violent forms of robbery.[11] Nearly one-fifth extended their range to all capital felonies, one writer being particularly keen to include duelists.[12] In addition to these twenty-nine we also uncovered other pieces of writing that addressed this issue without directly recommending the adoption of one particular form of aggravated execution practice. In 1735, for example, the *Derby Mercury* published an article that simply asked 'the Legislature' to find 'some punishment more terrifying' than the gallows in order to prevent the frequent robberies currently being committed, while in 1750 several papers demanded that 'additional pain' be added to the execution process for 'the vindictive or cruel murderer'.[13] Other publications either briefly discussed one or more of the torment-based execution techniques used on the Continent only to then completely reject their use,[14] or described a new aggravated punishment idea without overtly recommending it. At the beginning of 1752, for example, an article describing a new French proposal—that murderers be hanged alive in chains for two days on bread and water and then have the hand 'with which the murder was committed' chopped off before being executed—was published just before the Murder Act was debated in Parliament—suggesting, but not explicitly declaring, that the writer wanted the legislature to consider such a policy.[15]

Overall therefore, once these other publications are included, around thirty-five separate interventions within the broader pre-Murder Act debate about penal policy and capital punishment involved positive discussions of aggravated execution procedures and/or post-execution punishment in relation to murderers or property offenders. Well over half of these were published either in newspapers or in well-known periodicals such as the *Gentleman's Magazine* and the *London Magazine*, which alone gave space to four substantial contributions. Only ten of the twenty-nine interventions that specifically advocated one of these policies were published in pamphlet form. Some of the works advocating aggravated execution procedures had well-known authors such as Mandeville, Ollyffe and Defoe, but most were anonymous or were written under pseudonyms such as Plain Truth, Publicus or Philandros, which can make it very difficult to trace the background of the writer. Many of these pieces of writing can be found in more than one publication, either because some provincial newspapers reprinted articles that had already been published in London-based journals or newspapers,[16] or because a rival periodical reprinted the original but then added a response.[17] Some of them were written specifically in reply to other writers, but although a denser set of interrelated debates did develop immediately before the Murder Act, on the whole discussions about execution policies, and about the role of aggravated or post-execution punishments within them, were fluid and multi-vocal rather than being well-structured debates.[18]

The publication dates of these writings were not distributed regularly across the period 1694–1752. Given the fact that the first half of the eighteenth century witnessed a large increase in the number of outlets available for those who wished to publish their thoughts on penal policy, it is not surprising that our survey of the first half of the period (1700–1726) has yielded only six discussions advocating forms of aggravated execution or post-execution punishment, or that thirteen of the twenty-nine pro-severity publications we have identified were published in the two-and-a-half years immediately before the Murder Act. However, on closer inspection it becomes clear that these publications were mainly clustered into three groups of years, all of which coincided with periods of acute anxiety about crime in general, and about violent robbery and murder in particular, that is, 1694–1701, the 1730s (especially the period 1733–1736) and the final three years before the Murder Act. Nearly 80% of these writings were published during these periods, the remaining 20% being printed during two other brief windows of time, that is, 1725–1728 and 1744–1746.

Although Britain spent almost as many years at war as at peace between 1690 and 1752, all but one of these peak periods of debate occurred in peacetime, and there were good reasons for this. Post-war demobilization flooded the capital's labour market and brought home many of the marginal, and sometimes violent, young men who were swept off the streets and sent to fight overseas during every wartime period. This meant that, as Beattie has pointed out, 'peace abroad was commonly accompanied by violence at home'.[19] Indictment rates rose rapidly in each of these periods and the burgeoning London press, short of news now that the wars were over, tended to fuel the resulting fears by publishing increasing numbers of stories about murders, violent robberies, burglaries and other crimes.[20] Very occasionally the press also managed to create one of these moral panics about violent street crime during wartime, as Richard Ward's excellent article on the London crime wave of 1744 has recently shown, and as a result 1744–1746 was the only wartime period that witnessed the publication of even a small cluster of articles advocating aggravated execution policies.[21] Publications recommending, and often demanding, the introduction of new aggravated execution policies and post-execution punishments were not randomly distributed but came in clusters during key periods of anxiety about crime, when the existing capital punishment system was clearly perceived to be failing in its main role—as a deterrent against violent property crime and murder.

Many of the pamphlets and articles published in these key periods pinpointed the same three basic problems before going on to describe the different aggravated execution policies they wished to implement in order to solve them. A considerable number began by highlighting 'the lamentable increase of highwaymen and house-breakers among us', and emphasized that the use of lethal violence was on the increase by stressing that 'murders and robberies have been of late more frequent than has been known in the memory of man', or that 'the roads … swarm with thieves, and not only robberies, but murthers are more frequent than they were ever … before'.[22] Several of these publications then went on to argue vehemently that 'even the gallows cannot terrify' and therefore that the capital punishment system as it currently stood was simply not working.[23] 'Daily experience shows us' a correspondent of *Wye's Letter* argued, 'that hanging only signifies nothing, therefore the law in that particular is frustrated, and should be amended, as most laws are when they are found not to answer the ends intended'.[24] Thirdly, many of the contributors to the debate were concerned that the same punishment—death by hanging—was being given to very dissimilar crimes, 'there not being the least additional pain, or mark of infamy, to distinguish the vindictive or cruel murderer from the necessitous thief',—a theme we will discuss in more detail at the end of this chapter.[25]

As the number of executions rose rapidly in these key periods in response to rising indictments levels for robbery and violent crime, the sense that hanging was not working and that it was being used in an undifferentiated manner against too wide a range of crimes clearly increased. This in turn stimulated a wide variety of penal proposals. Some of these schemes tried to find suitably tough or terrifying non-capital punishments such as imprisonment with hard labour, work in dockyards or in public chain gangs, or tougher variations on the theme of transportation such as lifetime sentences to the galleys.[26] Others, by contrast, proposed keeping capital punishment but increasing the pain of execution, or the level of post-execution exposure of the corpse (and sometimes the amounts of time that both of these would be have to be endured) by advocating punishments such as breaking on the wheel, burning alive or starving to death on the gibbet. Because many of the proposals based on non-capital punishment options were adopted either during this period or after it, and became the core sanctions on which penal policy was based in the eighteenth and nineteenth centuries,[27] the writings that advocated them have received considerable attention from historians. The same is not true, however, for those publications that foregrounded ideas about aggravated and post-execution punishments. The implicit assumption that they were never serious possibilities because (with one or two exceptions) they were not eventually adopted by Parliament needs to be seriously questioned.[28] Those who felt that the condemned should either 'be made to feel himself die'[29] and/or face the prospect of his corpse being subjected to further humiliations after his death, put forward a range of proposals that appealed to a variety of audiences. When we look at the nature of these proposals, and at the particular sub-groups of aggravated execution and post-execution punishments that were advocated in each of the key periods between the end of the seventeenth century and the Murder Act, it becomes clear that these issues played a very significant part in contemporary penal debates.

3 The Types of Aggravated Execution and Post-execution Punishments Advocated

At least fourteen different types of aggravated execution and/or post-execution punishments found support in the twenty-nine writings we have identified (Table 1). Several of the writers who advocated increasing the severity of capital punishment wanted more than one new punishment introduced; Table 1 lists forty-one positive suggestions. However, the count presented in Table 1 excludes the negative references within these twenty-nine writings, several of which not only recommended a particular option or options, but also argued that other potential aggravated punishments should definitely not be introduced.[30] In these twenty-nine writings negative expressions were considerably outnumbered by positive recommendations but at least one policy option, breaking on the wheel, was so controversial that it attracted as many critical comments as it did recommendations. Nearly half of the fourteen forms of aggravated execution or post-execution punishments suggested in these writings between 1700 and 1752 were only mentioned once (Table 1) and a number of these involved highly exceptional methods of increasing the pain of capital punishment that do not appear to have gained much support from contemporaries. Two of the suggested options involved using animals to effect the punishment. One option (which achieved two recommendations) recommended that murderers be 'thrust bound hand and feet into the den of their kindred savages … the lions or tygers kept in the Tower', while the other proposed subjecting them to the bite of a mad dog—both of which would have resulted in a particularly painful death even by the high standards set by contemporary execution practices on the continent.[31] Another isolated proposal 'whipping them to death' built on an already existing punishment for felony and one which, when it was used by the army courts (where sentences of 1000 lashes were sometimes passed) could occasionally end in the death of the offender.[32] Two of the other options that were mentioned in only a single publication involved extending to murderers existing forms of execution that were particularly severe, but which were normally reserved for much more specific categories of offender. One pamphlet proposed that murder should be redefined as high treason.[33] The other, having pointed out that it was incorrect to say that 'our laws are strangers to tortures … for in the case of high treason you are to be emboweled being alive',[34] went on to mobilize a different tradition of torture by recommending that murderers should be subjected to *Peine Fort et Dure*, the punishment used by the courts when an offender refused to plead. This involved putting the prisoner on the 'equivalent to a rack' and then loading him with a huge weight of irons until he died.[35]

Almost all the remaining forms of aggravated or post-execution punishment found in these publications were mentioned several times and seem to have played a significant role in the debates about capital punishment during at least one of the periods we have listed. All but one of these forms clustered around a small group of fairly broad categories of punishments that were defined and visualized through their association with a particular specific mechanism/location: the wheel, the stake, the gibbet and the surgeon's table. The exception was discussed under the title *Lex Talionis*[36] and was based on a principle rather than a process, that is, on the retaliatory idea that violent offenders should suffer on their own bodies, before death, the same violent blows and pain at the hands of the executioner that they had inflicted on their victims.[37] 'Notorious robbers who desperately wound the persons they rob' were the main group targeted by most of the writers who favoured *Lex Talionis.*[38] One recommended very specifically that these severe retaliatory injuries should be inflicted well before the condemned was executed, and that they then 'be taken proper care of till their wounds are nearly healed and then hanged'.[39] Another wanted to confine *Lex Talionis* to those found guilty of premeditated murder, partly on the grounds of retribution, that is, that 'excess should be repaid with excess'. However, he also rather optimistically believed that forcing the condemned through the 'same process of pain and horror' as the victim would have a preventative role, because 'the deliberating villain, designing the murderous blow, would from a sudden recollection that he might afterwards feel the same painful stroke … stay his hand in the work of horror'.[40] Two of the authors recommending this punishment also suggested an alternative non-capital but extremely agonizing punishment—cutting off the hands of the prisoner—on the grounds that the offender's associates 'might be more awed by such an example ... than by an execution at Tyburn'.[41] It is worth noting at this point that all these three writings, along with another *Gentleman's Magazine* article (excluded from Table 1 because it advocated a non-capital sanction), which recommended the castration of all capital convicts, were not, as we might expect, published at the very beginning of the eighteenth century. Six out of the seven publications recommending *Lex Talionis* came out between 1744 and 1752—a clear indication of the survival right up to the Murder Act of writers willing to advocate punishments involving severe 'additions of torment' and 'a suitable degree of pain'.[42]

Directly retaliatory punishment apart, the options widely discussed in these pamphlets fell into six significant groups (Table 1). Dissection, breaking on the wheel, burning alive at the stake, burning after strangulation, gibbeting alive (with or without previous breaking/twisting of limbs) and gibbeting after hanging. All of these involved an element of post-execution punishment. Three of them, which between them constituted about one-third of all recommendations in Table 1, were simply and only post-execution punishments. Dissection was never performed (deliberately at least) on the living, while gibbeting after death by hanging and burning after strangulation were both punishments of the criminal corpse alone. However, the other three options, though they involved the infliction of pain on the condemned whilst they were still living, also had important elements of post-execution punishment written into them. Breaking on the wheel was usually designed to end with the long-term placement of the offender's corpse on a wheel in a public and highly visible place (often similar in location to the places where English offenders were gibbeted).[43] Burning alive ended in the complete obliteration of the criminal corpse, which some regarded as the ultimate post-execution punishment, and gibbeting alive was usually followed by the continued exposure of the criminal's corpse in chains after death. Almost all the main forms of aggravated execution advocated in the first half of the eighteenth century therefore had important consequences for, and tried to mobilize the power of, the criminal corpse. The role of the post-execution journey of the criminal's body was by no means always given centre stage in debates about increasing the severity of capital punishment, but with the exception of the discussions on *Lex Talionis* at mid-century, post-execution punishment was always a significant element whenever any of the other alternatives was discussed.

Dissection was the most popular aggravated execution option between 1700 and 1752, being recommended in eight of the twenty-nine publications we have identified (Table 1). Breaking on the wheel was recommended by seven different writers, while six argued for the introduction of burning at the stake (only two of whom wanted the condemned strangled first). Gibbeting alive (with or without the condemned being previously subjected to the breaking or twisting of limbs) was recommended four times and gibbeting after execution three. Although the vast majority of these proposals were based on similar foundational assumptions about the inadequacy of the existing capital punishment system and its failure to deter or to differentiate between offenders, some were also justified by more individual rationales.

Sending the prisoner's corpse to the surgeons for either public or private anatomization and dissection immediately after they had been executed was virtually the only option that was popular for both penal and non-penal (i.e. medical) reasons. Based in part on their belief in 'the superstitious Reverence of the vulgar for a corpse, even of a malefactor, and the strong aversion they have against dissecting them',[44] several commentators saw post-execution dissection as a very useful penal option. 'Death itself is hardly more terrible to the minds of criminals, than the apprehensions of being dissected', one suggested in 1733 'so were the bodies of all executed felons made liable for dissection, it would reduce the number of felons'.[45] Rather than confining this punishment only to murderers, some writers also recommended that 'every felon that shall be hanged at Tyburn' be then 'carried from thence to Surgeons Hall'.[46] This was true throughout the first half of the eighteenth century. In 1750 an article in the *London Magazine* recommended 'that all the bodies of executed criminals be given to the surgeons: because the generality of mankind have a great aversion to being anatomized: nay to many it is more terrible than death'. It then went on to point out that, 'by this means Surgeon's Hall will always be well supplied, without any need of robbing church yards'.[47]

Several other pamphlets were also concerned about the supply problems that the rapid development of anatomy was generating. The limited number of criminal corpses officially made available may previously have been adequate 'in that infant state of the chirurgical art', one writer argued, but 'the number of surgeons is so much increased, and the art itself arrived at so great a degree of perfection' that this was no longer the case. There were 'at least five or six lectures in anatomy read every night in the winter season' and every lecturer needed 'to be furnished with at least one fresh body a week'.[48] Some publications also showed an awareness of the problems that might be encountered in allocating criminals' cadavers between different groups of surgeons. One writer suggested that once the bodies reached Surgeons Hall, 'proper persons' should then distribute them 'among those gentlemen who are then reading anatomical lectures'.[49] Another recommended that the bodies of all 'doom'd to the gallows ... shall be liable to be purchased by any surgeon: That after the Surgeon's Company have chosen the body allowed them by law, any private surgeon shall be at liberty to purchase any other he shall pitch upon; paying twenty shillings, and that the first bidder, according to a register book kept for that purpose, be the buyer'. This writer then took the commodification of the criminal corpse to new heights by suggesting that if the relations of the hanged were willing to pay £5, they would be allowed instead to 'bury them themselves'.[50] The extent to which these writings were influenced by pressure from the surgeons, or even written in one or two cases by them, is difficult to determine. It is interesting, however, that one pamphlet, having recommended that all felons be anatomized, then went on to suggest that 'the governors of all the respective hospitals in England may be empowered to appropriate as many of the patients, who shall die in such respective hospitals, as they shall judge sufficient, for the service of the surgeons who belong thereto'—a policy that was only fully implemented in the nineteenth century.[51] Many of the advocates of dissection clearly understood the problems being experienced by the various institutions and private practitioners involved in the rapidly growing practice of anatomy, and in advocating that the bodies of all felons be subjected to dissection they would have known that this policy would make large number of corpses available. In the 1750s an average of thirty offenders a year went to the gallows in London and in peacetime crisis years such as 1749–1752 more than fifty a year were hanged.[52] Many of the writers who argued strongly for the potential effectiveness of dissection as a penal measure clearly also had in mind the potentially positive impact of such a policy on the supply of corpses.

In the first half of the eighteenth century dissection attracted hardly any direct critics as a potential means of aggravating the execution process, but the same was not true for the second most widely advocated option—breaking on the wheel. In Holland, France and Germany as well as elsewhere in North-Western Europe breaking on the wheel was the standard form of prolonged death penalty used during this period. It usually involved the convict being tied to a wheel or wooden cross-section with all his limbs exposed and then having each of them broken in turn with an iron bar by the hangman. Once he was dead, the corpse was usually then taken to the city's 'gallows field' where it was permanently displayed on a wheel.[53] Although the immense pain this process generated could be largely avoided by starting from the top, as it were, with blows to the heart or head, it was often effected from below so that the convict remained alive until the very end of the process, which was sometimes deliberately prolonged to increase the torment.[54] The nature of this punishment was fairly well known in England being described in many pamphlets, accounts of journeys abroad and newspaper reports from the continent.[55] Recommended by Ollyffe for the 'exquisite agonies' and the almost 'unconceivable torture' it involved, breaking on the wheel was popular with a number of writers as the most obvious and well-tried way to create pain in such 'an intense degree' that would be 'so terrifying' that it would dissuade others from offending.[56] 'Breaking on the wheel has been found in other countries to be the best expedient to diminish the number of malefactors', Nourse observed. 'Tis true this sort of punishment carries the face of cruelty … a man's bones are broken to pieces, and his nerves and sinews beaten to a pulp, which must needs be very dolorous and … very grievous to him'. However, robberies were said to have been reduced by 90% since its introduction in France, and fear of ending up 'in the same place of torment' was therefore thought to be effective 'in the prevention of the like offences'.[57] If they only faced a simple hanging some offenders might 'go fearless and ranting to the gallows, not in the least concerned at the approach of death', but 'they would hardly do so were they carrying to the wheel, where the pains of death would be so often repeated, before they would expire'.[58] This punishment was seen as a particularly appropriate response when offenders were thought to be showing 'a growing proneness to cruelty'[59] and, as we will see, it was still being widely proposed as a punishment for murder in the run up to the Murder Act.[60]

Opposition to breaking on the wheel was often strong, however. Some critics simply argued that the customs of the English would not stomach such punishments, quietly ignoring in doing so the fact that breaking on the wheel had occasionally been used against murderers in late-sixteenth and early-seventeenth-century Scotland.[61] 'Breaking on the wheel and other like torturing deaths, common in other Christian countries, the English look upon as too cruel to be used by the Professors of Christianity', Edward Chamberlayne wrote in *The Present State of Great Britain* in 1735.[62] Other writers argued more pragmatically that the negative effects outweighed the positive ones. 'In those countries where the breaking on the wheel is the form of execution, robberies are not so frequent but seldom or never committed without murder', one writer argued in 1726.[63] Twenty years later the author of a long article published in two prominent journals, while admitting reluctantly that there might be some justification for 'breaking on the wheel and other horrible executions' if they deterred 'others from committing the like crimes', argued that such spectacles of 'barbarity' would undermine the sensibilities of the audience, making them too familiar with violence and therefore more likely to accept its use.[64]

The third option—burning the condemned at the stake—although it also mirrored continental practice, may have appeared as a less radical departure because it had strong precedents in England. Until 1791 women accused of acts defined as petty treason (such as coining or the murder of a husband or master) could still be burnt at the stake and some writers wanted not only to extend the use of this punishment to thieves or murderers but also to make it much more painful by forbidding the executioner from following the customary practice of strangling the convict before burning her. After agreeing that it was only 'reasonable' that women burnt at the stake for coining 'are strangled first', the author of *Street Robberies Considered* (almost certainly Daniel Defoe) went on to advocate that 'in the case of Murder, both Male and Female should be burnt alive', because 'the fear of such dreadful punishments would correct the vicious minds, and make them less criminal'.[65] Hanging was 'too mild' for 'crimes of the blackest dye', the writer argued, and this was echoed ten years later by the author of a 'Scheme for Burning Malefactors at a Stake'. 'Even the gallows cannot terrify', he argued. 'A death without pain, or seeming pain, cannot be presumed to deter such people: moreover the many attempts of late to evade the cord, prove they do not believe it inevitably fatal. All hopes of evasion would be taken away by the awful stake; a punishment known to our laws, and not thought too severe for the softer sex.' In order to differentiate between crimes, he then went on to suggest that thieves who had not shed blood 'might be strangled' first, but that murderers should 'expiate their crimes in flames'.[66] The increasingly 'shocking barbarities' being committed by highway robbers caused another writer to argue that burning alive should be extended to some property offenders. Such offenders 'undoubtedly deserve a severer death than bare hanging', he argued, 'and methinks that burning alive or breaking upon the wheel, would not be at this juncture unseasonable'.[67]

The two pamphlets that advocated gibbeting the condemned whilst still alive and then starving them to death also recommended breaking on the wheel as another appropriate punishment. To the author of *Hanging not Punishment Enough* these two torment-based execution practices offered a finely graded method of dealing with murderers, highwaymen and arsonists. 'If hanging will not restrain them', he wrote, 'hanging them in chains and starving them, or (if murderers and robbers at the same time, or night-incendiaries) breaking them on the wheel', certainly would. Ollyffe, after rejecting burning as a 'quick dispatch', went on to suggest three different types of gibbeting, as well as breaking on the wheel, as particularly useful ways of creating 'lingering and terrifying torment'. Having pointed out that the 'ancient method of hanging such alive on gibbets till starved to death … could not fail of raising a suitable terror', he went on to advocate policies that mixed this option with other elements reminiscent of continental practice. 'Twisting a little cord hard about their arms and legs, which would particularly affect the nerves and sinews and the most sensible parts to produce the keenest anguish', was suggested as a prelude to fixing them on a gibbet within hearing distance of the highway, as was setting them 'on a gibbet in the like manner with their limbs broken'.[68]

Neither of these writers actively advocated the obvious, and less painful, alternative to these policies, that is, gibbeting the condemned person's corpse only after his execution. However, since (as we saw in Chap. 1) this policy was already being quite extensively used against particularly heinous male offenders, they did not need to advocate its use and their silence cannot therefore be automatically read as disapproval. The relative lack of writings suggesting a more extensive use of post-execution gibbeting may reflect a similar sense that, since the policy had already been adopted by the authorities, it did not need to be discussed. Only three of our twenty-nine writers explicitly indicated a positive attitude to hanging the offender's corpse in chains after execution, and one of these, who focused on murderers alone, was more descriptive than openly advocatory. Having contrasted the 'mild and gentle' approach of the English law with 'the most exquisite torments' inflicted on murderers elsewhere, the author noted that even in England the bodies of many murderers were 'denied even the burial of a Christian; and … exposed a prey to the ravenous birds of the air'. This he noted (apparently with approval) meant that 'his infamy is preserved as long as nature will admit, a gibbet exposes him as a terrible example to others, and he becomes the monument of his own shame, and of that of all his relations'.[69] Another article, which focused on the punishment of street robbers, contained a much more overt recommendation that this option be used. 'To let all their bodies remain upon the gallows in the manner they are hanged ... would be a perpetual memorandum of the dreadful consequences that attend such pursuits', it argued. 'Nothing is more terrible, even to these profligate men, than to be denied decent interment ... how very careful they appear that the dead may not be deprived of funeral rites'.[70] However, even though post-execution gibbeting had its advocates, it is difficult not to read the many demands for more 'tormenting' forms of execution that can be found in the majority of these twenty-nine writings as implicit critiques of this already existing practice. Indeed, at least one writer explicitly made this link as part of a broader critique of the policy of gibbeting after execution. 'What signifies hanging in chains after the breath is out of the body? As it gives no pain, it gives very little concern', he observed in 1752. 'In other countries ... executions are less frequent than with us; because when they punish they do it with great severity'.[71] Henry Fielding was also critical of gibbeting. In the *Covent Garden Journal* he told a fictional story of a man's conversation with a friend while visiting the latter's garden, where the fruit had been devastated by blackbirds. 'I have endeavoured all I can to prevent it ... I have hung up the carcasses of several of them in terrorem and you see the clacker there that the wind turns round all day long', his friend told him. 'It is visible enough', the main character replied, 'and so are four or five blackbirds, the wickedest of all felons who are playing just by it'.[72] This fictional account was probably given extra resonance by newspaper reports that described crimes committed within sight of the corpses of criminals still hanging in chains. *The London Journal*, for example, reported that a highwayman had robbed a coach 'just by the gibbet on Highgate road; one would have thought the remains of the two pendant criminals there should have struck some terror ... but it proved otherwise'.[73] Four years later another paper expressed equal surprise that despite the diligence of the Post-Master General, who had made sure that nine offenders were currently hanging in chains, others still attempted 'to rob the mails' even when 'there are so many dreadful objects in view'.[74] Despite the fact that post-execution gibbeting was the most widely used method of adding further sanctions to the execution process in the first half of the eighteenth century,[75] its efficacy was by no means universally accepted.

4 The Key Periods of Debate

Although a wide spectrum of aggravated and post-execution punishments can be found in the printed literature throughout the whole period from the late 1690s to 1752, the three key periods of debate—1694–1701, the 1730s and the two-and-a-half years before 1752—each exhibited their own particular mix of suggested penal measures. However, although there was a gradual increase in the advocacy of the post-execution punishment of dissection, this should not be allowed to obscure the fact that in all three of these periods the possibility of introducing new and more tortuous forms of execution was seriously debated not only in print but also in Parliament.

The first period when heightened anxiety about violent crime and robbery led to extensive discussions on these lines began in the mid-1690s and ended in 1702 when large-scale remobilization and a rapid fall in male indictment rates temporarily reduced the perceived need for changes in penal policy. In the mid-1690s the distress caused by harvest failures, the coinage crisis and wartime trade disruptions had been accompanied by rising crime rates in London, even though the wartime recruitment of many young men usually reduced indictment levels.[76] When peace returned in 1697 large numbers of soldiers and sailors were demobilized in London and the number of males accused of property crimes, nearly doubled reaching a peak in 1699–1700.[77] As alarming reports of robberies and violence multiplied rapidly, both contemporary writings and the limited parliamentary records that have come down to us indicate that a growing debate developed about how these offences should be prevented and punished. Facilitated, and in part stimulated, by the new regularity of parliamentary sessions after 1689,[78] discussions about capital punishment began to gain momentum.[79] As early as 1694 Parliament appointed a committee to consider the law on highway robbery[80] and in 1695 the House of Commons set up two separate committees to make the laws against highway robbery 'more effectual', as well as receiving a petition and further policy suggestions from two London citizens, which stressed that 'the frequent robberies' were a 'great grievance'.[81] Printed comments by contemporaries are relatively difficult to find at this point but at least one pamphlet published in 1695 directly addressed this issue. After arguing that hanging held 'little terror' because it was thought by offenders to be 'a most easie [sic] death', the writer called for either 'sharper deaths and more solemn' or 'loss of liberty by … perpetual imprisonment'.[82]Another pamphlet written by the Kent M.P William Brockman, but surviving only in manuscript, suggested that the corpses of highwaymen should be hung in chains near the scene of the robbery 'for a terrour', but this relatively mild solution was soon superseded.[83]

The further rise in robbery prosecutions and male property crime indictments that accompanied demobilization in 1697–1698, produced both another parliamentary debate and two important published writings (one of which was expressly addressed to the two Houses of Parliament) advocating much more painful forms of execution practice. A bill for 'the more effectual prevention of robberies and punishing such as shall be convicted' was considered by both Houses, was referred to two separate committees, and was subjected to various detailed amendments and debates in 1697–1698. We do not know precisely what was being proposed, because, although the bill got at least as far as a second reading, it failed to become law.[84] However it is interesting to note that at almost exactly the same moment Timothy Nourse was advocating in print that the law was 'too merciful' in punishing highway robbers and murderers, and recommending breaking on the wheel as a means of recreating the gallows as a 'place of torment'.[85] As robbery prosecutions and reports peaked in 1700–1701, Parliament was then directly addressed by another pamphlet —*Hanging Not Punishment Enough*—which advocated not only breaking on the wheel but also starving to death in chains and whipping to death, on the grounds that 'no argument will be so cogent as pain in an intense degree'.[86] We have no record of the content of the Parliamentary debates of the years 1694–1702, although it is clear from the *House of Commons Journals* that bills were written, committees appointed and amendments much discussed. However, it is more than possible that these pamphlets, which argued cogently for aggravated forms of execution designed to ensure that 'the pain' would 'much outbid the pleasure',[87] played a substantial part in these debates. The justification advanced at this point for greater severity—that 'any community may secure itself, as best it can, without the imputation of cruelty'[88] would almost certainly have overcome the scruples some MPs might have had about such policies. Branding the forehead, another policy advocated in these pamphlets, was actually introduced in 1699 and not repealed until 1706.[89] At the high point of anxieties about rising violence in the late 1690s extreme measures that might have introduced 'different sorts of death for different crimes'[90] were almost certainly discussed and may have come close to receiving Parliamentary sanction.

In the aftermath of the next demobilization crisis in 1714 mushrooming crime rates generated further debate, which centered mainly on the need for an effective non-capital sanction and resulted in the Transportation Act of 1717.[91] After this was passed transportation rapidly became the major punishment for most felonies,[92] but it was not long before it too came under serious scrutiny. Within a few years metropolitan magistrates were complaining that transportation was not working and that many transported convicts were quickly making their way back to Britain.[93] Three pamphlets published in 1725–1728, a period of particularly acute anxiety about violent robberies, not only criticized transportation as ineffectual and easily undermined, but also suggested the need for new additions to the current form of death penalty.[94] However, only one of these three writers was prepared to advocate adding torment to the execution process itself and his suggestion—that both male and female offenders be 'burned alive'—was confined to cases of involving murder'.[95] The other two whilst acknowledging that 'tortures have been mentioned by many as the surest means to extirpate these criminals' both confined themselves to suggesting the introduction of post-execution punishments. One advocated hanging street robbers in chains 'as a perpetual memorandum' while the other made the first detailed case for dissection on the grounds that it would not only put offenders in fear but also 'encourage the improvement of ... Surgery'.[96]

In contrast to the period 1725–1728, however, in the second major period of debate about the need to add further punishments to the execution process, the years 1731–1738, only one of the seven publications advocated post-execution punishment alone. Although this pamphlet did contain the first detailed plan to introduce the dissection of all capital offenders and to organize the distribution of the resulting cadavers amongst London's surgeons,[97] it was the exception. Almost all those who demanded that further punishment be added to the hanging process wanted to ensure that the convict 'felt his death'. Burning alive at 'the awful stake' and the equally cruel procedure of breaking on the wheel were each advocated by three of the seven writers,[98] while gibbeting alive, *Lex Talionis* and 'bringing the rack among us' by the introduction of pressing to death also received the backing of at least one writer.[99] The substantial wave of writings published in 1730s clearly focused almost entirely on ways to make the execution process more of a torment for the condemned.

Since many of those writings were addressed directly to Parliament or to individual MPs, it is not surprising that there is considerable evidence that Parliament was debating these issues during the 1730s. By that time male indictment rates for violent property crime had been at a very high level for nearly two decades, drawing the government into various policing and rewards-based initiatives.[100] In the early 1730s, however, fears of violent crime and the increasing space it was given in the newspapers, the *Old Bailey Sessions Papers* and a series of pamphlets had clearly sparked a broader debate not just about the prevention of violent property crime but also about the ways in which it was being punished.[101] A deep unease was already evident in 1731, the year in which Defoe observed that street robbery had grown to such a height that 'the cry against it is universal' and in which Ollyffe wrote his detailed pamphlet advocating a variety of torment-based execution methods.[102] By 1733 this wave of anxiety seems to have been reaching a climax. The newspapers reported that robberies were so frequent that travelling about the city was highly dangerous,[103] and after describing in considerable detail two robberies involving the murder of four victims, the *Gentleman's Magazine* published lengthy 'reflections' engendered by the 'barbarous murders lately committed'.[104] These fears led to pressure on Parliament to increase the severity of the capital code, which came to a head between March and May 1733. The House of Commons journals contain a series of references to 'a committee of the whole house to consider the laws in being with respect to the punishment of criminals and how the same can be made more effectual', and although those journals offer no evidence about the length or content of these debates,[105] there was a clear expectation in the newspapers and pamphlets of these months that aggravated forms of the death penalty were being given serious consideration. The first of these publications, which came out on 21st March, the day after the Parliamentary committee was first appointed, made the context very clear. 'There being a bill now depending in the House of Commons, to consider the laws … with respect to the punishment of criminals, it is thought proper to offer the following observations to the considerations of that Honourable House. The roads … swarm with thieves, and not only robberies, but murders are more frequent than were ever known before'. Execution alone, the author then argued, was clearly not working and 'the bodies of all executed felons' should therefore be 'made liable to dissection' in order to suppress crime and 'effectually supply the demands of our surgeons'.[106] The debate grew more intense in April both in Parliament and in the press. On the 10th April the newspapers noted that the House of Commons was about to receive the report of the committee for rendering the law more effectual against criminals and a week later the *Derby Mercury* noted that 'several schemes have also been printed on the punishment of criminals'.[107] The publication of at least three pamphlets on this subject was announced in the press during that month and although the text of only one of these appears to have survived the title of another—*Some Reasons, in a Letter to a Member of Parliament, setting forth the Defect of our laws in the Punishment of Execrable Murders, and for Changing that of Hanging into something more Severe*—suggests that it almost certainly advocated the introduction of more aggravated forms of the death penalty.[108] The surviving pamphlet, which was addressed to an MP, and which various newspapers announced was 'just published' on 26th April—the day before Parliament was again due to consider the issue—argued that 'Hanging only signifies nothing', and that in view of 'the many fierce and bloody assassins infesting our streets' it was necessary to ignore those who 'say tis inhuman to punish one of our own species in so tormenting a way' and introduce the torture-based punishment of pressing offenders to death.[109]

The debates of 1733 did not result in an Act of Parliament, nor has it been possible to trace the bill referred to in the newspaper reports.[110] The impact both of the pamphlets published in the early months of 1733 and of Ollyffe's 1731 demand for offenders to 'feel their death' is therefore impossible to measure. However, the introduction of aggravated execution methods was clearly discussed by Parliament that year. Nor did the issue then disappear. In April 1735 it was reported that since robberies remained frequent both in London and 'in distant parts' of the country, 'tis talked the Legislature will take cognizance of these proceedings, in order, by some punishment more terrifying to put a stop to them',[111] and these demands seem to have grown stronger as the year progressed. In August another newspaper argued that 'nothing but severity remains, such severity as may be felt',[112] and in early December 1735 it was announced that 'three different proposals are now before the Ministry for a law to be enacted by Parliament for altering the punishment of persons guilty of murder, burglary and other robberies'.[113] Another report published later that month made it clear, moreover, that at least one of those proposals involved the introduction of aggravated forms of the death penalty. 'Tis thought', it noted, 'it will be proposed to Parliament next Sessions to punish Murder, Robbery, Sodomy and other offences of the blackest Dye, with burning or breaking on the wheel, instead of hanging, a death which hardened villains perfectly laugh at'.[114] Having pointed out that 'all other nations' used aggravated punishments, 'the Dutch have their *Lex Talionis*, the wheel, the gallows, the sword; the French, Germans etc. have the St Andrew's cross, hot pincers, scalping; … the Spaniards have all these …' another 1735 writer went on to propose 'to the consideration of the Legislature' both the introduction of *Lex Talionis* for violent robbers and that murderers be fed to 'the Lions or Tygers kept in the Tower'.[115] However, despite further demands in 1736 that 'steps be taken next Session of Parliament' to introduce 'burning alive or breaking on the wheel',[116] there is no evidence that these writers succeeded in persuading Parliament to introduce a bill incorporating any of these aggravated punishments in either 1735 or 1736. Reflecting later on this recent period when the punishment of crimes was 'ordered by the House of Commons to be taken into consideration' one 1738 writer suggested that 'the just fear of verging to cruelty … prevented any resolution being taken',[117] but despite these fears various writers continued to advocate aggravated forms of the death penalty right up to the passing of the Murder Act.

During the brief crime panic of the mid-1740s[118] the balance between the advocacy of aggravated pre-execution practices and that of post-execution punishments changed in favour of the latter. Two of the three writers who published demands for the introduction of more severe forms of the death penalty in the period 1744–1746 advocated dissection as the best solution and specifically rejected breaking on the wheel.[119] However, in the next period of major debate—from the beginning of 1750 until the passing of the Murder Act in late March 1752—only four of the thirteen pamphlets, newspaper articles and brief indirect reports about discussions in Parliament that we have traced involved dissection.[120] The majority of the fourteen recommendations contained in these thirteen writings still involved aggravated pre-execution practices rather than post-execution punishments. Four advocated some form of *Lex Talionis*, two wanted the introduction of breaking on the wheel, one argued for death via the bite of a mad dog and another suggested that the punishments inflicted for high treason be extended to all murderers.[121] Growing fears about a particular kind of murder—parricide –prompted the suggestion that the punishment for petty treason (burning at the stake) be extended to it,[122] while only one writer advocated gibbetting after hanging.[123] The fact that the Murder Act only incorporated the two post-execution options of dissection and gibbetting does not therefore mean that other more severe policies were not still being powerfully advocated in the mid-eighteenth century.

5 The Making of the Murder Act

Unlike the extensive debates about pre-execution practices that took place in the years 1697–1701 and 1733–1736, the three years of debate leading up the 1752 Murder Act have been quite extensively discussed by historians. Since Richard Ward has recently written an excellent summary of both the historiography and of the main background elements that led to the Murder Act,[124] these will only be briefly summarized here. The coming of peace in 1748 and the consequent rise in recorded crime and especially in violent robbery formed the background. By 1751 anxieties had reached such a level that the King's annual speech to Parliament highlighted both the alarming growth of crime in London and the need for government action. In response the Commons rapidly set up a 'felonies' committee to look into the law relating to felony.[125] This began a period of extensive scrutiny by the legislature that initially focused on bills relating to issues not directly related to capital punishment—disorderly houses, pawn-broking and the possibility of using hard labour on the Thames as a sentencing option.[126] However, on the 10 February 1752 the Commons suddenly focused on capital punishment in relation to murder and ordered two MPs to bring in a bill 'for the better preventing the horrid crime of murder'.[127] In less than seven weeks this had passed into law as the Murder Act, having been hurried through both the Commons and the Lords with remarkable speed.[128]

Historians have highlighted various factors that may have brought about this sudden legislative initiative.[129] The influence of one possible factor, pressure from the medical community because of its need for cadavers, has not proved easy to substantiate due to the lack of any convincing evidence that they were directly involved.[130] Other historians have pinpointed Henry Fielding's influence—his formative *Enquiry into the Causes of the Late Increase of Robbers* came out two days after the King's initial speech in 1751. However, his tract was not addressed specifically to murder, focused mainly on the need to execute offenders behind closed doors (which was not adopted in the Act), and did not recommend adding either dissection or hanging in chains to the execution process.[131] Nicholas Rogers has recently highlighted another factor—the increasingly regular and violent battles at Tyburn between the surgeons' servants and their opponents over the disposal of the bodies of the condemned.[132] However, apart from the clause in the Murder Act that made any attempt to rescue a murderer's body into a transportable offence, the Act does not seem to have been aimed mainly at controlling the Tyburn riots and may have had little impact on them, since more than 80% of the bodies fought over at Tyburn belonged not to murderers but to property offenders—over whose bodies battles continued well after 1752.[133] The particular political situation in the late 1740s and early 1750s may well have been a more important contributory factor. As Richard Connors has pointed out, the atmosphere created by both the economic policies of the Pelham administration and the coming of peace in 1748 encouraged broader parliamentary discussion of a range of social issues including those related to the criminal law.[134] The Pelhamites control of the House of Commons and the fact that the early 1750s continued to be a period of peace gave the ministry an opportunity to 'embark on a variety of reformatory measures', a number of which (including the Murder Act) subsequently introduced major legislative innovations.[135]

While these background influences had a role to play, Ward's recent book has argued cogently that the main catalyst that generated a demand for legislation introducing new punishments for murder was a press-fuelled moral panic about the nature and frequency of murder in the Metropolis. His detailed research into reporting patterns in the press indicates clearly that in late 1751 and early 1752 murder became a 'crime theme', a core news story that was developed and exaggerated through various printed media.[136] Reports of robberies involving overt violence and the murder of the victims, combined with two specific and hugely publicized cases of parricide (or neo-parricide)[137] and a general sense that the number of murder prosecutions was rising,[138] clearly frightened London's propertied classes, who felt increasingly unsafe in both their houses and in the streets. The legislators responded by debating new ways to make the death penalty more effective and by rapidly passing the Murder Act.

The reasons why the Murder Act eventually took the specific form that it did are less easy to unravel. The minor clauses of the Act enforcing speedier executions, and solitary confinement on bread and water between sentencing and execution were clearly influenced by Fielding.[139] However, given that the majority of the publications we have uncovered in the period 1750–1752 did not favour either dissection or hanging in chains, but wanted the introduction of more aggravated pre-execution punishments, it is more difficult to understand why the Act chose the former two options. The precise conjunction of forces that shaped the final form of the Murder Act passed on 26th March 1752 remains very difficult to unravel, given the lack of direct Parliamentary reporting. However, the chronology of the general debate about what the Act should contain, as it was reported in the press during the six-and-a-half weeks that Parliament was engaged in creating and debating the Act, makes it clear that the argument for torment-based additions to the execution process, and especially for the introduction of breaking on the wheel, was very definitely put forward by members of Parliament.

Although four publications advocating Lex Talionis were published between January 1750 and 1 February 1752,[140] this option was not mentioned in any of the reports or pamphlets published during the six-and-a-half weeks of Parliamentary debate. Nor was gibbeting mentioned until the final two days. In the first five days after 10th February, the day that the Commons commissioned the Bill, the reports about what might be proposed focused mainly on the introduction of punishment by breaking on the wheel. On 11th February an initial article published in several newspapers simply noted that 'we are assured that a proposal is on foot for altering the punishment for murder from hanging to breaking on the wheel'.[141] Four days later, on 15th February, a report in the *London Evening* Post (which was reprinted in several provincial newspapers) suggested that this proposal had been well received. 'A scheme which has lately been proposed to the consideration of the public, for breaking on the wheel all murderers, has been warmly received and agitated amongst many persons of distinction; who form part of the Legislature', it noted, before going on to suggest that any juvenile offenders in the local prisons 'should be brought out … to witness the execution, that by seeing the tortures of the delinquent, they may be terrified into obedience of the law: for those criminals are not sufficiently deterred from the dread of hanging, as they have imbibed the notion that this is an easy death'.[142] Although the newspapers were not allowed to report parliamentary debates or speeches, they were still able to report discussions in the Commons indirectly, as they appear to have done in this case. It is clear moreover, that a debate on the introduction of breaking on the wheel was also taking place in the public sphere outside Parliament. The following day the *Daily Advertiser* announced that amongst other things there would be a discussion of 'the wheel or next day execution for murderers' at the Oratory by Lincoln's Inn Fields.[143] Reports of similar punishments being used abroad may also have been used to reinforce these arguments. A very pointed report from Italy published on 8th February in the *Read's Weekly Journal* or the British Gazetteer lauded the fact that the authorities' 'resolution to keep their roads clear of robbers' had led to 17 'banditti' being 'broken alive on the wheel' in Lucca for 'several horrid crimes'.[144]

It may never be possible to ascertain whether those who wanted to introduce breaking on the wheel had a brief period in early February 1752 when they believed that this could be achieved, but on the 15th February an alternative proposal was also published in another London newspaper, the *Old England, or, The National Gazette.* This suggested two very different procedures both of which were eventually adopted. 'We hear it's proposed', the paper reported, 'for the more exemplary punishment of Murderers, that they should be executed soon after Conviction, and their Bodies sent to Surgeon's Hall to be anatomized'.[145] When, five days later on 20th February, the whole Murder Act debate was subjected to an excellent satire in *The Drury Lane Journal* all the different sides received equally critical treatment—not only breaking on the wheel, dissection and one of the proposed forms of *Lex Talionis* involving the cutting off of the right hand,[146] but also the proposals of Charles Jones—whose pamphlet, published during this debate, suggested that murderers be treated as if they had committed high treason and therefore be disembowelled and beheaded.

The satirical article began like many other contemporary pieces by complaining about 'the most horrid, barbarous, bloody, cruel, and unnatural murders' heard about 'every day', and about the 'danger of being knock'd in the head by vile villains' when out in the streets. It then went on to observe that 'these desperate and bloody-minded fellows don't mind being hanged or going to the gallows a pin. A harder punishment is necessary to frighten 'em ... and therefore the following scheme has been thought on', and is 'humbly proposed to the consideration of Parliament'. The 'bill' then proposed first suggested that 'surgeons be appointed for every jail, to make ottomies of all the condemned's bodies', and second 'that all malefactors, within two days after sentence of death is passed ... be cut up alive in the prison yard; and that every one confined there for capital offences be obliged to stand by and see it done'. While the surgeons were 'thus ottomising', the offenders' mouths were to be gagged 'to hinder their horrible shriekings and groans', and after this process their flesh should be cooked and fed to the prisoners. Moreover 'all those found guilty of the horrid sin of murder' were to be 'immediately roasted by a slow fire, and basted with their own grease'. Street robbers should be flayed alive and their tanned skins used for the prisoners to lie on, while other property offenders were to get off comparatively lightly: pickpockets and shoplifters were merely to 'have their hands chopped off in open court' and nailed on the inside of the prison gate. 'This', the satire concluded, 'will have a greater effect upon the minds of the people' than 'the fear of being broken alive upon the wheel ... and the like, which is practis'd abroad in foreign countries and dominions'.[147]

The author of this satire is unknown and its impact cannot be gauged, but no further 'proposals' were reported in the newspapers until 5th March, the day when the Bill was formally presented to the House of Commons and given its first reading.[148] At this point the debate was briefly redirected to a new theme: the need to punish parricide more severely. Two cases involving women who had killed their fathers—the prosecutions of Mary Blandy and Elizabeth Jeffries—had exploded into public view late in 1751.[149] Both came to trial in March 1752 accompanied by a huge wave of publicity [150] and this included detailed reports highlighting the judges' comments at Blandy's trial, which pointed out that, unlike females who had murdered their master or their husband—who could be burned at the stake for petty treason—these two women could only be hanged.[151] This was followed on the day of Jeffries' trial by reports suggesting that 'a clause be inserted in the Bill, to prevent the horrid crime of murder, whereby parricide and some other species of murder, will be made Petit Treason'.[152]

Neither this proposal to extend the use of burning at the stake, nor those involving breaking on the wheel or treating murder as high treason were eventually adopted by Parliament. In the Commons between the 5th and 18th of March the Bill ran rapidly through first and second readings, through a committee of the whole house where several (unfortunately unrecorded) amendments were made, through its third reading and on to the Lords.[153] There it was ordered to be considered by a committee of the whole house, the vital role of the judges at this point being highlighted by the specific request that 'the Judges in Town do then attend'.[154] While the bill was in the Lords the panic about the prevalence of murder in the metropolis was further fuelled by the reports in many newspapers that a further six murderers had been convicted at the Old Bailey and were to be executed on the Monday the 23rd, and by observations that this was not just a metropolitan phenomenon, since there were 'no less than 40 prisoners under confinement in several goals in this Kingdom for the horrid crime of murder'.[155]

At this point reports of one final 'proposal' appeared in a range of newspapers. The edition of the tri-weekly *London Evening Post* covering the period 21st–24th March, for example, reported at length that 'for the better preventing the crime of murder it is proposed that all persons who shall be found guilty of willful murder, be executed on the next day ... and also that the body of such murderer be … dissected and anatomized by the … surgeons'. The article then reported that it was also proposed that the judges could order 'the body of any such criminal to be hung in chains'.[156] Other newspapers used different words—reporting that 'the following regulations are talked on' and then repeated the core proposal that the body of every convicted murderer was 'to be anatomized or hung in chains'.[157] This reported 'proposal' quoted almost verbatim parts of the draft that the Lord's committee considered on the 23rd—around the time when printed copies of the proposed bill would first have become available.[158] Presumably it was this printed draft that was used by the press when they outlined the so-called proposal. When the Lords' Committee announced its amendments on the 24th minor matters had been changed—the Parliamentary Journals reported, for example, that the Lords changed 'next day' to 'next day but one' giving the condemned a little more time before execution.[159] However, although the bill was more detailed than the proposal reported in the press its main clauses were very nearly the same. The Commons received and agreed all the Lord's amendments on the 25th March, and the royal assent was then given the next day, just before parliament was prorogued.[160] The pressure to introduce new aggravated pre-execution punishments had made no impact on the final legislation. From April 1752 onwards it would be compulsory for the sentencing judge in all murder cases to choose between one of the two already existing post-execution punishments of dissection and hanging in chains, thereby adding—as the Act announced—'some further terror and peculiar mark of infamy' to the execution process and ensuring that no murderer would henceforth receive an intact burial.[161]

6 Why Were Aggravated Pre-execution Punishments not Adopted in the Murder Act?

There can be little doubt that Richard Ward was correct in seeing the Murder Act as, in part at least, the outcome of a print-driven moral panic. As the Act's introduction announced 'the horrid crime of murder has of late been more frequently perpetrated than formerly, and particularly in and near the Metropolis',[162] and the government clearly felt that it had to react. However, the nature of the sanctions to be introduced was by no means preordained. During the debate ideas about the possibility of resorting to continental-style aggravated punishments such as breaking on the wheel were obviously given consideration, as were ideas about extending the current English punishments for petty treason (or even for high treason) to all murderers. There is every sign that breaking on the wheel in particular was seriously proposed by some MPs and may well have played an important part in the varied debates and discussions that occurred in February and early March 1752. It should be remembered at this point that the first half of the eighteenth century did not necessarily see a decline in the use of such punishments elsewhere in Europe. As Pieter Spierenburg's research on Amsterdam has shown, prolonged and torment-based death penalties were much more common in the period 1700–1750 than they had been between 1650 and 1700. Only four people were broken on the wheel in the half century before 1700, compared to thirty-six in the first half of the eighteenth century.[163] As late as 1748 a Dutch women found guilty of murdering a servant and her mistress was not only broken on the wheel but also had her right hand and legs cut off and displayed separately. A similar practice was still used in Scotland. Between 1750 and 1754 three Scottish offenders suffered the aggravation of having their hand cut off prior to execution—a practice that was continued until 1765.[164] One of these executions was widely reported in January 1752 just as the debate on the Murder Act was getting under way. Normand Ross, who had been found guilty of murder in Edinburgh, was sentenced to 'have his right hand cut off' before he was hanged and then to have his hand 'affixed on the top of the gibbet above his body'.[165] Two weeks later a French proposal that in future murderers were to be hanged alive for two days and then have the offending hand chopped off before being executed was widely publicized in several press reports and then recommended in an article advocating the introduction of *Lex Talionis* in England.[166] The execution of Damiens, which a number of historians have seen as a watershed in French attitudes to aggravated execution rituals, was still in the future[167] and in Germany the reforms under Friedrich II had only just begun. Prussian Law not only continued to allow for the use of breaking on the wheel but also enshrined it in the new Penal Code of 1794 as the appropriate gradation of punishment for murder.[168]

In this context therefore, the question needs to be asked: Why did the advocates of aggravated torment-based pre-execution punishments fail to persuade Parliament that they should be introduced in England? There were clearly at least three distinct periods in the first half of the eighteenth century when this particular range of penal options was considered—why were none of them ever adopted? Pride in being different from the torture- and torment-based practices used on the Continent was often mentioned as a key reason. A long and well-argued article advocating post-execution dissection, published in both the *Westminster Journal* and the *London Magazine* in 1746 began by announcing that 'it is a common observation of foreigners, to the honour of the English nation, that … we have abolished all sorts of racks and tortures, and every other circumstance that any way tends to cruelty'. It then discussed 'breaking on the wheel, and other horrible executions', concluding that, despite their potential to prevent crimes the author could not 'see that such executions are anything else than wanton barbarity'.[169] At the beginning of the eighteenth century torment-based executions were specifically linked to the threat posed by Catholic France. *The Observator* argued in 1705, for example, that a successful Jacobite rebellion and the overthrow of Queen Anne would inevitably lead to the introduction of the forms of execution favoured by French tyrants (and used widely by them against protestants), namely burning alive and breaking 'alive on the wheel'.[170] In general, however, the foreign torment-based penal 'other' against which the English defined their own approach to capital punishment included almost all the countries on the Continent—the Dutch and German examples being particularly frequently quoted. In a pamphlet addressed to an MP in 1751 on the 'Vigorous Execution of the Present Laws' another writer noted that 'the merciful spirit of our laws spares even the boldest and blackest invader of them from those terrifying circumstances that attend … capital punishments in other countries', where 'plain death is looked upon as a favour'.[171]

Fear of the negative effects of torment-based executions—on both the audience and the offenders—was a second inhibiting factor also mentioned by several writers. 'General tortures in time become familiar to the mind and not very terrible to the heart' one 1752 newspaper article pointed out.[172] 'The scenes of barbarity and torture, that are so often exhibited before the eyes of the people … extirpate and extinguish the soft and tender passions of the human heart', another commented in 1746, 'so that at the last, we may be brought to behold the breaking of bones, and rending of limbs, without any remorse'. He then went on to suggest that 'the publick stabbings, and private assassinations, among some of our weak and pusillanimous neighbours (i.e. on the Continent)' were due to the fact that 'these bloody scenes' at executions had undermined 'any abhorrence to the spilling of human blood'.[173] A more specific fear about torment-based executions was that they would change the behaviour of those committing robbery. 'Tortures have been mentioned by many as the surest means … to extirpate these violences', one article suggested. 'But then they would introduce more pernicious evils. In those countries where breaking on the wheel is the form of execution, robberies are not so frequent, but seldom or never committed without murder'—an argument repeated by a *London Magazine* article in 1750, which suggested that, if faced by the possibility of an excruciatingly painful death, robbers would 'always murder' their victims in order to avoid detection.[174]

A third factor inhibiting the introduction of new aggravated pre-execution practices was thought to be the innate conservatism of the English people in relation to legal change. 'The English nation', one pamphleteer wrote in 1751, 'cannot easily digest either sudden alterations in their laws, or unknown, or unusual ways of executing them'. Rapid change might therefore be destructive and might undermine 'the genius of the English nation, to love and respect the laws'.[175] 'It is the duty of every honest Englishman', another pamphlet argued in the same year, 'to aim at the preservation of every part of the original constitution' and 'to guard against any innovation'.[176] Even if every honest Englishman did not necessarily feel as concerned as this author suggested about the introduction of innovations in sentencing and punishment policies, the judges almost certainly did. Judges very rarely made their opinions known but there is little evidence that a significant proportion of them favoured the introduction of torment-based execution rituals. One judge, faced with a particularly heinous rape and murder by a black soldier did remark in 1750 that he would have liked, in this case, to have passed a heavier sentence than just hanging. However, he prefaced this remark by saying that this was an exception and that he had 'never before desired a power of extending legal penalties'.[177] The twelve judges, who manned the main Westminster courts and the Assize Circuits certainly proved to be innately conservative when criminal law reform was discussed in the late-eighteenth and early-nineteenth century[178] (see Chaps. 4 and 5). Before the 1770s no record of what they may have said in Parliament is available, but it seems very likely that the judges were also a conservative force at this point,[179] preferring to make compulsory the post-execution sanctions they were already making informal use of, rather than introduce new ones tainted by Continental overtones of torture and torment. The leading judge at this point, the Lord Chancellor, Lord Hardwicke, when later recalling the debates of the early 1750s, made it clear that in penal matters he was opposed to what he called 'rash theorists'.[180] His private papers indicate that he was deeply involved in shaping the Act as it finally came out, and it appears almost certain that he was one of the key government figures, and possibly the most influential government figure, who influenced the shaping and passing of the bill in February and March 1752, thereby insuring that post- rather than pre-execution punishments were the compulsory sanctions selected.[181] Although the lack of direct reports of Parliamentary debates or of intra-governmental discussions make it impossible to draw definitive conclusions, it appears that in 1751–1752, faced with pressure from the King, the public and a press-fuelled moral panic about murder, the government felt obliged to organize the introduction a new level of penalties for that offence.[182] Not being convinced that aggravated pre-execution penalties were appropriate in the English context, they therefore turned to two existing and already widely used post-execution punishments—dissection and hanging in chains.

7 Conclusion: Rethinking the Origins of the Murder Act

It would be dangerous, however, to see the Murder Act as simply a knee-jerk reaction to a moral panic or to other short-term circumstances. Certainly the immediate context in the early 1750s—the battles over bodies at Tyburn, the surgeon's need of cadavers, Fielding's demands for more solemn executions, the intense early 1750s legislative activity around related social issues,[183] and the press's tendency to fuel anxieties by extensive and exaggerated reports of every new murder—were important catalysts, but from another perspective the Murder Act can be seen in an entirely different way: as the almost inevitable solution to a long-term and growing penal problem.

As the number of property offences punishable by the death penalty continued to accumulate from the later seventeenth century to the mid-eighteenth century,[184] the fact that the punishment for murder was exactly the same as that for relatively trivial property offences came to be seen as increasingly anomalous and problematic. This disjunction in the legislation would have caused considerable disquiet even if those accused of violent or particularly heinous property crimes, such as robbery or burglary, had been the only offenders actually hanged rather than conditionally pardoned. However, in London and the South-East at least, a small but significant proportion of the property offenders that ended up on the gallows had committed relatively minor felonies, many of which had only recently been made capital.[185]

This theme played an important role in the debates that led up to the Murder Act. It was first aired as early as 1701 when the author of *Hanging not Punishment Enough* pointed out that 'If Death then be due to a Man who surreptitiously steals the value of five shillings (as is made by a late statute) surely He who … murthers me … and burns my house, deserves another sort of censure; and if the one must die, the other should be made to feel himself die'.[186] This reference to the fact that Parliament had just made shoplifting to the value of five shillings (and thefts of the same amount from stables or warehouses)[187] a hanging offence made a clear link between the growth of the capital code and the consequent need for heavier punishments for murder. So did Charles Jones's remark, published in 1752 in the middle of the Murder Act debate in Parliament, which also referred to an offence only added to the Bloody Code a few years before. 'Almost all nations but ours, adapt their punishments to the Nature of the Offence', he wrote. 'We make no difference in the sentence of our laws, between a poor sheepstealer that takes wherewith to feed his wretched Family, and the most inhuman and blood-mangling Highwayman or murderer'.[188] This demand for greater differentiation, which was reinforced by a growing range of different arguments and approaches, was heard with increasing frequency in the years immediately before the Murder Act, and came particularly to the fore between 1750 and 1752.

Several articles argued that the inequality of punishment actually created violent crime. 'The man who takes a shilling on the highway, shall meet with the same fate as if he had murdered half a score of people', an article in the *London Magazine* argued in the mid-1740s.[189] 'This inequality of punishment is the principal reason of the frequency of the crime. If murder was to be punished with greater severity, or theft or robbery with less, it would, in all probability have its desired effect'.[190] In December 1750 a widely published newspaper article about the 'barbarities committed of late by robbers' reinforced this view. 'We hear a bill will be brought in the next session of Parliament', it announced, 'to inflict a heavier punishment on offenders of this sort than what the Law now does, which making no difference in the punishment of these barbarous villains from others, in a great measure occasions the offence'.[191] In 1751 this argument was once again applied to murderers alone. 'Is it not the frequency of executions that is the principal cause of murder in England?' Sedgly's response to Fielding's pamphlet asked. 'Ought the pilferer of a few shillings to be punished with the severity due to a murderer? … Is it not from this indiscriminate execution of felons, that so many felonies have their source?' He then went on to argue that death should 'be more sparingly implemented' and confined to murderers and street robbers.[192]

Others pushed this argument even further generating a critique of capital punishment for property offences that was further developed by a range of penal reformers from the later eighteenth century onwards. In April 1751 a long journal article, reproduced in several provincial newspapers, highlighted the problem of 'the inequality of punishments to the offence' and demanded that capital punishment be reserved for murder alone, as part of a much more general critique of the unnecessary growth of the Bloody Code. 'It has always been the practice, when any particular species of robbery becomes prevalent and common, to endeavor its suppression by capital punishments. Thus one generation of malefactors is commonly cut off and their successors are frighted into new expedients', the article argued. 'The law then renews the pursuit in the heat of anger, and overtakes the offender again with death. By this practice, capital inflictions are multiplied, and crimes very different in their degrees of enormity are equally subjected to the severest punishment that man has the power of executing upon man'. The terror of death 'should therefore be reserved as the last resort of authority … and placed only before the treasure of life, to guard from invasion what cannot be restored. To equal robbery with murder is to reduce murder to robbery', which would 'confound in common minds the gradations of injury'.[193] This deep critique of the capital code was also not infrequently reinforced by references to Biblical arguments. As a journal article pointed out in 1750 'the law of God', while permitting the execution of murderers made it clear that 'it must be unlawful to take away the life of a man for … robbery or theft'.[194] In the following year another pamphlet argued even more strongly on the same grounds that it was

> a very unjust thing to take away a man's life for a little money … we ought not to approve of these terrible laws that make the smallest offences capital … as if there was no difference between killing a man and taking his purse … God has commanded us not to kill, and shall we kill so easily for a little money? … If by the Mosaical law … men were only fined, and not put to death for theft; we cannot imagine that, in this new law of mercy, in which God treats us with the tenderness of a father, he has given us greater license to cruelty than he did to the Jews. Upon these reasons … it is plain and obvious that it is absurd … that a thief and a murderer should be equally punished.[195]

This argument that murder alone should be punished with death was still the view of only a relatively small minority in the 1750s, but while it would take three-quarters of a century before Parliament would seriously countenance removing the death penalty from all property crimes, in the early 1750s the fact that such fundamental critiques were already being aired—both in Parliament[196] and outside it—would almost certainly have made the ruling elite aware that in order to preserve the Bloody Code it was important to differentiate the punishments inflicted for murder from those used against routine property crimes. Since they were clearly not yet willing to countenance repealing the property-crime-based capital statutes—indeed they went on adding to them in the second half of the eighteenth century[197]—the obvious solution to the problem of differentiation was to add further levels of punishment to the execution process in the case of murderers. This is precisely what the Murder Act did, and what its preface explicitly said it wanted to do. Faced with a moral panic about murder in the early months of 1752 the government turned to a policy which by then had a long pedigree, a good degree of backing from penal writings and an obvious grounding in what contemporaries would have seen as 'common sense'. 'It has long been the Opinion of many thinking People', one fairly typical and widely published article observed in 1750,

> that our laws are too severe with regard to the crimes for which capital punishments are inflicted, at the same time that they are too gentle in the manner of those punishments for crimes of the most atrocious nature. Thus a very small felony, attended with certain circumstances, brings the malefactor to the gallows; and the most barbarous murderer ... does no more; there not being the least additional pain, or mark of ignominy, to distinguish the vindictive or cruel murderer, from the necessitous thief.[198]

That article went on to suggest that 'the practice of other countries, in similar cases' should be 'sometimes attended to'[199] but even though the English government did not eventually take that road—choosing to introduce two post-execution punishments rather their Continental alternatives—by passing the Murder Act they explicitly accepted the argument for differentiation, as the preface to that Act made clear. In wording that was very similar to that found in the article just quoted, the first sentence of the Act's preface stated that since 'the horrid crime of murder' was now being much more 'frequently perpetrated', it had 'become necessary that some further terror and peculiar mark of infamy be added to the punishment of death, now by law inflicted' on that specific and particularly 'heinous' offence.[200]

Underlying the passing of the Murder Act, therefore, was the need to solve a well-recognized structural problem created by the growth of the Bloody Code. As the capital sanction was attached to more and more minor property offences—shoplifting, thefts by servants in a dwelling house, breaking and entering (to steal to the value of five shillings or more), stealing from bleaching grounds, thefts from ships on navigable rivers, sheep theft, cow theft and so forth[201]—so the need for a specific extra sanction to be available for the punishment of murder became more and more pressing, especially when a panic about rising murder rates occurred at the beginning of the 1750s. Many existing accounts of the Murder Act have implicitly or explicitly portrayed it as cutting across a more general trend away from severity, and from this viewpoint the imposition in the Murder Act of 'a more severe and exemplary form of punishment' seems aberrant, exceptional and difficult to explain.[202] However, the fresh perspective suggested by these contemporary writings casts a very different light on the origins of the Murder Act. The increasing sanctions imposed on murderers in 1752 no longer appear as a temporary reversal within what was otherwise a long-term movement towards a more humane penal code, but rather as a logical and necessary extension of the inhumanity of the Bloody Code, and another stage in its development.

Notes

1. L. Radzinowicz, *A History of English Criminal Law and its Administration from 1750* (London, 5 Vols., 1948–1986), 1, pp. 231–238.
2. J. Beattie, *Crime and the Courts in England 1660-1800* (Oxford, 1986) pp. 487–490, 524–530 also quotes Jones's 1752 pamphlet and mentions that similar ideas were frequently discussed in the press (p. 525). P. Smith, *Punishment and Culture* (Chicago, 2008), pp. 48–52 quotes only 2 pre-1750 pamphlets.
3. R. McGowen, 'The Problem of Punishment in Eighteenth-Century England' in S. Devereaux and P. Griffiths (eds.) *Penal Practice and Culture 1500-1900: Punishing the English* (Basingstoke, 2004), pp. 10–31.
4. Ibid., pp. 222–223.
5. Ibid., pp. 214–216.
6. Ibid., p. 222.
7. The poor quality of eighteenth-century type face means an unknown fraction of the relevant items are missed.

8. T. Nourse, *Campania Folix* (originally published London, 1700), 2nd edition (London, 1706), pp. 229–230; J. Beattie, *Policing and Punishment in London 1660-1750* (Oxford, 2001), pp. 42–43; Anon, *Hanging not Punishment Enough* (London, 1701), especially pp. 1–14; B. Mandeville, *An Enquiry into the Causes of the Frequent Executions at Tyburn* (London, 1725), pp. 26–27; Philandros, *British Journal*, 2 April 1726; Anon (attributed to D. Defoe), *Street-Robberies Considered: The Reason of their Being so Frequent with Means to Prevent 'em* (London, 1728), p. 54; G. Ollyffe, *An Essay Humbly Offer'd for An Act of Parliament to Prevent Capital Crimes* (London, 1731), pp. 3–11; *Derby Mercury, 3* May 1733; Eboranos (attributed to Thomas Rake), *A Collection of Political Tracts: Some Considerations for Rendering the Punishment of Criminals more Effectual* (London, 1735), pp. 42–45; Supplement by Philo Patriae—*Anon. A Full and Genuine Account of the Murder of Mrs Robinson by Elton Lewis* (London, 1735); *Caledonian Mercury*, 22 December 1735; *Derby Mercury*, 4 November 1736 and *Caledonian Mercury*, 8 November 1736; Verus, *Gentleman's Magazine*, 8 (June 1738), pp. 286–288; Justitia, *London Magazine*, 13 (1744), pp. 506–508—this includes passages from the 'Philo Patriae' piece 9 years earlier but then advocates a different post-execution punishment; Publicus, *The Daily Advertiser*, 19 October 1744; Publicus, *Westminster Journal*, 20 December 1746, reprinted with further remarks *London Magazine* (December 1746), pp. 637–639; *Derby Mercury*, 4–11 January 1750; 'Plain Truth', *London Magazine* (October 1750), pp. 452–453; *Newcastle Courant*, 22 December 1750 and *Derby Mercury*, 28 December 1750; *London Magazine* (February 1751), pp. 82–83; B. Sedgly, *Observations on Mr Fielding's Enquiry into the Causes of the Late Increase of Robbers* (London, 1751), pp. 49–69; C. Jones, *Some Methods Proposed to Put a Stop to the Flagrant Crimes of Murder, Robbery and Perjury* (London, 1752), pp. 7–14; *Old England or The National Gazette*, 1 February 1752; *London Evening Post*, 13 February 1752; *Salisbury Journal*, 17 February 1752 and *Newcastle Courant*, 15 and 22 February 1752; Beattie, *Crime*, pp. 525–526; *Derby Mercury*, 7–14 February 1752; *London Daily Advertiser*, 14 February 1752 and *Old England or The National Gazette*, 15 February 1752; *Newcastle Courant*, 15 February 1752; *London Daily Advertiser*, 13 March 1752, and *General Advertiser*, 13 March 1752; *Read's Weekly Journal or The British Gazetteer*, 14 March 1752; *London Evening Post*, 21–24 March 1752*; General Advertiser*, 24 March 1752*; Old England or The National Gazette*, 28 March 1752. Some of these reports note that people of distinction were discussing a particular policy and I have defined these as advocating that punishment since they record or imply this was happening in Parliament. Because it was published a week after the Murder Act, *Examples of the*

Interposition of Providence in the Detection and Punishment of Murder with an introduction and conclusion written by Henry Fielding (1752), is excluded from this analysis. It was positive about gibbetting, pp. 69–70.

9. *Gentleman's Magazine*, December 1750, pp. 532–533 and *Salisbury Journal*, 7 January 1751.
10. Anon, *Some Reasons … Castration Instead of Death may Prove to be the Most Effectual Method of Punishing Persons found Guilty of Robbery and Theft* (Dublin, 1731) reprinted in *Echo or Edinburgh Weekly Journal*, 8 December 1731 and Anon, *Britannia's Fortune-Teller: Humbly Dedicated to the People of England* (London, 1733), pp. 32–38.
11. Anon, *Hanging not Punishment*, p. 7.
12. On duellists—*Westminster Journal*, 20 December 1746. Another focussed on parricides *London Daily Advertiser*, 13 March 1752.
13. *Derby Mercury*, 17 April 1735; *London Evening Post*, 14 July 1750; *Caledonian Mercury*, 24 July 1750.
14. *Observator*, 23 May 1705.
15. Since the article did not actually ask for the introduction of this policy it is not included in the twenty-nine core pamphlets described above. *Penny London Post*, 25 January 1752.
16. The *Derby Mercury*, 3 May 1733 published a shortened version of an article from *Wye's Journal* (26 April 1733), and the *Caledonian Mercury*, 1 May 1733 inserted an even more truncated one.
17. The article by Publicus, *Westminster Journal*, 20 December 1746, was reprinted with further remarks *London Magazine* (December 1746), pp. 637–639.
18. R. McGowen, 'Making Examples and the Crisis of Punishment in Mid-Eighteenth-Century England' in D. Lemmings (ed.), *The British and Their Laws in the Eighteenth Century* (Woodbridge, 2005), p. 183.
19. Beattie, *Policing*, p. 321.
20. R. Ward, *Print Culture, Crime and Justice in Eighteenth-Century London* (London, 2014); N. Rogers, *Mayhem; Post-war Crime and Violence in Britain 1748-1753* (Yale, 2012).
21. R. Ward, 'Print Culture, Moral Panic and the Administration of the Law: The London Crime Wave of 1744'. *Crime, Histoire et Societes/Crime, History and Societies*, 16 (2012), pp. 5–23.
22. *London Magazine*, 13 (1744), p. 506; Anon, *Hanging not Punishment*, p. 1; Eboranos, *A Collection*, p. 42.
23. *Gentleman's Magazine*, 8 (June 1738), pp. 286–288; Anon, *Hanging not Punishment*, p. 6.
24. Reprinted in the *Derby Mercury*, 3 May 1733.
25. *London Evening Post*, 14 July 1750.
26. McGowen, 'The Problem', pp. 220–225.

27. Rogers, *Mayhem*, p. 10.
28. McGowen, 'The Problem', p. 223.
29. Anon, *Hanging not Punishment*, p. 5.
30. Twice new initiatives are reported that clearly were being advocated elsewhere and these are included in the count even when the article concerned makes no direct positive comment, *London Daily Advertiser*, 13 March 1752; *Old England or the National Gazette*, 28 March 1752.
31. *London Magazine*, 13 (1744), pp. 506–508; Beattie, *Crime*, p. 526.
32. Anon, *Hanging not Punishment*, p. 3; J. Dinwiddy, 'The Early Nineteenth-Century Campaign against Flogging in the Army'. *English Historical Review*, 97 (1982), p. 311.
33. Jones, *Some Methods*, p. 8.
34. *Derby Mercury*, 3 May 1733.
35. W. Blackstone, *Commentaries on the Laws of England* (4 volumes, Oxford, 1765–1769), 4, pp. 320–322. A. McKenzie, 'This Death Some Strong and Stout Hearted Man Doth Choose: The Practice of Peine Fort et Dure in Seventeenth- and Eighteenth-Century England' *Law and History Review*, 23 (2005), pp. 311–313.
36. Ibid., 4, pp. 12–15; *Old England or The National Gazette*, 1 February 1752.
37. Sedgly, *Observations*, p. 66; *Anon. A Full and Genuine Account of the Murder*, pp. 24–25; *London Magazine*, 13 (1744), p. 507; *Old England or The National Gazette*, 1 February 1752; *Daily Advertiser*, 19 October 1744; *Derby Mercury*, 4–11 January 1750; *Newcastle Courant*, 22 December 1750 and *Derby Mercury*, 28 December 1750. For continental examples of *Lex Talionis*—P. Spierenburg, *The Spectacle of Suffering* (Cambridge, 1984), pp. 73–74.
38. Sedgly, *Observations*, p. 66; *Daily Advertiser*, 19 October 1744; *Derby Mercury*, 4–11 January 1750.
39. *London Magazine* (1744), p. 507.
40. *Old England or The National Gazette*, 1 February 1752.
41. Sedgly, *Observations*, p. 67; *Derby Mercury*, 28 December 1750 and *Newcastle Courant*, 22 December 1750.
42. *Gentleman's Magazine*, 20 (1750).
43. Spierenburg, *The Spectacle of Suffering*, p. 57.
44. Mandeville, *An Enquiry*, p. 26 quoted again in a different argument *London Magazine*, 13 (1744), p. 508.
45. Eboranos, *A Collection*, p. 51.
46. *Westminster Journal*, 20 December 1746.
47. *London Magazine*, October 1750.
48. *Westminster Journal*, 20 December 1746.
49. Ibid.

50. Eboranos, *A Collection*, p. 49 parts of which later republished in *London Magazine*, 13 (1744), p. 508.
51. *Westminster Journal*, 20 December 1746; On the important role hospitals later played: E. Hurren, *Dying for Victorian Medicine: English Anatomy and its Trade in the Dead Poor c.1834-1929* (Basingstoke, 2012), p. 145.
52. *Parliamentary Papers*, (Henceforth *PP*) 1819, viii, p. 136.
53. Spierenburg, *The Spectacle of Suffering*, pp. 71–72.
54. Ibid., p. 72; For a classic seventeenth-century description of breaking on the wheel in Germany written by an English traveller see R. Evans, *Rituals of Retribution: Capital Punishment in Germany 1600-1987* (Oxford, 1996), pp. 27–29.
55. Anon, *Annals of the Universe; Containing an Account of the Most Memorable Affairs, and Occurrences* (London, 1709), p. 110.
56. Ollyffe, *An Essay*, p. 8; Anon, *Hanging not Punishment*, p. 5.
57. Nourse, *Campania Folix*, pp. 230–231.
58. Anon, *Hanging not Punishment*, p. 14.
59. *Derby Mercury*, 4 November 1736.
60. *London Evening Post*, 13 February 1752; *Salisbury Journal*, 17 February 1752 and *Newcastle Courant*, 22 February 1752.
61. D. Hume, *Commentaries on the Law of Scotland* (3rd edition, Edinburgh, 1829), p. 482.
62. J. Chamberlayne, *Magnae Britanniae: or The Present State of Great Britain* (London, 1735), p. 195.
63. *British Journal*, 2 April 1726.
64. *London Magazine* (December 1746), pp. 637–638: *Westminster Journal*, 20 December 1746.
65. Anon, *Street-Robberies*, pp. 53–54. Hanging was 'too mild' for male 'crimes of the blackest dye', Defoe argued.
66. *Gentleman's Magazine*, 7 (1738), p. 286.
67. *Derby Mercury*, 4 November 1736.
68. Ollyffe, *An Essay*, pp. 7–9.
69. Anon, *Examples of the Interposition*, pp. 69–70.
70. *British Journal*, 2 April 1726.
71. Jones, *Some Methods*, pp. 7–8.
72. B. Goldgar (ed.), *Henry Fielding, The Covent Garden Journal and A Plan of the Universal Register-Office* (1988, Middletown Connecticut), pp. 162–163.
73. *London Journal*, 2 December 1721.
74. *Newcastle Courant*, 20 March 1725.
75. S Tarlow, 'The Technology of the Gibbet'. *International Journal of Historical Archaeology*' 18 (2014), p. 670.
76. Beattie, *Policing*, pp. 47–68.
77. Ibid., p. 68.

78. J. Innes, 'Legislation and Public Participation 1760-1830' in Lemmings (ed.), *The British*, pp. 102–105, which also discusses the limited information available about early eighteenth-century parliamentary discussions.
79. Rosenberg's keyword publications search 1600–1750 for the percentage of titles including the words 'execution or executed' indicated the final quarter of the seventeenth century had much the highest proportion. P. Rosenberg, 'Sanctifying the Robe: Punitive Violence and the English Press 1650–1700' in Devereaux and Griffiths, *Penal Practice*, p. 160.
80. *General Index to the Eighth, Ninth, Tenth and Eleventh Volumes of the Journals of the House of Commons* (henceforth *GIJHC*, 8–11 or if the Lords *GIJHL*), p. 763.
81. *GIJHC*, 8–11, p. 93; *GIJHC*, 10, pp. 218, 229, 460; *GIJHC*, 11, pp. 26–27. The specific policies suggested by the petition were not recorded. The first committee was largely concerned with making local hundreds responsible for compensating victims but later committees clearly had wider remits.
82. Anon, *Solon Secundus: or Some Defects in the English Laws* (1695), pp. 6–7. Transportation the writer noted 'won't do the business'. p. 8.
83. Beattie, *Policing*, p. 321.
84. *GIJHC*, Index 11–17, p. 200; *GIJHC*,11, pp. 47, 72, 74, 77, 87, 91, 100, 132; *GIJHC*, 12, p. 22; see also *GIJHL*, Index 11–19, p. 339.
85. Nourse, *Campania Folix*, pp. 229–231. This was published in 1700 but since Nourse died in the middle of 1699 it was almost certainly written between 1697 and mid-1699.
86. Anon, *Hanging not Punishment*, p. 3.
87. Ibid., p. 13.
88. Ibid., p. 15.
89. Beattie, *Policing*, pp. 317–334.
90. Anon, *Hanging not Punishment*, p. 14.
91. Beattie, *Policing*, pp. 370–371, 427–432.
92. Beattie, *Crime*, pp. 487 and 507, 80% of London property offender punishments at the Old Bailey 1718–1750 involved transportation, Beattie, *Policing*, p. 473.
93. *Gentleman's Magazine* 8 (June 1738), pp. 286–287; *Derby Mercury*, 17 April 1733; Beattie, *Crime*, p. 540.
94. Ibid., p. 516; Mandeville, *An Enquiry*, pp. 26–27, 40, 46–48; *British Journal*, 2 April 1726.
95. Anon, *Street-Robberies Considered*, p. 54; D. Defoe, *Second Thoughts are Best; or a Further Improvement of a Late Scheme to Prevent Street Robberies … Offered to the Consideration of Parliament* (1729), p. ii; D. Defoe, *Augusta Triumphans* (London, 1729), pp. 47–57.
96. Mandeville, *An Enquiry*, p. 26; *British Journal*, 2 April 1726.

97. Eboranos, *A Collection*, pp. 49–50.
98. *Derby Mercury*, 4 November 1736; *Caledonian Mercury*, 22 December 1735; *Gentleman's Magazine*, 8 (June 1738), pp. 286–288; Ollyffe, *An Essay*, p. 8.
99. *Caledonian Mercury*, 1 May 1733; *Derby Mercury*, 3 May 1733; Ollyffe, *An Essay*, p. 9.
100. Beattie, *Policing*, pp. 68 and 391–402.
101. Ibid., p. 374.
102. D. Defoe, *An Effectual Scheme for the Immediate Preventing of Street Robberies* (London, 1731); Beattie, *Policing*, p. 375; Ollyffe, *An Essay*.
103. *London Evening Post*, 17 April 1733; *Daily Post*, 19 April 1733.
104. *Gentleman's Magazine*, 26 (February, 1733), p. 88. This journal covered two particularly violent robbery-with-murder cases in the first 3 months of 1733. One in Lincolnshire, pp. 43 and 154–155 and pp. 97–111 and the other involving multiple London murders by Sarah Marshall, pp. 97, 99–100, 108, 137, 151–154.
105. *GIJHC*, 22, pp. 97, 104, 115, 117, 123, 131, 139.
106. Eboranos, *A Collection*. Although this volume of essays was published in 1735 the individual essay quoted was published on 21 March 1733.
107. *Caledonian Mercury*, 10 April 1733; *Derby Mercury*, 19 April 1733.
108. *Gentleman's Magazine*, 26 (April 1733). The other work was announced in the *Weekly Miscellany*, 28 April 1733 under the short title 'Reasons, etc. for more effectually punishing criminals'.
109. *Derby Mercury*, 3 May 1733, quoting *Wye's Letter*. See also *Caledonian Mercury*, 1 May 1733.
110. However an act was passed the following year making assault with intent to commit robbery a transportable felony, 7 George II.c21.
111. *Derby Mercury*, 17 April 1735.
112. *London Daily Post*, 20 August 1735.
113. *Ipswich Journal*, 13 December 1735; *Derby Mercury*, 18 December 1735.
114. *Caledonian Mercury*, 22 December 1735.
115. Philo Patriae' in Anon, *A Full and Genuine Account*, pp. 24–25.
116. *Derby Mercury*, 4 November 1736.
117. *Gentleman's Magazine*, 7 (1738), p. 286.
118. For 1744 moral panic see Ward, 'Print Culture, Moral panic'.
119. *London Magazine*, 13 (1744), pp. 506–508; *Daily Advertiser*, 19 October 1744; *Westminster Journal*, 20 December 1746, reprinted with further remarks *London Magazine* (December 1746), p. 637.
120. *London Magazine* (October 1750), pp. 452–453; *London Evening Post*, 21–24 March 1752 and *General Advertiser*, 24 March 1752; *London Magazine* (February 1751), pp. 82–83; *London Daily Advertiser*, 14 February 1752 and *Old England or The National Gazette*, 15 February 1752.

121. *Old England or The National Gazette*, 1 February 1752; Sedgly, *Observations*, pp. 49–69; *Derby Mercury*, 4–11 January 1750; *Newcastle Courant*, 22 December 1750 and *Derby Mercury*, 28 December 1750; *London Evening Post*, 13–15 February 1752; *Derby Mercury*, 7–14 February 1752; *Salisbury Journal*, 17 February 1752 and *Newcastle Courant*, 15 and 22 February 1752; Jones, *Some Methods*, pp. 7–14; Beattie, *Crime*, pp. 525–526.
122. *London Daily Advertiser*, 13 March 1752, and *General Advertiser*, 13 March 1752; *Read's Weekly Journal or The British Gazetteer*, 14 March 1752.
123. *London Evening Post*, 21–24 March 1752; *General Advertiser*, 24 March 1752; *Old England or The National Gazette*, 28 March 1752.
124. Ward, *Print Culture*.
125. Ibid., p. 159 and R. Connors, '"The Grand Inquest of the Nation"; Parliamentary Committees and Social Policy in Mid-Eighteenth-Century England' *Parliamentary History*, 14 (1995), pp. 301–302.
126. Connors, 'The Grand', pp. 301–310.
127. *GIJHC*, 26, p. 426.
128. *GIJHC*, 26, pp. 426, 478, 482, 489, 493, 496, 499, 514–515, *GIJHL*, 27, pp. 692, 697, 699–702.
129. Well summarised in Ward, *Print Culture*, pp. 159–169.
130. Ibid., pp. 165–166.
131. Radzinowicz, *A History*, 1, pp. 399–424 and Ward, *Print Culture*, pp. 163–165. It did recommend other changes in the timing of the execution and the prisoner's treatment between sentencing and execution some of which were adopted.
132. Rogers, *Mayhem*, p. 57–61; Ward, *Print Culture*, pp. 165–167.
133. *London Evening Post*, 1 April 1758; Ward, *Print Culture*, p. 167.
134. Connors, 'The Grand', pp. 285–286.
135. Ibid., p. 300.
136. Ward, *Print Culture*, pp. 169–185. On the concept of a crime theme P. King, 'Moral Panics and Violent Street Crime 1750-2000: A Comparative Perspective' in B. Godfrey, C. Emsley and G. Dunstall (eds.), *Comparative Histories of Crime* (Cullompton, 2003), pp. 53–71.
137. The two outstanding and hugely reported cases, that is, the prosecutions of Mary Blandy and Elizabeth Jeffries, which involved women killing their fathers (or an uncle who had acted as a father), exploded into the public view late in 1751, Ward, *Print Culture*, pp. 169–185.
138. In one week seven people were hanged for murder in London, *London Daily Advertiser*, 19 March 1752.
139. Ward, *Print Culture*, p. 163.

140. *Old England or The National Gazette*, 1 February 1752; Sedgly, *Observations*, pp. 49–69; *Derby Mercury*, 4–11 January 1750; *Newcastle Courant*, 22 December 1750 and *Derby Mercury*, 28 December 1750.
141. *Derby Mercury*, 7–14 February 1752; *Salisbury Journal*, 17 February 1752 and *Newcastle Courant*, 15 February 1752.
142. *London Evening Post*, 13–15 February1752; *Salisbury Journal*, 17 February 1752; *Newcastle Courant*, 22 February 1752.
143. *Daily Advertiser*, 15 February 1752.
144. *Read's Weekly Journal or the British Gazetteer*, 8 February 1752.
145. *Old England or The National Gazette*, 15 February 1752.
146. *Old England or The National Gazette*, 1 February 1752.
147. *Drury Lane Journal*, Number 6, 20 February 1752, pp. 121–124.
148. *GIJHC*, 26, p. 478.
149. In Jefferies case although the victim was an uncle the press still treated it as parricide, *General Evening Post*, 6 July and 15 August 1751.
150. See, for example, *London Evening Post*, 3 March 1752; *General Advertiser*, 14 March 1752. Ward, *Print Culture*, pp. 169–185.
151. *Newcastle Courant*, 14 March 1752; *The Scots Magazine* (March 1752), pp. 106–107.
152. *London Daily Advertiser*, 13 March 1752; *General Advertiser*, 13 March; *Read's Weekly Journal or the British Gazetteer* 14 March 1752. Another attempted murder by a young women of the male head of her household was also reported at this point. *London Evening Post*, 12–14 March 1752.
153. *GIJHC*, 26, pp. 426, 478, 482, 489, 493, 496, 499. An attempt to delay its progress to the committee stage was unsuccessful, *Caledonian Mercury*, 16 March 1752.
154. *GIJHL*, 27, p. 697.
155. *London Daily Advertiser*, 19 March 1752; *General Advertiser*, 19 March 1752; *London Evening Post*, 17–19 March 1752; *Old England or The National Gazette*, 21 March 1752; *Derby Mercury*, 7–14 February 1752.
156. *London Evening Post*, 21–24 March 1752; The proposal seems to have been publicised on the 23rd as the Lords' committee met. *General Advertiser*, 24 March 1752; *Manchester Mercury*, 24 March 1752; *Caledonian Mercury*, 30 March 1752.
157. *Old England or The National Gazette*, 28 March 1752—the same edition of this weekly also reported elsewhere that the Act had been passed.
158. The bill was ordered to be printed by the Lords on the 18th of March—*GIJHL*, 27, p. 692.
159. *GIJHL*, 27, p. 701; *GIJHC*, 26, p. 514.
160. *GIJHC*, 26, p. 515; *London Evening Post*, 24–26 March 1752; *General Advertiser*, 26 March 1752; *Old England or The National Gazette*, 28 March 1752; *Read's Weekly Journal or the British Gazetteer*, 14 March 1752.

161. 25 Geo.II. cap 37.
162. Ibid.
163. Spierenburg, *The Spectacle of Suffering*, p. 74.
164. See R. Bennett, 'Capital Punishment and the Criminal Corpse in Scotland 1740-1834' (Leicester University PhD, 2015) for further discussion. *Ipswich Journal*, 19 May 1750.
165. *Read's Weekly Journal or the British Gazetteer*, 7 December 1751.
166. *Salisbury Journal*, 27 January 1752; *Penny London Post*, 25 January 1752; *Old England or The National Gazette*, 1 February 1752.
167. On the watershed in France see P. Friedland, *Seeing Justice Done: The Age of Spectacular Capital Punishment in France* (Oxford, 2012), pp. 176–191. For Damiens see M. Foucault, *Discipline and Punish: The Birth of the Prison* (London, 1979), pp. 1–5.
168. Evans, *Rituals*, pp. 121–135.
169. Publicus *Westminster Journal*, 20 December 1746, reprinted with further remarks *London Magazine* (December 1746), pp. 637–639.
170. *The Observator*, 23 May 1705.
171. Anon, *The Right Method of Maintaining Security in Person and Property … by a Vigorous Execution of the Present Laws* (London, 1751), p. 42.
172. *Old England or The National Gazette*, 1 February 1752.
173. *Westminster Journal*, 20 December 1746; *London Magazine* (December 1746), pp. 637–639.
174. *British Journal*, 2 April 1726; *London Magazine* (October 1750), p. 435.
175. Anon, *The Right Method of Maintaining Security*, pp. 3–4.
176. Sedgly, *Observations*, p. 84.
177. *London Evening Post*, 8 September 1750; *Derby Mercury*, 14 September 1750.
178. Radzinowicz, *A History*, 1, pp. 422 on the 1750s and 505–507 for the judges as a group opposing early-nineteenth-century reform.
179. In 1752 an act to substitute hard labour in the Government's dockyards for capital punishment was passed by the Commons but failed in the Lords, Connors, 'The Grand', p. 309.
180. Radzinowicz, *A History*, 1, p. 424.
181. For evidence that between the printing of the bill and its final amendment less than a week later Hardwicke went through and noted several changes on his copy that were then adopted British Library, HOL 35877 f.96-7.
182. We cannot be absolutely sure that the government was behind the Murder Act but what evidence there is concurs with Connors suggestion that 'major legislative initiatives like the Murder Act may have been orchestrated by the administration' Connors, 'The Grand', p. 312.
183. Connors, 'The Grand', p. 312.

184. D. Hay, 'Property, Authority and the Criminal law' in D. Hay et al. (eds.), *Albion's Fatal Tree* (London, 1975), p. 18.
185. For example, in the City of London alone between 1714 and 1750 twenty-five offenders were hanged for stealing in the dwelling house, shoplifting, or theft from a warehouse—all of which had fairly recently been made capital. A further five were hanged for picking pockets—an offence which had long been capital but which was regarded as so minor by the eighteenth century that the majority of those detected were informally ducked. Beattie, p. 457; D. Churchill and P. King 'Left to the Mercy of the Mob; Ducking, Popular Justice and the Magistrates in Britain (1750-1890)' in E., Delivre and E., Berger (eds.), *Popular Justice in Europe* (Berlin 2014) pp. 135–168. The Parliamentary returns, for both London and Middlesex, indicate that between 1750 and 1752 at least ten Old Bailey offenders were hanged for these four offences whilst a further five went to the gallows under other recent statutes for riot, or returning from transportation—*PP.*, 1819, viii, p. 136. However, these new statutes—like all capital statutes involving property offenders—were relatively unused in the North and West of England and in Wales. See P. King and R. Ward, 'Rethinking the Bloody Code in Eighteenth-Century Britain: Capital Punishment at the Centre and on the Periphery' *Past and Present* (2015), 228, pp. 159–205.
186. Anon, *Hanging not Punishment*, pp. 4–5.
187. Beattie, *Crime*, pp. 144–145.
188. Jones, *Some Methods*, p. 7. Sheep stealing was made capital in 1741, Beattie, *Crime*, p. 145.
189. *London Magazine*, 13 (1744), p. 506. Stealing privately from the person was capital if the goods stolen were worth a shilling as was highway robbery to even such a tiny value.
190. Ibid., p. 506.
191. *Newcastle Courant*, 22 December 1750; *Derby Mercury*, 28 December 1750.
192. Sedgly, *Observations*, pp. 64–65.
193. *Newcastle Courant*, 20–27 April 1751; *The Scots Magazine* (May 1751) p. 222–224; *The Rambler*, no 114 (April 1751).
194. *Newcastle General Magazine* (May 1750), p. 265—an extract from 'Whiston's Memoirs in relation to Public errors'—which Whiston published that year.
195. Anon, *The Right Method of Maintaining Security*, pp. 75–76. These views drew upon on a much older critique. In the 1650s several writers attacked those who had 'broken the statute laws of God' by executing a man 'merely for theft'. William Tomlinson, writing under the title 'Of hanging for theft, filling the land with blood', asked why Parliament both ignored 'the restitution that the wisdom of God thought good to allow in cases of

theft' and persisted in this 'most unjust and cruel law' even though God's law 'was not so cruel as to take away the life of the thief for goods'. W. Tomlinson, *Seven Particulars* (London, 1657) Section 4; S. Chidley, *A Cry Against … them who have Broken the Statute Laws of God by Killing of Men Merely for Theft* (London, 1652) which described this practice as 'inhumane, Bloody, Barbarous and Tyrannicall' p. 6; I. Gentles, 'London Levellers in the English Revolution: the Chidleys and their Circle' *Journal of Ecclesiastical History*, 29 (1978), pp. 295–296.

196. Connors, 'The Grand', p. 302.
197. For three examples from the 1750s and 1760s—see Hay, 'Property', pp. 20–21.
198. *London Evening Post*, 14 July 1750; *Caledonian Mercury*, 24 July 1750.
199. *London Evening Post*, 14 July 1750.
200. 25 Geo.II. cap 37.
201. All these were introduced in the later seventeenth and early-eighteenth centuries, Beattie, *Crime*, pp. 144–180. Others such as picking pockets and horse theft not to mention burglary had long been capital by 1689. To those offences made capital in the early-eighteenth century could also be added many more including those covered by the Black Acts and various forms of forgery.
202. Ward, *Print Culture*, p. 159.

3

Implementation of the Murder Act

1 Introduction

The Murder Act was very widely publicized immediately after it received the royal assent in late March 1752. It was very rare for the newspapers to print the text of an act in full, or even to describe its contents in detail, but a wide range of newspapers and periodicals did precisely that in the weeks following the passing of the Act. The *London Gazette*, for example, reprinted it in full. The *London Magazine*, the *General Advertiser* and the *Scot's Magazine* published a detailed description of every clause.[1] It was also very widely publicized in the provincial papers. Both the *Manchester Mercury* and the *Derby Mercury* dedicated half of their front pages to a detailed description of all the Act's main provisions, while a considerable range of other newspapers described the content of all its main clauses, praising it as a 'very good provision' and 'a very wholesome Act.'[2] This enthusiastic welcome did not necessarily continue, as we will see in Chap. 4 when we will look in detail at changing attitudes to post-execution punishment between 1752 and the early 1830s, which was the point at which Parliament decided to put an end to both the dissection and the gibbeting of executed offenders. In this chapter, however, the focus is not on discursive formations and legislative initiatives but on the actual decisions of the courts. Between 1752 and the early 1830s a large number of capitally convicted offenders were subjected to post-execution punishments and a few were sentenced to other aggravated forms of execution such as burning at the stake. This chapter analyses the ways these punishments were used by the courts and how that usage changed between 1752 and 1832.

Although this volume focusses primarily on the initial set of decisions that shaped the fate of the criminal corpse, that is, those made by the judges when they passed sentence in court—huge discretion was also given to various other actors in deciding precisely what post-execution punishment each criminal's corpse would actually receive. Since Elizabeth Hurren and Sarah Tarlow[3] have recently completed studies of the post-sentencing roles played by the surgeons in charge of dissection and by those responsible for the gibbeting of offenders, the decisions made by these actors, such as those made by the few surgeons who returned the bodies of executed criminals to their families rather than dissecting them,[4] are only discussed relatively briefly in this chapter. What is presented here is a detailed analysis of the first and most formative moment in the decision-making process that shaped the fate of a criminal's corpse, that is, the sentences pronounced by the trial judges and the semi-formal instructions that sometimes followed those sentences.

The core of this chapter will be a new and comprehensive set of statistics that enables us to map out the changing patterns of post-execution punishment that can be observed in the period between the passing of the Murder Act in 1752 and its effective repeal in 1832. The main focus will be on the dissection and gibbeting of murderers under that Act, but the chapter also includes an overview of the other much smaller groups of offenders who were sentenced to post-execution punishment or aggravated forms of the death penalty between 1752 and the early 1830s. This will include the relatively small sub-group of property offenders who were selected by the judges for gibbeting, the offenders subjected to either dissection or gibbeting by the Admiralty courts, and two groups who appeared to receive aggravated pre-execution punishments for different types of treasonable offences but who in practice almost always suffered only post-execution penalties.

Two main types of punishment were used against treasonable offenders. The first was burning at the stake for petty treason—which was a punishment reserved for women alone (the vast majority of whom had either murdered their husbands/masters or committed coining offences). To all intents and purposes this had turned into a post-execution punishment by the early-eighteenth century because by then it had become customary to strangle the offender to death before burning her.[5] The second type was disembowelling, beheading and so forth that continued to be used against those convicted of fully treasonable offences, but these also changed into what were effectively post-execution punishments as it became normal practice to hang the offenders until they were dead before cutting and beheading them.[6] Since these two exceptional treason-related punishments constituted less than 4% of the post-execution sanctions used in this period, the main focus in this chapter will be the changing ways that both the major courts and, to a lesser extent, the Admiralty courts utilized the two main post-execution punishments available to them: dissection and gibbeting.

2 The Sources for the Study of Post-execution Punishment 1752–1834

In analysing patterns of post-execution punishment in the period between the passing of the Murder Act in 1752 and the final abandonment of dissection in the 1832 Anatomy Act, and of gibbeting in the 1834 Act for the Abolition of the 'Hanging the Bodies of Criminals in Chains',[7] this chapter will begin by exploring four main aspects: the overall percentage of offenders given each type of post-execution punishment; changes across time in the use of dissection, gibbeting, and so on; geographical variations in sentencing policies; and the ways that the nature of the offence and of the offender may have influenced the courts' decisions about which post-execution punishment to use. It will also attempt to explain these patterns, but it will not explore the broader historiographical questions raised by these findings; these will be discussed in Chaps. 4 and 5.

As we saw in Chap. 1, the two main forms of post-execution punishment in use in the eighteenth century—hanging in chains, and dissection—had been part of the state's penal repertoire for centuries, being used against both murderers and other types of offenders such as violent highway robbers. We cannot be sure that the use of either of these two punishments peaked in the period between the 1752 Murder Act and the 1830s. Zoe Dyndor's recent work has shown, for example, that the State's desire to crack down on violent smugglers produced very high gibbeting rates in the 1740s,[8] and there can be no doubt that dissecting surgeons made extensive formal and informal use of the corpses of various types of offenders before 1752.[9] Lacking systematic sources for the first half of the eighteenth century, we are reliant on newspaper accounts of executions and there are certainly a substantial number of these that report the dissection of highway robbers, murderers and other serious offenders. However, it is very unlikely that the numbers subjected to post-execution dissection were greater before the Murder Act than in period between 1752 and 1832. Those 80 years were not only a period in which these two post-execution punishments were extensively used, but also the only era in which they played a formal role in sentencing and penal policy, and it is therefore very fortunate that systematic sources became available from the mid-century onwards that enable us to analyse the precise extent to which dissection and hanging in chains were used as formal sentences during this time.

One of the main reasons why historians have not analysed post-execution punishment in detail has been the apparent lack of systematic sources. Assize court records have not survived for several circuits or are available only for parts of the period. Moreover, even though they usually record the passing of a death sentence, they may not always have included an indication that the offender was to be hung in chains because, after a debate among the judges three months after the passing of the Murder Act, it was decided that this part of the sentence could be achieved not by formal announcement but 'by special order to the Sheriff', which was usually made at the end of the assizes.[10] Moreover, although the 1819 committee charged by Parliament with investigating the capital code collected a considerable amount of material on past execution levels, additional post-execution punishments were very rarely mentioned and were never systematically counted by those who compiled the report's statistics.[11] Fortunately the Wellcome Trust's funding of the 'Harnessing the Power of the Criminal Corpse' project enabled us to make an extensive search of hitherto unused sources and to exploit a largely neglected source: the Sheriffs' Cravings and the sheriff's assize calendars.[12] These sources were stored in the Treasury records rather than in the court archives and had therefore been missed by most criminal justice historians. They were created by the county sheriffs' regular requests to central government demanding reimbursement for the expenses incurred in inflicting on the condemned all the punishments imposed by the county assizes, including every hanging.[13] Although there are a few small gaps,[14] they offer an almost complete guide to the number of provincial hangings and to the proportion of offenders who were then either sent for dissection or hung in chains.[15] The resulting dataset, which covers every county in England and Wales, and nearly every sentence of dissection or hanging in chains that occurred between 1752 and 1834, forms the basis for all the tables and figures in this chapter.[16]

3 Patterns of Post-execution Punishment 1752–1834: An Overview

In homicide cases, if the jury had neither acquitted the accused nor avoided a capital sentence by bringing in a partial verdict of manslaughter, the judge had no choice but to sentence the convicted murderer to death. However, between 1752 and 1832, even after a full murder conviction had been brought in, the judge still had to make a further choice between three basic options: to recommend a pardon, to order the offender to be hung in chains or to sentence him/her to dissection. One other outcome was also possible: the convicted offender might die in gaol before the sentence could be carried out. However, when this outcome was the result of the convict's own choice—that is when he or she had committedsuicide before execution—the offender did not usually escape post-mortem punishment. Of the six murderers who took this route between 1752 and 1832 three were hung in chains or on the gallows, two were dissected and one was buried at a local crossroads.[17] A similar fate might also befall those who chose to take this way out whilst awaiting trial. In 1811, for example, the corpse of the man accused of the notorious Radcliffe Highway murders was paraded through the streets on a cart and buried at a crossroads with a stake through his corpse after he committed suicide in prison.[18]

As the review of all murder conviction outcomes in Table 1 makes clear, dissection dominated the post-execution sentencing choices of the assizes and of the Old Bailey judges. Between 1752 and 1832 just under 80% of murderers whose convictions we have been able to trace were sentenced to have their corpses anatomized and dissected. One eighth was hung in chains and about one in twelve escaped with a pardon.[19]

The main question that emerges from the pattern of post-execution sentences seen in Table 1 is why, in cases of murder, did trial judges in

Table 1 Outcomes of convictions under the Murder Act

	Number	*Percentage*
Dissected	923	79.2
Hanged in chains	144	12.3
Pardoned	97	8.3
Misc	2	0.2
Total	1166	100

Sources (for all tables) TNA E197/34, E389/242-57, t90/148-70, T207/1, Assi 2/19,21/9,23/7; p128/3-6; DUR 16/2-5

both the provinces and in London clearly regard dissection as a much more suitable post-execution sentence? However, before we look in detail at decisions about dissection or gibbeting, it is also important to understand the role that pardons played in these statistics. Almost all the murderers who were pardoned from post-execution punishment did so because they escaped the noose entirely. It was extremely rare for the post-execution part of the sentence to be formally removed unless the offender had also been pardoned from the death sentence itself. Petitions requesting this partial form of pardon were infrequent, partly because only two or three days were available before the offender was executed, and partly perhaps because they were so rarely successful.[20] However, some examples have come to light. In the mid-eighteenth century Lord Hardwicke, the Chief Justice, had to respite the gibbeting part of a sentence he had passed on a Cornish offender after being informed that the 'rabble' would undoubtedly 'cut him down', which 'would be a fresh insult to authority' and might offer them 'a new triumph',[21] and on another occasion the same judge left it to the Sheriff of Cornwall to decide whether or not to gibbet a man found guilty of three murders. The Sheriff decided to reprieve him of this part of the sentence because of 'the disturbed and lawless condition of the county', and Hardwicke agreed that 'the disposition of the common people would not allow it' and that 'it might have been very unfortunate … to have given the rabble an opportunity of striking the last blow'.[22]

A dissection sentence was virtually never respited by the assize judges[23] but this did not mean that some of those ordered to be dissected did not avoid this part of the punishment, despite the judges' refusal to pardon them. In some remote rural areas where county hospitals had yet to be established, the lack of appropriate medical men able and willing to dissect sometimes meant the sentence was not actually carried out,[24] while occasionally the surgeons took it upon themselves (without statutory justification) to hand a criminal's corpse over to his relatives for burial, either intact or after a few token incisions, thus enabling him or her to avoid this part of the sentence.[25] It remains unclear precisely why the judges used their pardoning powers so infrequently to remit the post-execution element of the sentences they passed. It is possible that they did not believe that the Murder Act gave them the right to do so. Indeed there were some late-eighteenth-century commentators who believed that the wording of the Act went further than this and also made it illegal for either the judges or the King to pardon anyone from the hanging part of the sentence.[26] Most judges clearly did not believe this. Over ninety murderers were pardoned between 1752 and 1832, usually because the evidence against them was flawed, there were questions about their sanity or they had friends in very high places.[27] However, murder was still regarded as an extremely serious crime and pardoning rates were therefore extremely low compared to those for other crimes—in Essex nearly three-quarters of capitally convicted property offenders were pardoned in this period compared to only 8% of murderers.[28] The main choice of punishment in murder cases therefore remained between dissection and gibbeting.

Before we move on to look at detailed patterns of post-execution sentencing, at how they varied over time and between regions, and then at why dissection was so much more frequently chosen compared to hanging in chains, it is important to note that dissection was not quite as dominant amongst the entire group of offenders subjected to post-execution punishments as it was among murder cases alone. This was because dissection did not dominate the sentences handed out in the five other (much smaller) categories of case that could result in a post-execution punishment (Table 2).

Table 2 Patterns of post-execution punishments 1752–1834; by court and type of case

		Hanged	*Burnt*	*Beheaded*		
	Dissected	*In chains*	*At stake*	*Etc.*	*Total*	*% of all*
Assizes & Old B; Murder Act convictions*	908	131	0	0	1039	87.3
Assizes and Old B; Property Offences	0	55	0	0	55	4.6
Admiralty court; Murder Act cases	15	13	0	0	28	2.4
Admiralty court; Non-Murder cases (Piracy etc.)	0	23	0	0	23	1.9
Assizes & Old B; Petty Treason (Murder/Coining)	0	0	22	0	22	1.8
Assizes Old B & Higher Courts: High Treason	0	0	0	23	23	1.9
Total	923	222	22	23	1190	99.9
Percentage of all post-execution punishments	77.6	18.7	1.8	1.9	100	

*Pardons excluded

The first of these—the burning of women found guilty of petty treason—never involved dissection. The twenty-two women who were found guilty of either murdering their husbands/masters or of coining between 1752 and 1790 (when this punishment was abandoned by Parliament) were all burnt at the stake. Burning was effectively a post-execution punishment because by the mid-eighteenth century it was a tradition that the person was always strangled first. The second category centred on the relatively small number of capitally convicted property offenders whom the assize or Old Bailey judges decided not only to sentence to death but also to hang in chains. Since the courts could not formally sentence these offenders to dissection, the fate of these fifty-five men (women were never hung in chains) also reduces slightly the proportion of post-execution sentences that involved a visit to the surgeon's table.[29] The third category of cases—the twenty-three executions that resulted from convictions for high treason—had the same effect. These might sometimes involve the disembowelling and beheading of the offender after they had been hanged, but they did not involve a formal sentence of dissection. Because the Admiralty Court heard both murder cases and those not involving homicide, it used both dissection and gibbeting. However, since nearly half of the capital sentences it passed involved piracy, theft on the high seas, or mutiny (for all of which dissection does not seem to have been an option) and since it only used dissection against just over half of those convicted of murder (Table 2), this court also reduced the overall proportion of post-execution punishments that involved dissection. However, because these five minor groups of cases accounted for only one-eighth of the post-execution sentences passed between 1752 and 1832, their impact on the proportion of offenders subjected to dissection remained minimal. Overall in this period well over three-quarters of the offenders whose corpses were subjected to post-execution punishment were sent to the surgeons table, while less than one-fifth were ordered to be hung in chains (Tables 1 and 2).

4 Changing Patterns of Post-execution Punishment 1752–1832

The pattern of post-execution punishments used by the courts had its own distinct chronology and geography. Over the period 1752–1832 as a whole, once the small number who received pardons are excluded,

13.5% of murderers were hung in chains compared to the 86.5% who were dissected. However, the degree to which dissection dominated post-execution sentences did not remain static over time. As Table 3a makes clear the role of dissection became more dominant after 1800. Although the figures oscillated considerably, overall in the first half century after the Murder Act (1752–1801) just under 20% of murderers were gibbetted (Table 3b). However, after 1801 there was a drastic collapse in the proportion of murder sentences that involved gibbeting. Between 1802 and 1832 less than 4% of murderers were gibbeted. Clearly the early years

Table 3 **a** Number of Murder Act Sentences involving dissection/gibbeting by decade 1752–1832; Assizes and Admiralty courts (pardons excluded). **b** Proportion of Murder Act Sentences involving hanging in chains (HIC). By decade 1752–1832. Assizes and Admiralty courts (pardons excluded)

(a)

Period	*Ass Mur; Diss*	*Adm Mur; Diss*	*Both Crts Mur; Diss*	*Ass - Mur; HIC*	*Adm- Mur; HIC*	*Both Crts Mur; HIC*
1752–1761	114	1	115	28	0	28
1762–1771	102	1	103	27	0	27
1772–1781	97	0	97	18	2	20
1782–1791	122	0	122	28	3	31
1792–1701	110	6	116	23	0	23
1802–1811	75	2	77	2	0	2
1812–1821	168	5	173	2	8	10
1822–1832	120	0	120	3	0	3
All years	908	15	923	131	13	144

(b)

Period	*All Mur puns*	*% HIC both courts*	*% HIC assizes only*
1752–1761	143	19.6	19.7
1762–1771	130	18.9	19.0
1772–1781	117	14.0	12.7
1782–1791	153	21.7	19.7
1792–1801	139	16.1	16.2
1802–1811	79	1.4	1.4
1812–1821	183	7.0	1.4
1822–1832	123	2.1	2.1
All years	1067	13.5	12.6

of the nineteenth century witnessed a major change in attitudes towards hanging offenders in chains.

Although Table 3a, b appears to suggest that there was a brief revival in the use of hanging in chains in the second decade of the nineteenth century, this was almost entirely due to the fact that the Admiralty Court gibbeted eight offenders for murder on the high seas between 1814 and 1816 (Fig. 1 and Table 3a, b).[30] When these cases are excluded it becomes clear that the Old Bailey and assizes judges changed their sentencing policies fundamentally after 1801. Although they sentenced five murderers to hanging in chains between 1800 and 1801, they only used this option twice in the following decade and did not use it at all between 1816 and 1826. Indeed in the entire three decades before the 1832 Anatomy Act the assizes courts sentenced only five murderers to hanging in chains compared to the 363 whose corpses they subjected to dissection.[31] Thus the proportion of murderers hung in chains by the assize and Old Bailey judges suddenly and irreversibly declined from just under 1 in 5 between 1752

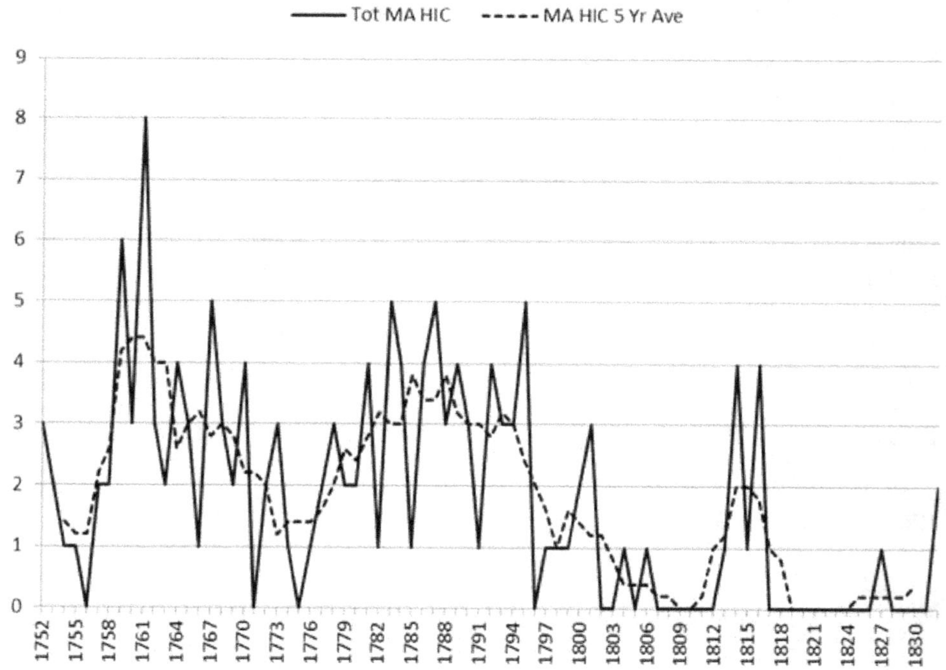

Fig. 1 Corpses hung in chains under the Murder Act, 1752–1832 (including Admiralty cases)

and 1801 to less than 1 in 50 between 1802 and 1832. Having peaked between 1782 and 1791, when it constituted nearly 22% of sentences for murder (Table 3b), after 1801 hanging in chains became an extremely rare sentencing option.

This sudden change in sentencing policies is even more evident when we look at the patterns of post-execution punishment in relation to non-killing offences (primarily property crimes) seen in Fig. 2. Here the change was extremely sudden at both the assizes courts and the Admiralty Court. In 1803 the assize judges, who, on average, had gibbeted a dozen property offenders per decade in the 1780s and 1790s, and had used this punishment against nine such offenders in the 4-year period 1799–1802, suddenly decided to completely abandon the use of hanging in chains in property crime cases. It was never part of a non-murderers sentencing after 1802. In the Admiralty Court the change was equally sudden and came a few years earlier. In the 1780s that court sentenced an average of one person a year to hanging in chains for mutiny, piracy or stealing,[32] and a similar number received the same sentence for non-killing offences

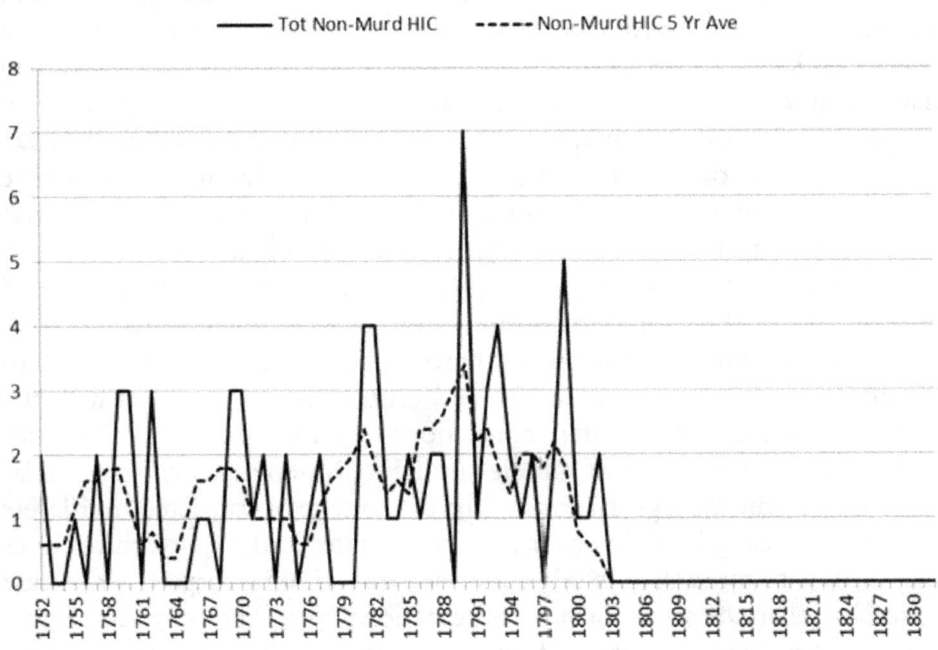

Fig. 2 Corpses hung in chains for non-killing offences, 1752–1832 (including Admiralty cases)

between 1790 and 1798. However, after gibbeting two offenders in 1798 for serving on a French ship while Britain was at war with France, the Admiralty Court completely stopped using hanging in chains for non-killing offences. Like the assizes they still very occasionally resorted to gibbetting for murder (in 1814 and 1816 only) but they abandoned the use of hanging in chains for non-killing offences 4 years before the assizes judges made the same choice in 1802.

5 The Geography of Gibbeting

Patterns of post-execution punishment not only changed over time, they also varied between regions (Table 4). Although overall between 1752 and 1832 only 13.5% of executed murderers were hung in chains, in ten of the fifty-one counties of England and Wales, as well as in the Admiralty Court, more than one-quarter had their corpses gibbeted rather than dissected. The geography of the courts' dissection/gibbeting preferences is complex but four features stand out. First, the four very large counties that had the highest numbers of convicted murderers—the only four that averaged at least seven full murder convictions per decade—all gibbeted significant but smaller than average proportions of their corpses. London (6.3%) Devon (5.4%) Yorkshire (7.0%) and Kent (7.5%) between them averaged less than half the gibbeting rate of the country as a whole. Having lots of potential corpses to gibbet does not appear to have encouraged the judges to make this part of the punishment. Indeed, in relative terms, it seems to have discouraged them, perhaps because only a certain number of gibbetings were deemed to be either necessary, useful or socially acceptable.

Secondly, by contrast, the four highly exceptional counties that gibbeted at least 50% of their murderers were all places were few convictions took place. The counties with the highest percentages of murderers sentenced to be gibbeted were the two southern and central English counties with the smallest number of murder convictions—Huntingdon and Rutland. Thirdly the vast majority of middle-sized English counties clustered relatively near to the average in terms of the percentage of convicted murderers punished by being hung in chains. Gibbeting rates in the fourteen counties that dealt with more than two but less than five criminal corpses per decade varied less than 9% above or below the national rate. The only region that seems to have had more than double the average gibbeting rate was East Anglia. The average rate in the counties of Suffolk, Norfolk and

Table 4 Sentences under the Murder Act—dissection or hanging in chains—by county 1752–1832

County	*Diss*	*H in Ch*	*Total*	*% H in Ch*	*County*	*Diss*	*H in C*	*Total*	*% H in C*
Bedfordshire	4	0	0	0.0	Leicestershire	16	2	18	11.1
Breconshire	5	0	5	0.0	Northumberland	8	1	9	11.1
Cardiganshire	5	0	5	0.0	Surrey	32	6	38	15.8
Cornwall	18	0	18	0.0	Nottinghamshire	10	2	12	16.7
Denbighshire	2	0	2	0.0	Warwickshire	33	7	40	17.5
Flintshire	3	0	3	0.0	Derbyshire	9	2	11	18.2
Merionethshire	1	0	1	0.0	Staffordshire	22	5	27	18.5
Monmouthshire	14	0	14	0.0	Hampshire	42	10	52	19.2
Montgomeryshire	3	0	3	0.0	Lincolnshire	20	5	25	20.0
Oxfordshire	11	0	11	0.0	Worcestershire	12	3	15	20.0
Sussex	15	0	15	0.0	Suffolk	22	6	28	21.4
Westmorland	3	0	3	0.0	Gloucestershire	31	9	40	22.5
Devonshire	53	3	56	5.4	Dorset	6	2	8	25.0
Lancashire	35	2	37	5.4	Herefordshire	9	3	12	25.0
Somerset	33	2	35	5.7	Pembrokeshire	3	1	4	25.0
London	148	10	158	6.3	Carmarthenshire	5	2	7	28.6
Essex	27	2	29	6.9	Caernarvonshire	2	1	3	33.3
Yorkshire	53	4	57	7.0	Norfolk	10	6	16	37.5
Northamptonshire	13	1	14	7.1	Radnorshire	3	2	5	40.0
Kent	49	4	53	7.5	Cambridgeshire	4	3	7	42.9
Durham	12	1	13	7.7	Cumberland	4	3	7	42.9
Hertfordshire	11	1	12	8.3	Admiralty Sessions	15	13	28	46.4
Wiltshire	32	3	35	8.6	Berkshire	4	4	8	50.0
Buckinghamshire	10	1	11	9.1	Glamorgan	5	5	10	50.0
Shropshire	19	2	21	9.5	Rutland	1	2	3	66.7
Cheshire	16	2	18	11.1	Huntingdonshire	0	1	1	100.0
					Total	923	144	1067	13.5

Cambridgeshire, all of which dealt with less than two murderers' corpses a decade, was 29.4%. However, a considerable number of the counties with very small numbers to deal with exhibited the final outstanding feature of the geography of judicial decision making under the Murder Act: they did not gibbet any murderers at all during the entire 80 years (Table 4). Many of the twelve counties that fell into this category were very small. Half of them dealt with three corpses or less during the entire period that the Murder Act was in operation. Two others dealt with only five. The average among this group was well under one per decade, presenting a huge contrast to the average of seven per decade seen in Yorkshire, Devon and Kent and the twenty per decade seen in London. In contrast to the smaller counties such as Huntingdonshire and Rutland that went the other way and made hanging in chains their main response, the majority of these twelve non-gibbeting counties were on the western periphery of England and Wales: including Cornwall, Westmoreland and seven Welsh counties. This tendency for the western parts of the country to avoid gibbeting murderers should not be overemphasized—although the absolute numbers involved were always small, at least a few Welsh counties gibbeted above average percentages. However, when we move on to look at the geography of gibbeting polices for non-murder convicts it becomes clear that the western periphery did indeed have a much greater reluctance to hang offenders in chains than the rest of the country.

Gibbeting for property crime had a very specific geography (Table 5). Nearly half of the fifty-five gibbetings ordered by assize judges took place in London or on the Home circuit, while the far Northern and Western counties of England—Cornwall, Northumberland, Cumberland and Westmoreland—along with the whole of Wales only saw a total of two non-murderers hanged in chains in the entire 80 years. This was mainly the result of the refusal of most areas on the western periphery to hang more than a tiny number of convicts for property crime, an aspect of the history of capital punishment which, as Peter King and Richard Ward have recently shown, created a very different penal regime on the periphery.[33] The Cornish examples already quoted—in which the crowd, by threatening to triumphantly rescue the offender's body from the gibbet, persuaded the judge to cancel this part of the sentence—suggest, however, that the almost complete absence of gibbeting on the periphery was not merely a function of the lack of capitally convicted property offenders in these areas. The minimal use made of hanging in chains in non-murder cases was almost certainly also a function of the lack of support in many of these areas

Table 5 Number hung in chains, non-killing offences by county 1752–1832

County	*Non-murd HIC*	*County*	*Non-murd HIC*
Admiralty crt	23	Breconshire	0
London	8	Caernarvonshire	0
Sussex	7	Cambridgeshire	0
Hertfordshire	5	Cardiganshire	0
Lancashire	4	Carmarthenshire	0
Cheshire	3	Cornwall	0
Devonshire	3	Cumberland	0
Hampshire	3	Derbyshire	0
Kent	3	Dorset	0
Yorkshire	3	Glamorgan	0
Essex	2	Gloucestershire	0
Wiltshire	2	Herefordshire	0
Buckinghamshire	1	Huntingdonshire	0
Denbighshire	1	Leicestershire	0
Durham	1	Lincolnshire	0
Flintshire	1	Merionethshire	0
Norfolk	1	Monmouthshire	0
Nottinghamshire	1	Montgomeryshire	0
Northamptonshire	1	Northumberland	0
Oxfordshire	1	Pembrokeshire	0
Rutland	1	Radnorshire	0
Shropshire	1	Staffordshire	0
Somerset	1	Suffolk	0
Surrey	1	Warwickshire	0
Bedfordshire	0	Westmorland	0
Berkshire	0	Worcestershire	0

for the use of gibbeting against anything except particularly heinous murderers. Courts in the London area, by contrast, made extensive use of gibbeting in non-murder cases. If we add the twenty-three gibbetings ordered by the Admiralty court for non-murder offences, almost all of which took place on the Thames estuary, courts based in London or in the five Home Circuit counties between them initiated forty-nine gibbetings of non-murderers, that is, three-fifths of the total for the whole of England and Wales. Sussex alone gibbeted seven such offenders, partly because, as Zoe Dyndor's work has shown, a pattern of using hanging in chains against violent smugglers had been established in the county during the 1740s.[34] By contrast only ten counties outside London and the Home Circuit gibbeted more than one property offender during these 80 years and most of these only did so two or three times.

When it came to hanging the corpses of offenders in chains, the inhabitants of the capital and the counties immediately surrounding it would have witnessed a vastly greater density of gibbeted corpses than any other region. If we include the thirteen gibbetings for murder ordered by the Admiralty court (Table 2), and the twenty-three murderers gibbeted by the Old Bailey and Home Circuit judges a total of eighty-five corpses were put on gibbets in the area around London. In the Metropolis alone more than fifty corpses—between six and seven per decade—were left to rot 10–12 metres above the ground in their specially designed iron cages. Since, as Tarlow has pointed out, these gibbets could remain standing for several decades,[35] this meant that visitors to the metropolis would have found it difficult to avoid seeing a gibbeted offender. If the average gibbeted corpse remained in situ for 20 years [36] this would have meant that on average around fifteen such sights could be found in London at any one time between 1752 and 1832. These fifty or so corpses would have been shared fairly equally between the various Admiralty sites on the Thames approaches, and the well-established gibbeting sites used by the Old Bailey on the major roads out of London (at Hounslow Heath, Finchley Common, Kennington Common, Hangar Lane, Shepherd's Bush, Mile End, and on the Edgware Road).[37] Despite the fact that the Old Bailey judges gibbeted a lower proportion of convicted murderers than some provincial assizes, London was very much the epicentre of gibbeting especially in the third quarter of the eighteenth century. Between 1759 and 1772 around twenty offenders were hung in chains in the capital.[38] Given that the words gallows and gibbet were often virtually interchangeable in contemporary discourse,[39] it is not surprising that London was known as 'the city of the gallows'.[40]

The judges of the Admiralty court played a large role in creating this reputation, both by ordering around two-thirds of London gibbetings, and by placing their gibbets in very prominent positions, which most of those entering the capital by water could not have failed to see. The judges did not usually record their reasons for using gibbeting so widely, but hanging executed offenders in chains at prominent points on the Thames estuary almost certainly appealed to the Admiralty Court judges because it offered both the opportunity to display their authority, and the possibly of deterring potential pirates, or mutinous/murderous crews. The court's disparate jurisdiction over crimes committed on 'the high seas' made it particularly important to physically establish its authority, and these overt expressions of its power to execute offenders and then to punish their corpses would have done just that. Britain's large and rapidly expanding empire made it vital that trade links with the Americas, the West Indies, Africa, the East Indies and beyond be made as secure as possible from piracy, robbery and mutiny, and it was the function of the Admiralty Court to protect British shipping from these different depredations; no easy task in a period when Great Britain was more often than not at war. Given that London was the key port of the empire in the eighteenth century and that huge numbers of sailors therefore passed up the Thames each year, the assembly of gibbets that they saw each time they visited the port gave substance and immediacy to the power of the Admiralty Court and the fiscal/military state whose interests it guarded. It may also have been easier for the court's officers to ferry the corpses of executed criminals from the Admiralty Court's gallows at Execution Dock to a gibbeting site further up the Thames, than it would have been to transport them across London to the Surgeon's Hall surrounded all the way by jostling crowds.[41] However, their need to make expressive and long-lasting statements about their power to execute was almost certainly the main reason why this court made only a small contribution to the supply of criminal corpses sent to London surgeons.

6 The Prevalence and the Geography of Dissection

The number of convicted murderers subjected to dissection also varied considerably both across time and between regions.[42] Although nearly 80% of fully convicted murderers were dissected (Table 1), the number of corpses this made available to the surgeons was relatively small. In all 923 criminal corpses were ordered for dissection in these 80 years, an average of less than twelve per year. This is a very small number when compared with the needs of the metropolitan and provincial surgeons. For example, 592 bodies were used by the London's anatomy schools in 1826 and at least 450 in 1828, both being years in which there was only one full conviction under the Murder Act at the Old Bailey. Nor was the supply reliable or predictable for two main reasons. First the pattern of convictions under the Murder Act fluctuated very considerably, the lowest annual figure being three and the highest twenty-six (Fig. 3). These fluctuations were sometimes completely random but after 1775 the number of cadavers made available by the courts tended to be lower in wartime and higher in peacetime. Between 1775 and 1825 the 5-year moving average in Fig. 3 exhibits significant troughs during the American War of Independence

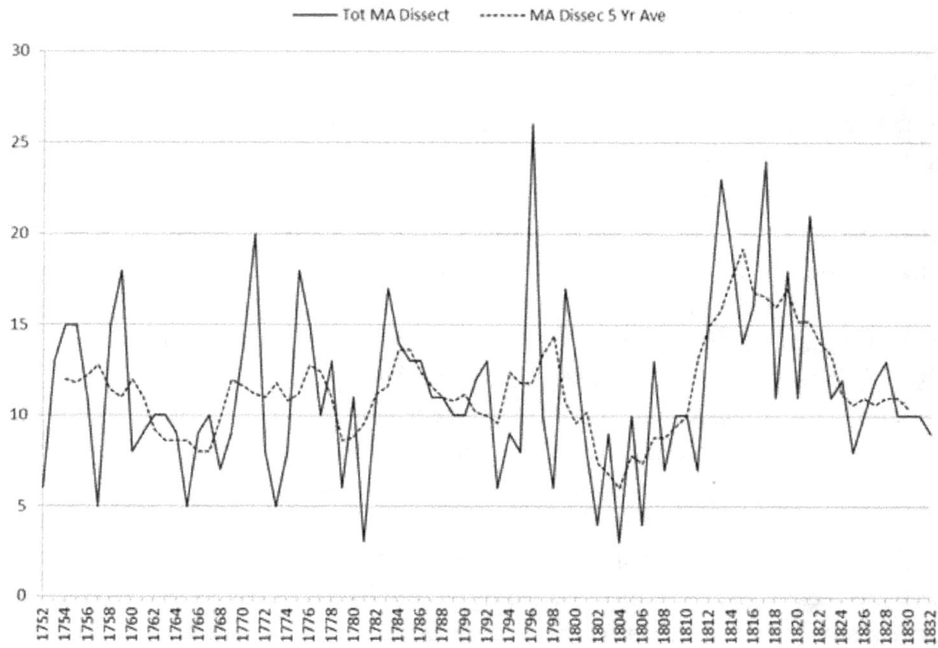

Fig. 3 Corpses made available to the surgeons under the Murder Act, 1752–1832 (including Admiralty cases)

(1776–1782) and the French Wars (1793–1815) and rises significantly in two periods that immediately followed the end of those two wars (1783–1785 and 1815–1818), probably because a significant percentage of young men, who formed the main demographic group accused of murder,[43] would have been absent abroad during these wars, but would have returned at the coming of peace.

In addition, as Hurren's work has also shown, the availability of corpses varied massively between areas. In London (if the Admiralty Courts contribution is included) around twenty per decade were available. In twenty out of the fifty-one counties of England and Wales less than one per decade was the norm. A variety of factors influenced the numbers of corpses made available for dissection under the Murder Act. The size of each county's population is the most obvious. The propensity of any particular county's inhabitants to commit acts that could be indicted for murder was also vital and was greatly influenced by the nature of the area. Murder indictment rates were six times higher in rapidly urbanizing areas like Lancashire, for example, than they were in the more remote rural regions of western

England and Wales.[44] The proportion of murderers who were detected and prosecuted was also important, but even more influential were the various factors that drastically reduced the proportion of indicted murderers that were actually sentenced to death.

Between 1791 and 1805—a period for which calculations are made easier by the existence of detailed calendars—only fifteen out of more than one hundred men and women accused of murder at the Old Bailey were actually executed. One in ten were left to remain in gaol or were released because their prosecutor failed to appear, one in eight had their indictments 'not found' by the grand jury, and well over one-third were found not guilty by the petty jury. Thus only just over two-fifths were actually convicted. Moreover, two-thirds of those convictions were not for murder but for the lesser, non-capital, offence of manslaughter.[45] A very similar pattern can be found outside the Metropolis. In Cornwall the assizes records indicate that between 1770 and 1824 only 12% of murder indictments ended in a sentence of death; 10% were not found, 45% were acquitted and 33% were found guilty only of manslaughter.[46] In Durham between 1780 and 1819 just under 15% of those indicted for murder were actually sentenced to death.[47] Many murder indictments in the eighteenth century arose either from cases in which the victim had been killed unintentionally during a fight or from other contexts in which there had been no premeditated intention to kill, and jurors were therefore very reluctant to bring in full convictions (or often any conviction at all) in such cases. It was therefore remarkably difficult to get yourself hanged for murder in any region of eighteenth-century England and Wales and the relatively small number of cadavers made available by the Murder Act mainly reflected that fact, although it was also affected to some extent by each county's gibbeting-to-dissection ratio.

Given that the population size of any given county and the degree to which it was experiencing industrialization and/or urbanization were such key factors, it is unsurprising that (as column 1 of Table 4 indicates) the largest counties containing major cities, such as Middlesex, Yorkshire, Lancashire and Warwickshire, and the few rural counties with very high populations, such as Devon, produced the highest numbers of criminal cadavers, as did the semi-metropolitan counties of Kent, Essex and Surrey. One-quarter of all those dissected for murder were executed in London, Surrey, Kent and Essex. Another eighth were sent on to surgeons in Warwickshire, Lancashire and Yorkshire, but in most Welsh counties, in Cumbria and in some other small English counties such as Bedfordshire and Berkshire one dissection every 20 years (or less) was the norm between 1752 and 1832. As Hurren has shown this did not prevent the development in most counties of elaborate and often highly public dissection rituals in specially assigned venues, the nature of which varied between regions.[48] Nor did it prevent London surgeons from developing very public rituals of anatomization and so on, which were accompanied by large crowds and involved a considerable degree of public participation.[49] However, prosecutions under the Murder Act were clearly utterly inadequate as a means of meeting the surgeon's needs for cadavers, and this was the main reason why some members of the medical profession pressed in 1786 for compulsory dissection to be extended to other types of capital convict.[50] However, even these limited numbers could be, and in many counties were, used to create periodic spectacles of post-execution punishment that were witnessed by large numbers of local inhabitants.[51] Although these dissection rituals only lasted a matter of days, rather than the many years of exposure to public gaze that were intrinsic in sentences of hanging in chains, both these post-execution options attracted huge crowds and provided an opportunity to demonstrate the law's power over a convicted murderer's body even after his or her execution.

7 The Impact of the Nature of the Offence and the Offender

It is a lot easier to describe the geography and chronology of the courts' decisions about sentencing murderers to either dissection or hanging in chains, than it is to analyse the impact that the nature of the offence and the character of the offender had on those decisions. The Sheriff's Cravings do not contain systematic information on the age, previous character, physical condition or occupation/social status of the offender, and unfortunately the vast majority of the assize records are also silent on these matters. Moreover, it is often not possible to obtain precise information on the type of murder for which the accused was convicted. However, the offenders' first names make it relatively easy to analyse the impact of gender. No women were hung in chains. None of the fifty-five non-murderers gibbeted for property crimes between 1752 and 1832 were women and no female murderers appear to have been gibbeted rather than dissected. This may have been because, to quote Blackstone, 'the decency due to the sex forbids the exposing ... their bodies,' but this did not prevent women's corpses from being sent for public dissection and the precise thinking behind this policy therefore remains unclear.[52] What is clear, however, is that it was only in cases involving males that the courts saw themselves as having a choice about which post-execution punishment to use.

How did the crimes and the characteristics of the male condemned affect the kind of post-execution punishments they received? The types of offences they had committed were clearly the major factor in the fifty-five cases where non-murderers were hanged in chains. As Tarlow's more detailed analysis has shown, more than three-quarters of those who were gibbeted had been convicted of highway robbery, the great majority of whom made the mistake of robbing the mail in an era when Post Office officials often made a point of asking assize judges to use this additional sanction.[53] Another 13% had been convicted of burglary, while the remaining 10% were hung in chains for shooting with intent to kill (two cases), arson, animal theft and riot (one case each).[54]

Lacking systematic data on the social status and age of convicted murderers, the impact of these variables on sentencing decisions about post-execution punishments can rarely be assessed, but some clues can be obtained from two small samples that can be extracted from the Old Bailey records. Unfortunately the last London murderer to be hung in chains went to the gallows in 1789, 2 years before the brief period (1791–1805) when details of the age and backgrounds of offenders were fairly systematically recorded in the Newgate Calendars. The Calendars do, however, give us information on fourteen London men and one woman dissected for murder during this period, and we can compare this sample of dissected offenders with the limited information Julian Raynor has managed to obtain on the occupations of a different, but similarly sized, group of London offenders gibbeted in the much longer period 1740–1789.[55] Not surprisingly perhaps the occupational backgrounds of the two samples are very similar. The dissected 1791–1805 convicts whose occupations are listed include a selection of unskilled and semi-skilled workers—a labourer, two mariners, a retired soldier, a soap-maker and a drover, as well as four from fairly skilled artisan backgrounds—a watchmaker, a bookbinder, a printer and a harness-maker. A fairly similar pattern emerges amongst Raynor's sample of gibbeted offenders, which included a sailor, a soldier, a husbandman, a saddler's apprentice, a journeyman gunsmith, a chocolate-maker, an attorney's clerk and three servants. In both cases half of the convicts were London born and between 20 and 26% were born outside England. The age ranges covered in the sample were also fairly similar: 73% of the dissected offenders were aged under forty, as were 78%

of the gibbeted. Both samples contained one convict over age seventy. One difference did stand out, however. While none of those who were dissected were aged under twenty, three of the nine gibbeted offenders fell into that category and two more were only twenty. However, this should not be taken to indicate that young offenders were more likely to be hung in chains simply because they were young. The younger age structure of these gibbeted offenders mainly reflected the very specific types of murderers that the Old Bailey judges chose to have hung in chains.

Unlike the dissected offenders, most of the gibbeted offenders in the 1740–1789 sample had committed murder during an act of robbery (ten out of fourteen), and since highway robbery was very much a young man's occupation, this meant that a much higher proportion of those hung in chains were young. Between 1752 and 1805 the Old Bailey judges also gibbeted at least six highway robbers who had not murdered their victims and it is possible that this regular practice also influenced their decisions in murder cases, since they confined the use of hanging in chains primarily to murders committed during acts of property crime.[56] The fate of three offenders convicted of murder at the July Old Bailey sessions in 1753 provides a clear illustration of these attitudes. One was found guilty of murdering his wife, the other two were convicted 'for the murder of the postman' during a robbery. The corpse of the former was 'carried to Surgeons' Hall', but the two robbers were eventually gibbeted 'in pursuance of an application from the Postmaster General'.[57]

Provincial practice followed a fairly similar pattern, although murders during robberies did not dominate to quite the same extent.[58] In 70 of the 131 murder cases across England and Wales that ended in a gibbeting the Sheriff's Cravings indicate roughly what types of murder resulted in a gibbeting sentence, and much the largest category, once again, were murders committed during a robbery or violent burglary (40%). A further 10% involved the murder of an official: a magistrate, bailiff, excise officer or gaoler.[59] Another 17% involved a husband killing his wife or a father killing his child.[60] Other murderers deemed suitable for gibbeting rather than dissection included three masters who murdered their servants, two servants who murdered their masters, a man who beat a woman to death after his proposal of marriage was turned down,[61] a stalker who constantly followed the victim and 'told her that if he could not have her he would end her'[62] and the 'Congleton Cannibal' (a butcher who cut the victim's body to pieces and then ate them).[63] Lacking the equivalent information for all murder convicts, it is difficult to draw definite conclusions, but it appears that a large proportion of those selected for gibbeting had committed forms of homicide that were regarded as particularly cruel and premeditated. Murders committed during robberies were certainly regarded as especially callous forms of homicide and it is not therefore surprising that this group dominated sentences of hanging in chains in the capital and were the much the largest subgroup across the whole of England and Wales. Overall, therefore, it appears that the type of murder the convict had committed almost certainly had a much greater influence on the judge's decision to sentence him to gibbeting than his age, status or migration history/ethnicity did. It should be remembered, however, that if the court had decided to send the corpse of a convict for dissection factors such as class, gender, age and ethnicity might well play a role in decisions about how the surgeons would handle the cadaver and what level of damage they would eventually inflict on it, a theme investigated in Chap. 4.

8 Reasons for Dissection's Dominance Amongst Sentences Passed Under the Murder Act

Why was dissection the dominant post-execution sentencing option under the Murder Act? There are, of course, no definitive answers to this question. Those who made these decisions almost never recorded their reasons and the attitudes and motives that lay behind their actions can therefore be interpreted in a variety of ways. The most obvious influence, if not necessarily the most important, was gender. Given that the courts had decided that it was not appropriate to hang women in chains, this automatically excluded 15.7% of those convicted of murder between 1752 and 1832 because they were female. If we look at the men only, the proportion subjected to gibbeting rather than dissection then rises from 13.5 to 16.0%. This would have meant that in the years before 1802, that is, the sub-period when gibbeting was still a major option, the courts chose to gibbet nearly one in four of the male murderers convicted before them. Until the beginning of the nineteenth century, therefore, the decision not to hang female convicts in chains made a significant, albeit minor, contribution to the ratio of dissections to gibbetings. However, this does not explain why, even in the pre-1802 period when hanging in chains was at its height, three out of every four males were sent for dissection. To explain the judges clear preference for dissection we need to investigate a number of potential contributory factors.

First, although the majority of criminal cadavers went to the surgeons, their influence on the sentencing process may well have been small. While the surgeons of cities where there were established anatomy schools, or where a good income could be obtained from public anatomy lectures,[64] would have been keen to get hold of criminal corpses, it is very difficult to find evidence of surgeons successfully demanding that the judges allow their need for cadavers to be the deciding factor in the sentencing process. Virtually the only recorded instances in which the surgeons decided the nature of the post-execution punishment were the very limited number of occasions when surgeons in remote provincial towns refused to take the offender's corpse, thus forcing the trial judges to hang the offender in chains.[65] Overall, however, these occasions appear to have been rare and in most parts of England the surgeons were not only willing to dissect the bodies of executed murderers, but were also very keen to do so. The surgeons increasing need for cadavers in places like London or Leeds may have had some influence, and this may partly explain why the gibbeting rate was lower than average in the capital. However, the courts could not have supplied a significant proportion of the numbers required by the anatomy teachers even if they had sent all convicted murderers on for dissection, and the vast majority of the judges do not seem to have been interested in making the surgeon's needs their main sentencing priority. On balance, therefore, it seems unlikely that the demand for cadavers was the main reason why sentences of dissection were used much more frequently than those involving gibbeting.

A second and probably more important factor may have been penal sensibilities—the desire of the judges not to overdo the gibbeting option, which if used regularly for a high percentage of murderers would, overtime, have populated the landscape of some areas with relatively large numbers of rotting corpses. It is interesting that the six exceptional counties that gibbeted at least 50% of their murderers were all places were very few convictions took place. It is no coincidence that the two English counties with the highest percentages of murderers sentenced to be gibbeted were the two smallest—Huntingdon and Rutland—which each averaged just one convicted murderer every 40 years, and therefore only gibbeted one murderer during the entire Murder Act period. The Old Bailey, by contrast, hung in chains a ten times smaller proportion of its convicted murderers, but despite this it still managed (with help from the Admiralty Court) to generate so many gibbets that London was perceived by many contemporaries as a major centre of gibbeting punishments. It is possible that in areas where murder convictions were relatively frequent judges deliberately cut back on their use of this punishment in order to keep the currency of hanging in chains high.[66] Overuse would have crowded certain parts of the urban landscape with rotting gibbets and stinking corpses and they may have thought that this would become counter-productive. Gibbeting in urban areas like London also tended to generate complaints from local inhabitants who disliked the stench, the noise and the visual proximity of the resulting gibbets, while often remaining doubtful about their deterrent value.[67]

A third factor that may have affected the courts' decisions to dissect rather than hang in chains was cost. Gibbeting was extremely expensive. The wood, the iron work, and the problem of creating a gibbet high enough and well protected enough to prevent rescue made gibbets very costly to build.[68] According to the Sheriffs' Cravings the average gibbet cost around £16.00 and some cost more than £50.00 (more than a year's wages for a labouring man).[69] By contrast the sheriffs could usually sell the body to the surgeons for a fee at least equal to the cost of organizing the dissection and were often, therefore, in profit at the end of the process. The sheriffs who, as members of the local elite, dined with the circuit judges regularly during their visit to the county, would have been very keen to avoid a gibbeting since their Cravings indicate they were rarely reimbursed for most of the costs they incurred.[70] The assize judge's habit of pronouncing an initial sentence of dissection on all convicted murderers and then announcing before they left the town at the end of the assizes week which of them (if any) had been selected to be gibbeted instead, gave the sheriffs an opportunity to work on the judges and it is possible that this operated to reduce still further the proportion of murderers hung in chains.

The sheriffs may also have been keen to avoid offenders being sentenced to hanging in chains for another reason. The gibbeting process was inherently difficult to organize and control. The same might be said of public dissection. As Hurren has shown large crowds were involved in the anatomization process and in viewing the dissected body, and crowd control could therefore be a problem.[71] However, the spaces in which dissection took place—surgeons' halls, county hospitals, shire halls, dispensaries—were relatively constricted and easier to control than the heaths and other public open spaces where gibbetings were staged.[72] As Tarlow has pointed out gibbetings often attracted vast crowds and there was no possibility of limiting the numbers or types of people involved. Thousands often attended.[73] Gibbet sites quite frequently became temporary recreational centres. Booths were set up, picnicking crowds often gathered in close proximity and local publicans not infrequently made a killing out of the gibbeting of a killer.[74] By contrast, although the dissection process might last for several days, it had a definite beginning and end. The venues were closed to the public after a limited period and the remains disposed of.[75]

Gibbets, on the other hand, could and did last for many decades. Crowds certainly gathered for an extended period after the initial gibbeting and their interactions with the corpse and the gibbet were almost impossible to control.[76] By climbing the gibbet and offering the corpse some food, a pipe or a one-way conversation, members of the crowd could undermine the solemnity of the punishment.[77] They might also rescue the corpse. During the second half of the eighteenth century we know of at least ten gibbeted bodies that were illegally removed. Some rescues took place in remote locations where they were relatively easy to achieve without discovery. In 1784, for example, two murderers' corpses were taken down from a gibbet in Whichwood Forest and carried off,[78] and several of the corpses gibbeted by the Admiralty Court along the remoter parts of the Thames estuary were also 'stolen and carried away'.[79] However, rescues also took place in urban locations. In 1763, for example, it was reported that 'all the gibbets on the Edgware Road, on which villains hung in chains, were cut down by persons unknown.'[80] Since there were almost certainly a number of other rescues that were not reported in the newspapers, it seems likely that somewhere around 10% of the criminal corpses gibbeted in this period were deliberately removed prematurely.[81]

The evidence already quoted, of Lord Hardwicke twice having to remit the gibbeting part of the sentence for fear of reprisals from the unruly inhabitants of Cornwall, clearly indicates the crowd could undermine this form of post-execution punishment. Was it just coincidence that no murderer or property offender was ever gibbeted in Cornwall in the period under study here, that is, in precisely the county where the crowd openly opposed its use and threatened to rescue the corpse? The authorities in other western counties faced similar problems. When William Skull was sentenced to be hung in chains at Wells Assizes 'the colliers rose in a body' and pulled down the gibbet before the corpse was brought there. The gibbet 'being again put up' and the body 'fixed in chains thereon' the authorities may have thought they had won the day but they were soon proved wrong. The colliers simply waited till nightfall when 'the body and chains were entirely carried off, so as not to be found'.[82] The long drawn out nature of the gibbeting process could also create other management problems. Corpses might fall down and have to be put back on the gibbet. Gibbets were sometimes blown down or destroyed by lightning.[83] Local residents sometimes petitioned successfully for the resiting of a gibbet and there were increasing worries that the corpses were a health hazard, especially in hot weather.[84] While dissection was a discreet, time-limited process (unless the convict was among the few who were allocated a niche at Surgeon's Hall), hanging in chains was an open-ended and much less controllable process.

Given that dissection was so much cheaper and easier to manage while extensive use of hanging in chains was probably seen as counter-productive, for the authorities to use gibbeting as frequently as dissection the former option would have needed to have had substantial, obvious and believable advantages that dissection did not possess. In reality, however, although the use of the gibbet had some outcomes that dissection did not have, both sentencing options shared several key features and conveyed a number of similar messages. Both aimed at deterring crime by creating a vivid public mark of infamy on top of the original execution rituals. Both drew large crowds to what could be (though it not always was) a ceremony of communal retribution. Both demonstrated the power of the state. Both denied a respectful, intact, burial to the criminal's corpse and relied on the belief that the lack of such a burial would have a deep impact on potential offenders. To some extent hanging in chains was a rather different process and perhaps a more punitive one in certain respects. While dissection, Tarlow has pointed out, obliterated the memory of the convict, gibbeting perpetuated the memory, notoriety and possibly (if the onlookers were antagonistic) the infamy of the accused—cementing that memory across periods of time that could span the generations and linking it to a prominent place in the everyday landscape of the local inhabitants.[85] Gibbeting also denied the criminal corpse even the semblance of the burial rites that were sometimes afforded to what remained of the post-dissection corpse.[86] However, many contemporaries (and many historians after them) had severe doubts both about whether either of these punishments was effective and about whether the add-ons offered by hanging in chains made post-execution punishment any more successful as a deterrent or any more effective as a means of delivering the messages that the state wished to get across.

Is it possible that the judges used dissection more frequently because they believed that it was more feared by the populace and therefore more useful as a deterrent? It is very difficult to find any concrete evidence to support this view. Although it is true that some contemporaries believed that 'the superstitious reverence of the vulgar for a corpse … and the strong aversion they have against dissecting them' made dissection an effective punishment, the same would have been true of hanging in chains.[87] If, as Linebaugh has argued, 'the formalized customs of bereavement, depending as they often did on the integrity of the corpse and the respect shown to it, were brutally violated by the practice of dissection',[88] this was surely even more true of the process of hanging the convict's corpse in chains, which ended without even the possibility of burying what remained of the corpse and meant that the offenders only place of memorial was a gibbet. Unfortunately it is almost impossible to ascertain how the criminals themselves saw these two options. All we have is a collection of brief statements drawn from newspaper coverage and court reporting indicating that some offenders showed great anxiety either because they were being sentenced to dissection or because they would soon be hanging in chains.[89] However, other convicts appeared to be relatively untroubled by the prospect of undergoing either one of these post-execution punishments[90] and it is possible that the remarks they made were much less widely reported than the more fearful expressions uttered by a minority of offenders. The Recorder at the Old Bailey certainly believed that very few murderers minded being anatomized 'as it is attended with no pain to them',[91] and some highway robbers were obviously equally immune from the fear of dissection, since they willingly sold their future corpses to the surgeons to fund their last days in prison.[92] Hanging in chains sometimes produced a similar reaction. One offender, faced with the prospect of gibbeting, joked calmly about being 'made Overseer of the Highways'. Another ordered beer for the blacksmith sent to measure him for his irons saying 'he always treated his tailor when he took his measure for a suit of clothes'. More typical perhaps was the stoical remark, 'I know my body must turn to corruption, and therefore it is all one to me, whether it rots above or below ground.'[93]

Not all of the murderers who were reported as having a fear of post-execution punishment regarded hanging in chains as the worst option.[94] However, in the majority of cases Radzinowicz may well have been correct when he suggested that offenders would be 'still more (terrified) that they might be hung in chains' than 'at the idea that their bodies might be dissected'.[95] Usually offenders were only recorded as being afraid of either one or the other of these sentences, but occasionally they have left some comparative evidence. A Suffolk murderer, for example, was reported to have specifically expressed a deep regret about 'the sentence being altered from dissection to hanging in chains', while a Bristol murderer who showed a great concern at being hung in chains, also made it clear that 'he did not care if they quarter'd his body' as long as 'it was not hung up in the air for prey for the birds.'[96] It remains unclear, however, whether the vital decision-making group, the judges, would have regarded one of these two options as more feared by the populace than the other. Unsurprisingly, therefore, given the practical disadvantages of gibbeting already listed and the fact that dissection could be seen as having a positive function in supplying the ever-growing needs of anatomy, sentences of hanging in chains were only resorted to in a relatively small sub-group of cases.

It is possible, as Richardson argued, that dissection was regarded by the courts as the more severe punishment in murder cases.[97] However, it seems more likely that in a significant range of circumstances the judges regarded gibbeting as the heavier punishment. They certainly used it against murderers such as the 'Congleton Cannibal', whose actions were deeply repulsive to the community. It is also possible to find a few occasions when the courts, faced with a group of offenders convicted of murder, chose hanging in chains for the offender they thought most culpable and dissected those they saw as less so. In 1764, for example, John Croxford, who had stabbed and killed a travelling pedlar whilst in the act of robbing him, was hung in chains on Hollowell Heath, Northamptonshire, whilst his two fellow highwaymen, who had only assisted him by burning the corpse in a local oven, were dissected.[98]

The courts also seem to have reserved hanging in chains mainly for two categories of cases that particularly mattered to them. They used it against the sub-group of murderers that were seen by the propertied elite as particularly heinous and dangerous, that is, those who had deliberately murdered someone during an act of robbery—and they used it to punish groups such as smugglers, pirates and mutinous crews who threatened the lifelines of the fiscal/military state. 'Crimes against the state', Tarlow has cogently argued, 'were more likely to lead to the spectacular punishment of hanging in chains than private, personal or domestic ones'.[99] However, since these crimes only formed the background to a relatively small number of executions, in the vast majority of cases the cheaper, more easily manageable and less cumulatively problematic option—dissection—was the sentence of first choice for most assize judges, most of the time, as well as being their only choice when the convict was a woman. Until around 1800 some of them still made reasonably extensive use of gibbeting in cases involving males, but from that point onwards dissection came to completely dominate sentencing policies, for reasons we will investigate more fully when we look in Chap. 4 at the discursive frameworks that dominated discussions of post-execution punishment between 1752 and 1832 and the ways that they changed across that period.

Notes

1. *London Gazette*, 7–11 April 1752; *London Magazine*, (April 1752), pp. 177–178; *Scot's Magazine*, 14 (May 1752), pp. 242–243; *General Advertiser*, 13 April 1752; *London Evening Post*, 24 March 1752.
2. *Manchester Mercury*, 21 April 1752; *Derby Mercury*, April 17–24 1752; *Salisbury Journal*, 20 April 1752; *Newcastle Courant*, 18 April 1752; It was also described as 'very wholesome' in *General Advertiser*, 13 April 1752. *London Evening Post* offered similar praise—R. Ward, *Print Culture, Crime and Justice in Eighteenth-Century London* (London, 2014) p. 200.
3. E. Hurren, *Dissecting the Criminal Corpse: Staging Post-Execution Punishment in Early-Modern England* (London, Palgrave, 2016) and S. Tarlow, *Hung in Chains: The Golden and Ghoulish Age of the Gibbet in Britain* (London, Palgrave, forthcoming).
4. For an example see D. Gray and P. King 'The Killing of Constable Linnell: The Impact of Xenophobia and of Elite Connections on Eighteenth-Century Justice' *Family and Community History*, 16 (2013).
5. The last known example of a woman burned alive was in 1726, S. Devereaux, 'The Abolition of the Burning of Women in England Reconsidered' *Crime, Histoire et Societes/Crime, History and Societies*, 9 (2005), p. 88.
6. V. Gatrell, *The Hanging Tree* (Oxford 1994) p. 317; Tarlow, *Hung*, pp. 12–15 provides an overview of punishments for treason.
7. 2 & 3 William IV, c.75, and 4 & 5 William IV, c.26.
8. Z. Dyndor, 'The Gibbet in the Landscape: Locating the Criminal Corpse in Mid-Eighteenth-Century England' in R. Ward (ed.), *A Global History of Execution and the Criminal Corpse* (Basingstoke, 2015) pp. 102–125; for the problematic evidence of the incidence of gibbeting S. Tarlow, 'The Technology of the Gibbet' *International Journal of Historical Archaeology*, 18 (2014), p. 670.
9. P. Linebaugh, 'The Tyburn Riot against the Surgeons' in D. Hay et al. (eds.), *Albion's Fatal Tree* (London, 1975) pp. 71–78.
10. M. Foster, *A Report of Some Proceedings … and of Other Crown Cases*, (Dublin, 1791, 2nd Edition) p. 107; National Army Museum Archives Ref 6510-146(2)-24 7 May 1752; Tarlow, *Hung*, pp. 21–22.

11. *Parliamentary Papers* (henceforth *PP*) 1819, viii.
12. The National Archives, London (hereafter TNA), Sheriffs' Cravings, T 64/262, T 90/148-166, and Sheriffs' Assize Calendars, E 389/242-248.
13. When submitting their Cravings the sheriffs included assize calendars as supporting evidence. They therefore represented 'the only warrant that the sheriff has, for so material an act as taking the life away of another.' W. Blackstone, *Commentaries on the Laws of England,* 4 vols. (Oxford, 1765–1769), 4, 369.
14. The Cravings do not cover London, Wales or certain special jurisdictions such as Durham, but extensive work on the court records of these areas, and the availability of Simon Devereaux's and Julian Rayner's work on the Metropolis enabled these gaps to be filled. I am grateful to Simon Devereaux for providing us with his database of London capital convictions and to Julian Raynor for data offered from his forthcoming Leicester Ph.D. thesis on Murder in London 1730–1900. The only remaining gap in the cravings data arises from the nineteen urban areas that could sentence offenders to death outside the county assize. Executions in these places were not included in the Cravings.
15. Sources for these areas were; National Library of Wales (hereafter NLW), Great Sessions 4 (county Gaol Files), as in the *Crime and Punishment in Wales* online database http://www.llgc.org.uk/sesiwn_fawr/index_s.htm (accessed 7 Nov. 2013); TNA, PL 28/2-3, CHES 21/7, DURH 16/1-2; *PP.*, viii (1819), pp. 236–250.
16. Sources on which this data set is based are TNA, E197/34, E389/242-57, T90/148-70,T207/1, Assi 2/19,21/9,23/7; P128/3-6; Ches 21/7; DUR 16/2-5; Devereaux database on London; NLW 4/188-1020; For pardons—TNA, SP 44/86-96, HO 47/6-71, HO 13/1-3. Admiralty—HCA 1/61, 85, 87,111–112. When Sheriff's Calendars were not available Sheriffs Cravings were used. Other gaps were filed from assize gaol or minute books.
17. E389/251/269; E197/34; E389/246/41; E389/246/77d; E389/245/602; t90/160. For post-mortem punishment of suicides and of staked highway/crossroads burial, Tarlow, *Hung,* pp. 16–18.
18. Gatrell, *The Hanging Tree*, pp. 84–85.
19. Given that the information available for London, Wales and Durham is not based on Sheriff's Cravings, there may have been a few cases where offenders were not described in the records as hung in chains but still suffered that punishment. It has been difficult to trace any such cases, however, despite a newspaper keyword search, and the data appears to be very nearly completely accurate. If a homicide by a woman was tried as petty treason she was not punished under the Murder Act and is therefore excluded from these statistics.

20. J. Beattie, *Crime and the Courts in England 1660–1800* (Oxford, 1986) p. 528 quotes two examples. For a wife petitioning that her husband's body not be hanged in chains for murder TNA SP 34/36/49 and for a rare successful petition against a mail robber being hanged in chains *Leicester and Nottingham Mail*, 30 March 1782.
21. D. Hay, 'Property, Authority and the Criminal Law' in Hay, *Albion's Fatal Tree*, p. 50. For discussion of post-gibbeting petitions for the removal of a gibbet and other ways corpses escaped long-term gibbeting—Tarlow, *Hung*, pp. 47–48.
22. G. Harris, *The Life of Lord Chancellor Hardwicke* (London, 1842) pp. 299–302.
23. In 1788 the Admiralty Court appears to have respited 3 offenders due to be gibbeted as they were described as interred. HCA 1/85, *The World*, 15 January 1788.
24. Hurren, *Dissecting*, for more detail.
25. Gray and King 'The Killing' and discussion below.
26. *London Evening Post*, 30 June 1770 for a long letter arguing that 'no discretionary power is reserved by this Act to the Crown.' By contrast in 1811 doubts were expressed about the execution of a murderer during 'the indisposition of his majesty' because the possibility of pardon was thereby undermined, *The Examiner*, 20 January 1811.
27. For prisoners respited because their sanity was doubtful—*World*, 18 December 1787; TNA HO 47/15/20, HO47/63/9 and in HO 47/32/12 because the murderer thought the victim was the 'Hammersmith Ghost'; for doubts re guilt or the legality/quality of the evidence TNA SP 37/8/15, HO/16/6; for murder in a duel pardoned because the accused was not the one issuing challenge HO 47/53/29.
28. P. King, *Crime, Justice and Discretion in England 1740–1820* (Oxford, 2000), p. 274. Essex and the Home circuit followed similar patterns.
29. A number of offenders executed for non-killing offences were taken informally by the surgeons for dissection, but we have no systematic evidence of how many.
30. These were originally sentenced to dissection which was then changed to gibbeting.
31. Two more were gibbetted immediately following the Anatomy Act—see Chap. 4; A similar pattern of decline can be seen in Scotland but the key change came earlier, R. Bennett's 'Capital Punishment and the Criminal Corpse in Scotland 1740–1834' (Leicester Ph.D. 2015).
32. HCA 1/85 -Three were interred rather than gibbeted but ten were sentenced to hanging in chains.

33. P. King and R. Ward, 'Rethinking the Bloody Code in Eighteenth-Century Britain: Capital Punishment at the Centre and on the Periphery' *Past and Present* 228 (2015) pp. 159–205.
34. Dyndor, 'The Gibbet', pp. 102–125.
35. Tarlow, *Hung*, pp. 32–34.
36. Ibid.
37. Julian Raynor's database indicates that at least one or two murderers were gibbeted in each of these places 1752–1832. Provincial gibbetings were less likely to be in previously used locations, *General Evening Post*, 21 July 1787. On the high proportion of scene of crime executions involving hanging in chains—S. Poole, '"For the Benefit of Example": Crime Scene Executions in England 1720–1830' in Ward, *A Global History*, p. 78.
38. Probably twenty-one if we include the two ordered to be gibbeted by the Surrey assizes.
39. Tarlow, *Hung*.
40. L. Radzinowicz, *A History of English Criminal Law and its Administration from 1750*, (London, 5 Vols., 1948–1986) 1, p. 200; D. Rumbelow, *The Triple Tree; Newgate, Tyburn and the Old Bailey* (London, 1982) p. 181.
41. For problems posed by crowd-packed streets see *Bell's Weekly Messenger*, vol. 4, 1809, p. 213.
42. See also Hurren, *Dissecting*, pp. 175–182.
43. Only 8.5% of murderers indicted at the Old Bailey 1791–1805 were female. 54% were aged 17–30, 85% were 17–40. TNA HO 26 1–11 For discussion of the Newgate Calendars and the precise periods covered in the sample see P. King, 'Ethnicity, Prejudice and Justice; the Treatment of the Irish at the Old Bailey 1750–1825' *Journal of British Studies*, 52, (2013) pp. 390–414.
44. P. King, 'The Impact of Urbanization on Murder Rates and on the Geography of Homicide in England and Wales 1780–1850.' *Historical Journal*, 53 (2010) pp. 1–28.
45. Based on TNA HO 26 1–11.
46. The 10% figure may be an underestimate as not founds were not always systematically recorded in the first part of this period. TNA, Assi 23/4-10.
47. *PP*, 1819, viii, pp. 245–250. A similar pattern can be found in 1757–1779 Ibid., pp. 242–244.
48. Hurren, *Dissecting*, p. 16.
49. Hurren, *Dissecting*, for detailed analysis.
50. R. Ward, 'The Criminal Corpse, Anatomists, and the Criminal Law: Parliamentary Attempts to Extend the Dissection of Offenders in Late Eighteenth-Century England' *Journal of British Studies*, 54 (2015) pp. 76–79.
51. Hurren, *Dissecting*, pp. 14–15 describes crowds of 10,000 people following the body and of thousands walking past the corpse when it was exposed for public view.

52. Devereaux, 'The Abolition', p. 77.
53. As early as the 1720s the Postmaster General was extremely diligent in obtaining sentences of hanging in chains *Newcastle Courant*, 20 March 1725.
54. Tarlow, *Hung*, Table 1.2 and p. 19.
55. Julian Raynor's Ph.D. research at Leicester University includes a survey of all London murder trials.
56. This tendency to gibbet those who had committed homicides during a robbery or burglary did not simply reflect the overall structure of executed murderers. In London 1780–1794, less than two-fifths of executed murderers fell into this category.
57. *Public Advertiser*, 25 July 1753; *Read's Weekly Journal*, 28 July 1753. For similar requests from the Post-Master General in 1770 and 1772—TNA, SP 44/89/350 and 44/92/38.
58. For a provincial hanging in chains for a non-robbery-related murder Anon, *The Trial of John and Nathan Nichols for the Wilful Murder of Sarah Nichols*, (Bury St Edmonds 1794) p. 8.
59. TNA, Durh16/5/86.
60. It is possible that men killing women were slightly more likely to be gibbeted, but the victim's gender does not seem to have been decisive.
61. NLW, 4/617/1-38.
62. TNA, E389/250/79 and t90/168/137.
63. TNA Ches21/7/53.
64. Ward, 'The Criminal', pp. 63–87, and Hurren, *Dissecting*.
65. *General Advertiser*, 4 August, 1752 and TNA T90/148; TNA E389/250/79, E389/245/186; *Lloyd's Evening Post*, 30 March 1767; Tarlow, *Hung*, p. 21.
66. Ibid.
67. For a criminal corpse removed from a Stamford Hill gibbet because of the heat and the stench—*Old England*, 15 August 1747; Tarlow, *Hung*, pp. 46–47.
68. Tarlow, 'The Technology.'
69. Tarlow, *Hung*, p. 58.
70. Some sheriffs also managed to recover the costs of delivering bodies to the surgeons.
71. Hurren, *Dissecting*, pp. 14–16.
72. Ibid., p. 130; Tarlow, *Hung*, p. 62.
73. Ibid., pp. 42–43.
74. Ibid; *Evening Mail*, 17 April 1799.
75. Hurren, *Dissecting*.
76. Tarlow, *Hung*, pp. 42–43.
77. Ibid., p. 43.

78. *Gloucester Journal*, 8 November 1784.
79. *London Chronicle*, 31 March 1759; *London Gazette*, 14 February 1786.
80. *Lloyd's Evening Post*, 4 April 1763; *London Magazine*, 1763, p. 223. For another London rescue *London Chronicle*, 23 December 1760.
81. Tarlow, *Hung*, p. 48.
82. *Monthly Chronicle*, September 1729.
83. *Public Advertiser*, 2 May 1768; *London Evening Post*, 29 June 1745; *Gazetteer and New Daily Advertiser*, 26 March 1765.
84. TNA SP 36/32/115 and 162; Tarlow, *Hung*, p. 49.
85. Ibid., pp. 64–68.
86. In Derbyshire many of those sent for dissection were later buried in St Peter's churchyard, P. Taylor, *May the Lord have Mercy on your Soul: Murder and Serious Crime in Derbyshire 1732–1882* (Derby, 1989) p. 20.
87. G. Durston, *Crime and Justice in Early Modern England: 1500–1750* (Chichester, 2004), p. 668.
88. Linebaugh, 'The Tyburn', p. 117.
89. Hurren, *Dissecting*, pp. 254–255; Tarlow, *Hung*, p. 62 on offenders trembling while being measured for their gibbeting irons.
90. For two offenders 'without emotion' and 'unmoved' when sentenced to dissection, *Evening Mail*, 17 March 1800.
91. *Bingley's Journal*, 6 June 1772.
92. *The Times*, 10 January 1787; Linebaugh, 'The Tyburn', p. 71.
93. W. Tutty, *A Sermon Preached … before the Execution of … Thomas Bilby for Robbing the Chester Mail* (London, 1748) p. 50; *The Times*, 9 January 1786.
94. M. Turner, *Crime and Murder in Victorian Leicestershire 1837–1901* (Blady, 1981) p. 15 for a Leicestershire murderer who asked for gibbeting 'to avoid falling into the hands of the surgeons' and another example see Radzinowicz, *A History*, 1, p. 192.
95. Radzinowicz, *A History*, 1, pp. 215–216.
96. *General Evening Post*, 29 March 1792; *Lloyd's Evening Post*, 4 April 1792 and 26 August 1749.
97. Richardson, *Death*, pp. 35–36 argued dissection was a more powerful exemplary punishment. Beattie, *Crime*, p. 528 was more balanced arguing 'dissection was perhaps the greatest indignity that could befall a condemned man' though hanging in chains was feared almost as much.
98. *Public Advertiser*, 1 September 1764 and *Northampton Mercury*, 6 August 1764. If a father and son committed a crime together, the former was sometimes hung in chains while the latter was dissected, *The Trial of John and Nathan Nichols*, p. 8. However, sometimes the opposite was the case, *London Evening Post*, 16 August 1759 and it remains unclear whether those held especially culpable were gibbeted.
99. Tarlow, *Hung*, p. 20.

4

Post-Execution Punishment 1752–1834: Debate and Criticism

Having analysed both the debates that occurred in the period prior to the Murder Act and the sentencing patterns that resulted from that Act, this study will now focus on the complex ways that attitudes towards post-execution punishment developed and changed during the period between 1752 and 1834. Although the many, largely unintegrated, strands of contemporary discourse that we have access to in the second half of the eighteenth century make it clear that extended debates were occurring, it is difficult at times to identify which of these ideas were most influential. As Devereaux has pointed out in his essay on capital punishment in London during this period, 'the substance of "public opinion" as historians are capable of reconstituting it from contemporary sources, often seems both too various in its content and too inconsistently asserted to provide us with any straightforwardly measurable or unidirectional influence on the course of events'.[1] However, as parliamentary proceedings began to be at least partially recorded towards the end of the eighteenth century and as systematic recording of all the speeches made in both Houses developed in the early decades of the nineteenth, more detailed analysis of the main points being debated and of the structures of ideas behind them becomes possible.

One thing is immediately clear from these sources. Changing attitudes and policies towards post-execution punishment cannot be explained by any simple unidirectional model. Rather than a pattern of general long-term decline in support for the use of post-execution punishments throughout the period 1752–1834, detailed study reveals a much more complex pattern. In the first four or five decades after 1752 the two main forms of post-execution punishment formalized in the Murder Act, dissection and hanging in chains, were sometimes criticized but rarely fundamentally challenged, and although they did not necessarily fulfill all that had been expected of them, they were seen by most commentators as a functioning and useful part of the criminal justice system. However, attitudes became much more complex at the end of the eighteenth century. As identified in Chap. 3, in the first 3 years of the nineteenth century the judges suddenly abandoned the use of hanging in chains except in a few highly exceptional circumstances. Dissection therefore became the main post-execution punishment, but, unlike hanging in chains, its popularity did not decline significantly—at least amongst those involved in making penal policy. Indeed proposals advocating the extension of dissection to other categories of offenders continued to be made both inside and outside Parliament until the early 1830s. Although the use of penal dissection was never extended in this way, this particular form of post-execution punishment continued to be seen as an important means of differentiating between different types of capital crime, and penal dissection for murderers alone was still being vigorously defended as such on the very eve of its repeal in 1832. Thus while some forms of post-execution punishment became so unpopular that they were largely abandoned around the turn of the century (burning at the stake after strangling was also ended in the early 1790s), the main form used under the Murder Act—dissection—had a much more complex history and was still regarded by many as a very useful component of the penal system 30 years after hanging in chains had been effectively set aside as unsuitable.

In exploring changing attitudes to post-execution punishment between 1752 and 1834 this chapter will look at a range of issues: at initial discussions about how the Act should be embedded in legal, medical and administrative practice; at how the surgeons responded to their new quasi-penal role; at the various aggravated and post-execution punishments that continued to be put forward as alternatives to, or supplements of, the Murder Act in the mid to late eighteenth century; at the criticisms levelled at hanging in chains, at dissection and at the Murder Act more generally; at the commentators who argued, by contrast, that many parts of the Act were proving useful and functioning well in practice; and at the various suggestions and parliamentary initiatives (such as those of 1786 and 1796) that attempted to extend the use of dissection to the corpses of those found guilty of other crimes apart from murder. It will then focus on the ideas and discussions that dominated the final 30 years of the Murder Act period, when the collapse of gibbeting made penal dissection the dominant post-execution punishment. Here it will explore the gradual privatization of penal dissection between 1808 and 1828; the extensive parliamentary debates in relation to three separate legislative initiatives that took place between 1828 and 1832, and which reveal the reluctance of Parliament even at this late stage to end post-execution punishment; the reasons why the penal dissection clause of the Murder Act was finally repealed in 1832, and the final demise of public post-execution punishment through the anti-gibbeting act of 1834.

1 The Judges' Initial Discussions About the Interpretation of the Murder Act

The 'careless manner in which many Acts of Parliament are drawn up' was the subject of extensive criticism in this period and, like many other eighteenth-century statutes, the Murder Act left much to be desired as a piece of legislation.[2] Written and passed through both houses of Parliament in a matter of weeks, it was not as complex or convoluted as some eighteenth-century acts,[3] but its relative brevity brought other problems. It did not, for example, clarify important areas of legislative overlap, such as the relationship between the new act and previous legislation on the punishment of murderers indicted for petty treason. Nor did it make clear precisely how those involved in dissection should perform their new role as 'penal surgeons' or how much discretion they could exercise in doing so. In the years immediately after the act the assize judges, the surgeons and the government's legal officers therefore attempted to clarify exactly how it would work in practice. The twelve judges, who met regularly in London between assize circuits, fairly quickly established how the act should be interpreted by those responsible for sentencing. The surgeons on the other hand had no such central body and no experience in the development of mutual rulings. They therefore continued to interpret and reinterpret their role in diverse ways, often on an individual or regional basis, throughout the Murder Act period.

The assize judges met a couple of months after the Act was passed to consider a number of legal issues raised by it. Some were relatively easily resolved. Accessories before the fact were not deemed to be within the Act, nor could female murderers pleading their belly hope to avoid this new part of the death sentence after their babies were born.[4] After considerable debate and disagreement about whether 'hanging in chains might ever be part of the judgment', the judges decided by a fairly narrow majority that 'the judgment for dissection and anatomizing only should be part of the sentence: and if it should be thought advisable, the judge might afterwards direct the hanging in chains by special order to the sheriff'. It was also agreed by 'the greater part of the Judges', that 'the judgment for dissecting and anatomizing … ought to be pronounced in cases of petty treason' but 'more as to men in *toto* but in women only in respect of the time of execution, because they are to be burnt'. The judges were unanimous, however, that with the above exception 'the sentence directed by the Act extends to women as well as men'.[5] Following these initial debates in May 1752, the judges do not appear to have discussed the Murder Act again until 1760 when 'Some doubts having arisen in the House of Lords' about how far the Murder Act 'ought to be put in execution in the case of Earl Ferrers now under sentence of death', they decided that a peer should receive the same judgment as a commoner under the Murder Act. In addition, this case (which, as we will see, also caused problems of interpretation for the surgeons) produced another ruling: that reprieves under the Murder Act could be granted 'as often as the King shall think fit'.[6]

2 The Surgeons' Interpretations of the Murder Act

The sheriff's role as the official responsible for organizing the gibbeting of offenders sentenced to hanging in chains did not change after the Murder Act, and if dissection was the sentence chosen by the court the same official was merely ordered to convey the body of the executed murderer 'to the Hall of the Surgeons' Company or such other place as the said Company shall appoint'.[7] The major new actors introduced into the penal process by the Murder Act were therefore the surgeons themselves, but it left their role almost completely undefined. The Act simply stated that 'the body so delivered … shall be dissected and anatomized by the said surgeons, or such persons as they shall appoint for that purpose' and that a parallel procedure should also occur in the provinces.[8] The Act did not therefore stipulate that anatomization/dissection had to be performed in public. Nor did it define what those two processes involved, or lay down any particular procedure that should be followed, leaving all the key issues—such as whether the surgeons could chose to make only a token incision—completely unaddressed by the formal law. Beyond the preamble's vague statement that the Act was designed to add 'some further terror and peculiar mark of infamy'[9] to the punishment of death, nothing was stipulated.

Richardson suggested that 'the surgeons were regarded by law as agents of the crown, and protected as such', but while it is true that the Murder Act did try to protect the surgeons from losing the criminal corpses allocated to them, by making it a transportable offence to rescue those corpses, the Act set up no mechanism for controlling the surgeons, for ensuring that a minimum level of dissection took place, or for disciplining them if they failed to perform as required.[10] If they were agents of the crown they were agents given immense freedom of operation. Sawday's description of the post-execution process, or 'penal dissection' as he called it, suggests that the Murder Act 'delineated the full, ferocious, outlines of the practice of "penal anatomy"'.[11] In reality, however, the Act failed to delineate anything. Elizabeth Hurren's excellent study of the Murder Act period, *Dissecting the Criminal Corpse*, which offers a detailed analysis of the diverse and innovative ways in which the surgeons fulfilled this role, makes it clear that the Act placed 'a high degree of discretionary justice' in their hands.[12] The journey from gallows to grave, which the surgeons were responsible for whenever a dissection sentence was passed, was shaped by many complex and regionally variable factors. As Hurren points out, this 'post-execution spectacle did not always have an undeviating medical logic', nor was 'the legal narrative of the punishment drama' staged by the surgeons 'necessarily linear'.[13] What is clear, however, is that the surgeons oversaw a 'spectacular post-execution encore' in which large crowds could be involved at various stages. Many thousands, for example, sometimes walked past the corpse when it was exposed to public view, both in London and at many of the diverse types of venue used by the provincial surgeons.[14] These audiences often witnessed a variety of post-execution rites drawn out over several days that involved, Hurren argues, a strong element of 'immersive theatre'.[15] Within these rituals, however, she has identified two distinct stages. After 1752 the surgeons redefined the general legal term 'dissected and anatomized' as two separate punishment procedures. In the process they not only reversed the order—putting anatomization first—but also informally created what Hurren terms 'the clandestine side of the Murder Act'.[16] The first procedure, anatomization, involved determining whether medical death had actually occurred, and then acting to ensure that it had. Since a considerable proportion of criminal bodies were not medically dead on arrival at the surgical venue this made the surgeons, Hurren argues persuasively, not one step removed from the penal sentence but actually part and parcel of the execution itself. Unlike anatomization, which was primarily about getting the body to become a corpse,[17] the second procedure, dissection, represented the core of the post-execution punishment to which that corpse was subjected. The degree of post-mortem harm inflicted varied tremendously, but in many cases it involved cutting the body 'on the extremities to the extremities' and a degree of dismemberment that 'despoiled' the murderer as a human being.[18] Since 'over two-thirds of the human material was generally disposed of' this process resembled 'a macabre showcase … a public drama of the unsavoury', which Hurren explores in detail in her book.[19]

The degree to which the various surgeons who found themselves placed at the centre of this dissection drama consciously took on the role of 'penal surgeons' remains unclear. A fairly large proportion of surgeons performed only one or two criminal dissections in their professional lifetimes—especially if they lived in one of the smaller provincial counties. Many of them therefore approached the task with relatively little experience to draw on. Did they see themselves as penal surgeons? The records suggest that individual surgeons reacted in very different ways and that it is possible to find some who completely spurned the role, and others who enthusiastically embraced it. At one extreme the courts were occasionally forced to hang offenders in chains because the local surgeons refused to dissect or anatomize their corpses. On other occasions the surgeons accepted the corpse but then made little or no attempt to make incisions upon it. At the other extreme there were those who fully embraced the role of penal surgeon, seeing themselves as responsible for the 'completion of the sentence'.[20] When the case involved a relatively low profile provincial murderer the surgeons may often have been free to take a relatively minimalist approach to the dissection process, if they chose to do so. However, when some of the London surgeons involved in the dissection of Earl Ferrers suggested an approach that would minimalize the post-mortem harm done to his corpse their decisions were heavily scrutinized in the press and subjected to considerable criticism. This forced them to seek advice from the government's leading lawyer, a process that created sources that give us important insights into the administration's own interpretation of this aspect of the Murder Act.

In May 1760 it was reported in the newspapers that the prospect of having to dissect a member of the aristocracy had created 'a dispute among the surgeons about what parts, and how much or how little shall be anatomized; some say a scratch is sufficient others affirm that only the bowels are to be taken out and then returned'. The reports then went on to note that 'this morning a court of the assistants of the Surgeons' Company will meet to consider the letter of the law.'[21] Under pressure both from some of the popular press, who demanded that Ferrers be treated like all other convicted murderers, and from other public figures who felt that a full-scale dissection was not warranted,[22] the surgeons court immediately sought the opinion of the Attorney General. While warning that 'they must be careful not to evade the Act', he largely handed the decision about the degree to which they were obliged to carry out a dissection back to them, saying that he thought that they would be better judges than him on the issue and adding that 'he did not think that anyone would ever question whether the body had been sufficiently dissected. They could dissect the whole or any part of the body as they thought fit'.[23] By reacting in this way and pointing out in addition that the surgeons 'were not directed to make the dissection in public or to exhibit the body',[24] the government's key legal representative effectively gave the surgeons *carte blanche*. In the Ferrers' case the London surgeons eventually compromised, anatomizing the noble Lord but not dissecting his corpse to the extremities and then permitting the public to view it.[25]

Class was not, however, the only criteria that might lead the surgeons to minimalize their penal role. In the 1780s, faced by what many considered to be the wrongful murder conviction and hanging of an army surgeon's son in Northampton, the local surgeons simply handed the corpse straight back to the family to bury as they wished, without cutting it at all.[26] Other surgeons made only token incisions, usually because they had sympathy with the executed man. In 1799 a Flemish-born 'Man of property' who had been found guilty of murder for neglectfully causing the death of an 8-year-old servant under circumstances that would have normally led only to a manslaughter conviction, was only subjected to 'a few incisions in order to fulfil the sentence' by the Welsh surgeons to whom his body had been delivered by the court. His near intact corpse was then 'given to his friends who had it put in a decent coffin and conveyed to his wife and family'.[27] Four years earlier, after William White had been hanged for murder at Bath, the surgeons followed a similar course, only making a few incisions before handing the body over to relatives for burial.[28]

Some surgeons also refused to dissect the criminal corpses sent to them by the courts for medical reasons. In 1762 the Surgeons of York refused to take such a corpse 'on account of its being full of ulcers'.[29] On several other occasions—in 1759, 1767, 1772 and 1797 for example—the reasons for the surgeon's refusal is less clear, the sheriffs records simply noting that the corpse was gibbeted because the surgeon was not willing to dissect it.[30] Throughout the second half of the eighteenth century, therefore, it is possible to find at least a few surgeons who refused to take on the role of 'penal surgeon' at all, and others who chose to minimize the impact they made on the criminal's corpse when being required to play that role. Moreover, although it is unclear whether they knew about it or not, the Attorney General's response in 1760 suggests that they were quite within their rights to do so.

However, this should not be taken to indicate that this minimalist approach was the norm. Systematic records do not exist but it is probable that the great majority of surgeons in all but the most remote regions willingly took on the task both of anatomizing the criminal corpses sent to them and of subjecting them to a substantial process of dissection. The surgeons' desperate need of cadavers for teaching and anatomical investigation was much publicized and many surgeons also stood to make financial and reputational gains from being involved in public dissections.[31] William Hey, for example, netted profits for his hospital of over £80 from one dissection process alone—the equivalent of two-years wages for a labourer.[32] A considerable proportion of these surgeons may have performed dissections despite the fact that they were troubled by the harshness of the Murder Act and the dehumanizing processes it prescribed.[33] However, there were undoubtedly others who embraced the role of penal surgeon wholeheartedly.

In 1759, for example, 'one of the Masters of Anatomy for that year' gave two powerful speeches as part of his lectures at Surgeons' Hall over the body of the murderer Richard Lamb. His first lecture began by praising the government for passing the Murder Act seven years before and thereby adding this additional punishment, 'it being well known in how great horror dissection was held by almost all mankind' and especially by the lower class who 'shuddered at the thoughts of being made an otomy'.[34] After acknowledging that 'curiosity more than improvement' had 'drawn the greater part of this audience together', he suggested that they would still benefit considerably from coming. 'Happy it would be', he announced, 'if this publick occasion, this sight of death, may prove a monitor to every individual here, and by them be repeated to their acquaintance (especially those prone to wrath) always to have in their eye this table whenever they find themselves urged by the passions of malice and revenge ... Let therefore the anatomical table in the Surgeons' Theatre be a preacher to all, and should their passions run high ... may this dread table present itself to their view and restrain their arm, raised to deprive a fellow creature of life'. Two days later, after the dissection and desecration of Lamb's corpse he returned to this theme. 'These lectures were not intended solely for anatomical benefit', he reminded his audience, but 'to strike greater terror into the minds of men, not by inhuman tortures on the living subject, as in other countries, but by denying the murderer the privilege of having his bones rest peacefully in the ground ... I think few who now look upon that miserable, mangled object before us, can ever forget it. It is for this purpose that our doors are opened to the publick, that all may see the exemplary punishment of a murderer and that it may be impressed on their minds, and be a warning to others to avoid their fate'.[35]

Clearly at least some surgeons revelled in the role of 'penal surgeon' and in London in particular their Company also used the bones of a small minority of criminal corpses to add a further level of post-execution punishment, which was effectively their own local form of gibbeting. On these occasions the surgeons not only dissected to the extremities but also sent the bones to be reconstructed as a skeleton and then hung it (with a name plate attached) in one of the niches created for public display around the dissection room at Surgeons Hall. This not only meant that a public reminder of their names and crimes remained for many years, but also that, unlike others who were dissected, they had no chance whatever of having what was left of their remains decently interred.[36] The selection of corpses/skeletons for this further punishment seems to have been largely done by the surgeons themselves, although they were no doubt influenced by the views of others, and were very occasionally specifically requested to consider this option by the trial judge.[37] They usually resorted to this procedure when the murder committed by the executed offender was particularly heinous and/or notorious. In 1767, for example, Elizabeth Brownrigg, who had gradually whipped her apprentice to death, had her skeleton reconstructed and displayed 'in the niche opposite the front door in the Surgeons' Theatre ... in order to perpetuate the heinousness of her cruelty in the minds of the spectators'.[38] Four years later the surgeons gave the same treatment to another highly notorious offender, Levi Weil, the leader of a violent Jewish gang who had murdered a servant during a robbery. Levi was a trained physician and had a degree in physic from Leiden University, but this did not save him from the ultimate destination for the dissected—his own niche at Surgeons' Hall.[39] The particularly cruel and violent robberies and murder committed by his gang had been widely reported in the newspapers and had led to a major wave of anti-Jewish feeling, and he was therefore a prime candidate for this strange combination of dissection and long-term public display.[40] His wife had pleaded with the surgeons after his dissection 'earnestly begging the body of her husband for internment' but the decision had already been made to hang his skeleton 'in Surgeons Hall'.[41]

The small sub-group of dissected offenders selected for this punishment included a considerable range of different types of convicts. Thomas Wilford, a one-armed workhouse inmate who had murdered his wife (also a workhouse inmate) three days after they were married, appears to have had his skeleton put in a niche simply because he was the first convict to be dissected under the Murder Act.[42] However, celebrity status was clearly a particularly important criterion. A few years before the Act James Maclean was given a niche mainly on the basis of his widespread reputation as a well-dressed and well-connected 'gentleman highwayman', while the selection of the violent highway robber James Field was almost certainly due to his reputation as a prize fighter.[43] The selection criteria remain obscure, but it is possible that in choosing which offenders to display as skeletons the surgeons may sometimes have given preference to those who were not only notorious murderers but were also members of ethnic minorities. In 1786 the black offender, John Hogan, who had murdered a young servant girl because she would not 'submit to his unchaste desires'[44] was also given a niche in Surgeons' Hall. The selection process was not always given extensive coverage in the newspapers but if any contemporaries were initially unaware that Hogan had been a given a niche they would have been in no doubt after reading the reports a year later concerning the huge crowds that had gathered to see the body of Henrietta Radbourn, who had been dissected at Surgeons' Hall after being executed for murdering her mistress. 'A vast concourse of people were in the gallery around the amphitheatre' the *Morning Chronicle* reported, when 'one of the skeletons, which was placed in a niche, fell down, and caused a consternation better conceived than described. The women fainted, and the men were frightened.' Hogan's posthumous revenge was short lived. 'In a short time the panic subsided, the place was soon cleared and the skeleton replaced', the newspaper reported, 'which was that of the black who was executed some time ago for the murder of the maid-servant'.[45] We should not necessarily assume that the surgeons were prejudiced against, rather than simply interested in, the skeletons of ethnic minorities but it is possible that the surgeons were particularly keen, for what they would have seen as scientific reasons, to preserve the skeletons of dissected offenders whom they conceived to be members of specific racial groups.[46]

Overall, however, even though the criteria they used are difficult to unravel, what is clear is that the surgeons, both in London and to a lesser extent in the Provinces,[47] had the discretionary right to subject the corpses of particular offenders to a potent combination of post-execution punishments—dissection followed by skeletal display—which combined public dismemberment and many of the elements of gibbeting, that is, long term exposure to public gaze and the denial of decent interment. Since, at the other extreme, the surgeons could also show mercy by effectively enabling selected corpses to avoid all, or almost all, the elements of public dissection, these medical men played an extremely important role in deciding what actual treatment each criminal corpse received, even though these powers were in no way spelt out by the Murder Act itself. Dissection and discretion went hand in hand and the surgeons were given huge power to decide the fate of each of the criminal corpses given to them, making them yet another potent example of the way justice was remade from the margins in the eighteenth and early-nineteenth centuries.[48]

3 Initial Reactions to the Murder Act in Operation, 1752–1759

Broadly speaking the immediate reaction of contemporaries to the 1752 Murder Act seems to have been a positive one. The widespread publication of the main clauses of the Act, which was a feature of both the London and the provincial newspapers in the early spring of 1752, was frequently accompanied by remarks suggesting that the Act was welcomed and was expected to have positive results.[49] In early July the Ordinary of Newgate, John Taylor, while admitting that the Act could not be expected to put an end to murder altogether, was praising the legislature for being 'willing to do all in their power' to curb it, by denying murderers a Christian burial and subjecting them to dissection, this being 'the utmost stretch of rigour that humanity can allow'.[50] A newspaper article published a few days earlier also lauded 'the several acts passed last session against murder and robbery', but went on to suggest that, 'like all human institutions, they were not without defects'.[51]

By the second half of 1752 the Murder Act was getting a much more mixed reception. Faced by two convictions and executions for murder in early September, John Taylor was forced to conclude that 'despite the late endeavours of the legislative power', this 'fresh instance … so soon after so wholesome a Law enacted, seems to shew that it yet wants to be impressed on the minds of men'.[52] Other commentators, who were not hindered (as Taylor was) by being government employees, were much less deferential in their criticisms. The author of *A Warning Piece Against the Crime of Murder*, for example, made the cogent point that even though the Murder Act had introduced a more severe punishment 'than was ever practis'd before by the *English* laws', the Act would not prevent murder because the perpetrators usually believed they could keep their crimes secret.[53] By 1754 there had clearly been 'many debates about the expediency of dissection' and the King himself was asking the legislature to 'try to find out some new laws for putting a stop to robberies and murders'.[54] Romaine's pamphlet on the frequency of murders, published that year, was also far from positive about the Act. 'The legislature has been lately alarmed at their prodigious increase', he wrote, 'and has been trying to find out some effectual remedy: but what has been hitherto attempted has not met with the desired success … murders are still as common as ever … The heart is the cause of all, and no act of parliament can touch the heart'.[55] In the following year the *Gentleman's Magazine* openly criticized 'the late laws' for failing to have an impact on 'the frequency of murder', and the *London Magazine* carried two articles criticizing hanging in chains and pointing out that robberies were being committed 'almost under the very gallows where some former highwayman hangs in chains'.[56]

As the 1750s came to a close there was still optimism in some quarters. The 1759 London surgeon's speech already quoted in detail argued that the Murder Act 'still promises success', basing this view on the fact that only two offenders had been executed for murder 'in this large and populous city … for upwards of two years'.[57] Others were more sanguine, however. After reporting an attempt to remove a gibbeted body from a Salford gallows in 1759 the local newspaper observed that murder had clearly 'puzzled the legislative power' since Parliament had failed 'either to put a stop to it, or to find out a punishment adequate to the offence'.[58] In the early years of its operation, the Murder Act therefore gained both a level of acceptance—there were no calls for its repeal and it was usually acknowledged to have been well-intentioned—and generated a considerable degree of pessimism about its likely impact and effectiveness. Between the late 1750s and the penal crisis of the mid-1780s this mixture—considerable criticism combined with broad acceptance—continued to dominate discussions of post-execution punishment but these themes were intermingled with two other related, but essentially opposite, strands of opinion—those that wanted to see the development of alternative punishments and those that wanted to see the Murder Act extended to a number of other crimes.

4 Acceptance, Debate and Criticism: The Murder Act in Operation Mid-1750s to the Mid-1780s

As we saw in Chap. 3, the period between the 1750s and the capital punishment crisis of the mid/late 1780s witnessed both the establishment of post-execution punishment as part of the normal penal response to murder, and the continued use of hanging in chains against some major property offenders and Admiralty Court convicts. Yet although these four decades witnessed the establishment of dissection and hanging in chains as accepted and taken-for-granted parts of the English criminal justice system, the same period also saw the development of broader critiques of capital punishment, which had important long-term implications for the role of post-execution punishment. In the two decades leading up to the mid-1780s English authors such as Eden and Blackstone, Dawes and Dagge, Howard and Hanway[59] had begun to question both the usefulness and the morality of capital punishment and to suggest various alternatives and, although those who wanted to reform the capital code made no significant progress until the nineteenth century, these writings gradually began to have an increasing impact.

In creating this critique these English authors called on the influential ideas already published by continental writers such as Beccaria and Montesquieu.[60] By calling for moderation and denouncing punishments based on terror or extreme intimidation; by arguing that the long-term deprivation of an offender's liberty had a greater impact than the terrible but momentary spectacle of death; and by stressing that certainty of punishment was much more effective than severity,[61] these writers began to undermine the foundations of the capital punishment system on which the extensive use of post-execution punishment in Britain was based.

Beccaria's writings also contained brief critical comments on aggravated and post-execution punishments and on the punishment of murder. The degree to which the poor might be 'deterred from violating the laws by the gibbet or the wheel' was very limited, he suggested.[62] 'In proportion as punishments become more cruel, the minds of men … grow hardened and insensible; and … in the space of an hundred years the wheel terrifies no more than formerly the prison'.[63] Moreover 'the impossibility of establishing an exact proportion between the crime and punishment' raised other problems 'for though ingenious cruelty hath greatly multiplied the variety of torments, yet the human frame can suffer only to a certain degree … be the enormity of the crime ever so great'.[64] Unlike many writers Beccaria also extended his critique of capital punishment to include its use in cases involving murder. 'Is it not absurd', he argued, 'that the laws, which detest and punish homicide, should, in order to prevent murder, publicly commit murder themselves?'[65]

Continental writers such as Beccaria were primarily concerned with attacking the capital punishment system as a whole, rather than focusing on its aggravated and post-execution forms, and since dissection was rarely used as a formal punishment on the continent they did not discuss it. Some English writers also gave these issues only passing attention. Dawes, for example, confined himself mainly to pointing out that punishment was made effectual more 'by its certainty than severity, and makes a stronger impression on the mind, than if attended by torment or cruelty'.[66] However, writers such as Eden and Blackstone did include some discussion of post-execution punishment, as we will see, and a range of different newspaper reports, magazine articles and other commentaries also included aggravated and post-execution punishments in their discussions of the criminal code and their suggestions about the need to reform it. Many of these writers aimed their comments and criticisms mainly at particular forms of post-execution punishment or suggested alternatives to, or extensions of, the sanctions imposed on the criminal corpse by the Murder Act. However, two of the core arguments that can be found in the works published between the 1750s and the mid-1780s involved more general and fundamental critiques of the Murder Act and the assumptions on which it was based.

The most direct of these two critiques, and the only one that was based on empirical evidence about the impact of the Murder Act, was published by the Recorder of London in 1772. This compared the number of murder convictions in London and Middlesex in the 20 years before the Murder

Act (80) with the number of murderers convicted between 1752 and 1772 (75), and concluded that 'in all that period there are only five difference, which I think may serve to show that our laws against murderers are not severe enough'.[67] Dissection was not working as a penal sanction, he argued; 'The murderer is anatomized, but very few of them mind that, as it is attended with no pain to them.'[68] The Recorder also suggested that 'the murders committed since the Act took place were attended with more barbarity than any I can find before'.[69] However, neither of these arguments was unproblematic. His theory that a qualitative change had occurred after 1752 in the nature of the murders being committed was unsubstantiated and highly subjective. His calculations that the Act had had no effect on murder conviction levels failed to allow for the fact that the London population increased rapidly in this period which meant that, as Shoemaker's recent work has confirmed, murder rates were actually declining.[70]

The Recorder also drew on the other general critique of the Murder Act that can be found in the post-1752 literature. The law against murder was not severe enough, he argued, because 'the man who robs me of a few pence to keep his family from starving is liable to the same punishment as the villain who breaks open my house in the night and murders me in my bed'.[71] This theme was also taken up by several other commentators in the early 1770s as part of a more general wave of criticism of the English criminal law. In November 1770 Sir William Meredith, during his speech in the House of Commons calling for a parliamentary enquiry into the capital code, pointed out 'that a man who had privately picked a pocket of a handkerchief worth thirteen pence, is punished with the same severity as if he had murdered a whole family of benefactors'.[72] A *London Magazine* article published in the same year similarly argued that 'the greater part of mankind' could never accept that 'to pick the pocket and to pierce the heart, is equally criminal' or that both should therefore be subject to the death sentence'.[73]

This view that under the existing capital code the degree of punishment was 'by no means proportionable … to the degree of guilt'[74] echoed similar arguments made in the run up to the passing of the Murder Act (Chap. 2) and in doing so they implicitly criticized much of the logic and purpose of that Act. These comments implied, or in some cases directly stated, that the compulsory addition of a post-execution punishment to the sentence passed on all convicted murderers had had a negligible effect and could not be regarded as creating a meaningful differentiation in the depth of punishment imposed. In arguing that the murderer and the pickpocket were 'doomed to the same punishment'[75] these critics effectively wrote off (or perhaps deliberately ignored) both the idea that dissection or hanging in chains could be seen as an extra layer of punishment, and the underlying logic that partly lay behind their imposition, that is, that they might be an effective deterrent.

This dismissal of the Murder Act by some of the more radical early criminal law reformers was not representative of broader opinion, however. As we will see, many judges and penal commentators were still arguing that the post-execution sanctions mobilized by the Murder Act did create differentiation in punishment right up to the early 1830s. These eighteenth century reformers seem to have been mainly arguing against the effectiveness of post-execution punishment in order to strengthen their core argument—which was a critique of capital punishment per se, rather than a direct attack on the punishments imposed on the criminal corpse. In particular, several of them wanted to use the argument that only murder should be punished with death[76] as a means of introducing a major reform in the ways the criminal justice system punished non-violent offenders. If hanging was largely confined to murder, Meredith argued, 'capital punishment, as it would be less common, would operate more forcibly in *terrorem* and consequently more effectively answer its end'.[77] This theme can also be found in several publications produced in the early and mid-1780s. 'It ought … to be the study of the legislature, not to impose death as a punishment except for murder', Dawes wrote in 1782, quoting both Beccaria and the Old Testament in support of his views, and a few years later Lord Gordon argued controversially that that the word of God did not allow the death sentence for theft and therefore that 'no man ought to suffer death without he spilt blood'.[78] It would take the reformers another half century to achieve this change and it would also only be at that point that post-mortem punishment under the Murder Act was finally done away with. However, it is clear that as early as 1770 there were already some commentators who did not see either of the two post-execution punishments introduced by the Murder Act as capable of producing the differentiation between punishments that they felt was required, and this theme came to the fore once again during the capital punishment crisis of the mid-/late 1780s, 'Cruel punishments are inflicted upon crimes with which they bear not the least proportion' *The Times* argued in 1786, before publishing several other more specific articles abhorring the equal punishment given to poor thieves 'pinched by want …

and cruel murderers'; to sheep thieves and those committing 'shocking … robbery and murder'; and to 'the poor thief who steals a coat and the hardened villain who attacks you by night, turns you naked to the storm, mutilates your limbs and deprives you of life itself'.[79] However, this critique of the lack of differentiation in the use of capital punishment, with its implication that the post-execution punishments introduced by the Murder Act had failed to remedy this, was by no means dominant. Several commentators, including the influential penal reformer William Eden, continued to analyse, and often to praise, the role of either dissection or hanging in chains as separate sentencing options.

Eden's important book *Principles of the Penal Law* published in 1772 was broadly, if slightly reluctantly, positive about the role of the surgeon's in post-execution punishment. 'To the dissection of criminals', he wrote, 'it is impossible to offer any solid objection'. However, his views on hanging in chains were very different. 'We leave each other to rot, like scarecrows in the hedges', he observed, 'and our gibbets are crowded with human carcasses. May it not be doubted, whether a forced familiarity with such objects can have any other effect, than to blunt the sentiments … of the people?'[80] Five years later a generally positive evaluation of the development of post-execution punishment also singled out dissection as the best current option. 'The chief end of punishment is example', it argued.

> Hence legislators frequently change the mode of punishment. When one becomes familiar, and has lost its terror, another is adopted. Hanging in chains has had a superior effect when the simple execution at Tyburn has made no impression, and when the horror of being exposed in chains has lost its force, the change from a gibbet to Surgeons' Hall has created new terrors in the most hardened villains.[81]

Occasionally the newspapers carried reports that suggested that these 'new terrors' could have a real impact, at least on the minority of potential offenders who attended dissections. In 1785 one offender was reported to have been 'more shocked at the idea of being dissected at Surgeons' Hall than with death itself', because 'the horrid spectacles he had seen there of several murderers … made a deep impression upon his mind'.[82] In one sense, this was precisely what the surgeon who spoke of the deterrent value of public dissections in 1759 had hoped would be the effect on the audience, except, of course, that despite the fear this spectacle engendered the offender still went on to commit murder.

Other newspaper reports and magazine articles tended to be less positive about dissection. 'The murderer will indeed have some marks of disgrace put upon his body after it is dead' one newspaper observed in 1786 'but the person, in fact, suffers no more for this enormous crime than the other who has committed a trifling offence'.[83] Other writers went further suggesting that public dissection was having a negative effect. 'The exposing the bodies of murderers', they suggested, 'has not appeared to have the salutary effect expected by the Act of Parliament; but from being frequently repeated tends to harden the minds of the vulgar and familiarize them with spectacles of horror'[84]—a sentiment echoed by the *Lady's Magazine* in 1782, which suggested that viewing such shocking scenes 'hardens the human mind'.[85] Hanging in chains also had its critics. Eden was not the only commentator to reflect negatively on its role. Blackstone pointed out that it was 'quite contrary to the express comments of Mosaic law'[86] and the *London Magazine* paralleled the Recorder of London's comments on dissection by arguing that 'hardened criminals … think that, because there is no corporal sufferance in it … being gibbeted … makes no part of the punishment'.[87] Other commentators disagreed, arguing that 'the stoutest of villains have trembled at the imaginary evil of hanging in chains',[88] and gibbeting was sometimes specifically recommended as more effective than dissection. In 1773, for example, the dissection of a Yorkshire murderer led the local paper to comment that 'it is a pity he was not gibbeted … as the remembrance would have existed these twenty years, whereas now, in a month, it will be forgotten'.[89] Penal commentators therefore had very mixed feelings about these two post-execution punishments in this period. Some favoured dissection, others preferred hanging in chains while a considerable number remained ambivalent about both options whilst still broadly accepting their introduction under the Murder Act. Another relatively small group suggested various alternative aggravated or post-execution punishments, implying by doing so that the sanctions introduced by that Act were inadequate.

5 Suggestions for Alternative Aggravated and Post-execution Punishments 1752–1786

Although there were still occasional calls for 'a more terrifying punishment' than the gallows,[90] few of the aggravated execution options proposed and debated in years before the Murder Act were given serious consideration in the second half of the eighteenth century. Three were at least briefly mentioned. One newspaper article got close to recommending *Lex Talionis* in 1770. 'The late horrid frequency of murders would tempt one to wish for a revival of the ancient *Lex Talionis*', it suggested, 'let him who shoots another be shot; who strangles his fellow creature be strangled',[91] and a year earlier Blackstone mentioned in passing the lack of 'an exemplary punishment' for parricide[92]—an issue that was also debated in the run up to the 1752 Act. In the mid-1780s William Paley, in searching for a way to 'augment the horror of punishment without offending … public sensibility' mentioned a recent proposal which involved privately 'casting murderers into a den of wild beasts'.[93] In general, however, the other forms of aggravated execution—breaking on the wheel, gibbeting alive or burning alive and so forth—that were quite frequently advocated before 1752 (Chap. 2) found no place in these later debates. In 1762 the Tyburn crowd did create its own brief form of post-execution punishment by stoning the bodies of two women who had just been executed for murdering their apprentice, whilst they were still hanging on the gallows.[94] However, the only major post-execution sanction proposed in these years centred on the method of burying the offender's corpse. In 1775 Hanway advocated the burial of the hanged in a special, well-marked and 'strongly walled in … malefactors burial place' by 'a road near the entrance to a city, such as Tyburn', which he believed 'could not fail of making some impression' on the minds of likely offenders.[95] Ten years later *The Times* despite pointing out that 'criminal executions should be as much avoided as possible', went on to suggest that in 'particular atrocious cases' it would create 'a greater terror' if the offender was 'hanged in secret and then thrown immediately into a private hole dug for them in a part of the prison … and quicklime thrown over the dead body'.[96]

In the third quarter of the eighteenth century two other death penalty-related punishments were also discussed, both of which involved subjecting capital convicts to the danger of dying whilst still offering the possibility, or even the probability, of survival. One of these, suggested by a Norwich correspondent of the *Gentleman's Magazine*, involved a bizarre form of half-hanging, which all felons apart from murderers would be eligible for. 'The convict should be hanged', the article suggested, 'but instead of being suspended for an hour let it be only for one minute, or less, in which time he will be as dead to his own sense of feeling, and as much punished, as if he were kept hanging the usual time … Would not a man thus brought again on the stage of life become … a more useful member of society?'[97]

There is no evidence that this proposal was ever actually considered by government, but the other death-penalty-related punishment suggested in this period was taken much more seriously and came within days of being put into practice in London.

This punishment was first mooted just a few years after the Murder Act, as a reaction to its lack of success. In 1755, a letter to the *Gentleman's Magazine* argued that since 'the late laws' had had so little impact on 'the frequency of murders ... instead of giving the murderer's body to the surgeons when it is dead, he should be put into their hands alive and subjected to such experiments as can only be made on a living subject'. Several diseases, the correspondent argued, 'might possibly be cured by chirurgical operations so dangerous that the experiment is not likely to be made, even in our hospitals'. Surely, the writer argued, 'notorious criminals might justly be reserved for these operations' provided that they were not 'wantonly mangled to gratify mere curiosity', and as long as these experiments were only done 'under the direction of persons properly appointed'.[98] Eight years later this was precisely the role that Thomas Pierce, who wished to test 'a styptic capable of stopping the most violent bleedings', petitioned the government to allocate to him. The styptic having been 'tried with success on brute creation', he asked that he now be allowed to experiment on the 'amputated limb' of a criminal under sentence of death, one of whom, George Clippingdale, had agreed to be subjected to the operation.[99] George was temporarily reprieved while the government consulted 'His Majesties serjeant surgeons', and was eventually transported when the latter advised the King against the experiment.[100] However, Pierce did not give up. Four years later he tried again and obtained the King's permission to perform the same experiment on another capital convict, John Bonham.[101] The 23rd June was appointed as the day for the experiment, and the newspapers not only announced the granting of a royal pardon on condition that Bonham undergo the operation but also carried an advertisement informing the 'gentlemen of the faculty' that if they wished to witness the amputation they needed to obtain tickets.[102] However, the King changed his mind at the last minute, and Bonham became the second convict to avoid the gallows by this route.[103]

The debate did not end there. In his *Observations on the Statutes*, published in 1769, Barrington praised the idea that criminals 'should be pardoned on condition that some hazardous experiment for the promotion of medical knowledge may be tried upon them'.[104] Three years later, however, Eden, while recognizing the 'seeming liberality' of subjecting 'certain classes of criminals to medical experiments for the benefit of mankind', argued that 'such a plan can never with any propriety receive ... legislative sanction', and it never appears to have done so.[105] Like the pre-1752 proposals that criminals should be subjected to castration this punishment was not strictly speaking an aggravated form of the death penalty, because the convict had at least some chance of recovery, but it was put forward as an alternative to the Murder Act and seriously considered by the government even though it was ultimately rejected. During the period from 1752 to the penal crisis of the mid/late 1780s the structure of post-execution punishments created by the Murder Act therefore came under considerable criticism, and although the alternatives suggested were relatively limited compared to earlier periods, thought was also given to new methods of punishment that might augment the Act. However, the repeal of the Murder Act was never seriously suggested in this period and the broad acceptance that the Act received was also indicated by the wide range of proposals that were made to *extend* dissection or hanging in chains (or both) to other types of offender apart from murderers —proposals that came nearest to reaching the statute book during the debate on the government-backed bill of 1786.

6 Proposals to Extend the Post-execution Provisions of the Murder Act to Other Offences

In the first three-and- a-half decades after the Murder Act a considerable number of commentators advocated a variety ofextensions to the Act and to post-execution punishment more generally, which suggests that, although the Murder Act was often criticized, it was also by this point a very broadly accepted plank of penal policy—and could therefore be seen as a plank that was worth building on. Three specific types of extension to the Murder Act were proposed during these years. The first involved the punishment of suicides. Debates about the potential usefulness of dissection in the mid-1750s produced a proposal that those who committed suicide should be delivered to the surgeons for dissection, and ten years later—faced by what was perceived to be the daily increase of suicides— another writer suggested that since 'no terror ought to be omitted' to suppress such a crime, 'exemplary shame should be inflicted on them' by their being publicly dissected.[106] In 1769 an article in the *Middlesex Journal* went a stage further suggesting not only 'that the bodies of suicides should be publicly anatomized' but also that their skeletons should be 'hung up in Surgeons Hall'.[107] That venue would not, however, have provided enough niches and another commentator suggested a way round this—that the bones of suicides should be exhibited in a special 'charnel-house' 'in which monuments should be erected giving an account of their deaths'.[108] As late as 1790 other commentators, including John Wesley, were still suggesting hanging in chains as an alternative, 'if nothing else be likely to deter men from so heinous an offence against reason',[109] but (with the exception of capital offenders who committed suicide in prison) no record has been uncovered of suicides being gibbeted anywhere in England.[110] Nor was dissection, or dissection followed by the public exhibition of the suicide's skeleton, ever enacted in England in relation to suicides. However, the latter combination was very actively advocated for several other types of offender.[111]

This double-pronged approach, involving both dissection and gibbeting, constituted the second major extension of the Murder Act proposed in this period. In 1761, after a sentence of hanging in chains had been handed down against a Swiss painter who had killed his landlady, it was suggested that since gibbeting rather than dissection 'may appear to some people not an increase but a mitigation of the punishment' it would be best to join both these punishments together by 'having the body first anatomized and dissected, and the skeleton afterwards hung in chains'.[112] This double punishment was also advocated during the 1760s in two angry articles that demanded further penal sanctions against particular types of murder. The first, published in 1768 after the Wilkite riots, suggested that magistrates responsible for 'firing upon innocent persons' and 'wantonly murdering' them should be punished 'not merely by hanging and sending their bodies to a surgeon, but by being hung in chains near the spot where they issued their … bloody orders'.[113] The other article, which focused on murders in duels, suggested not only that the surviving duelist be hanged and dissected under the Murder Act but also that the man killed in the duel should be hanged upon a public gibbet for a certain time (presumably short) and then given to the surgeons.[114]

This latter suggestion incorporated an element of the third type of Murder Act extension advocated in this period, that is, those that advocated including new categories of criminal corpse in its provisions. The public gibbeting and dissection of the corpses of men who had been murdered during the very small proportion of duels, which came to the notice of the courts, would not have significantly increased the numbers subjected to post-mortem punishment. However, the various commentators and potential legislators who advocated the extension of the Murder Act's provisions to many other types of capital offenders would, if they had been successful, have achieved precisely that.

The mixture of motives that lay behind these suggestions is not always easy to unravel but two main strands can be identified. First, the surgeons' need for more cadavers, and the desire to discourage the growing body-snatching trade that the unfulfilled need had generated, were undoubtedly important. 'Anatomy is certainly of great advantage to the community', a newspaper noted in 1766, but 'the great number of professors of anatomy in this vast metropolis cannot be supplied with a sufficient number of subjects ... What the gallows supplies are but few'. Grave robbery was therefore, he argued, bound to be prevalent.[115] A decade later in 1776 a letter to the *Middlesex Journal*, having pointed out that body-snatching had reached 'an enormous height', put forward the same arguments about the great increase in surgeons and about the 'few bodies' that the law gave them, to support the idea that the anatomy teachers should petition Parliament for an act stipulating 'that the bodies of all housebreakers, robbers, forgers, coiners' and all other capitally convicted convicts 'be immediately after execution delivered to the surgeons for dissection ... as the bodies of murderers have usually been'. 'I have not the least doubt', the writer confidently concluded that this 'praiseworthy measure ... would be granted' if the case was properly made.[116] Anger at body-snatching continued to grow. In 1777 two 'resurrection men' were nearly 'pelted to death' by the London crowd, prompting calls for a new method to be found 'to procure a sufficient number of subjects' for the surgeons.[117] By the early 1780s a major crisis about body snatching was brewing in London and in May 1785 one of the capital's main surgeons was prosecuted for conveying away dead bodies for dissection'.[118] In October that year disgust 'at the means taken to procure bodies for dissection' led one correspondent of *The Times* to suggest that 'as it is essential ... that lectures should be held on the bodies of the dead' a law should be passed enabling 'the bodies of executed felons' to be sold to the surgeons.[119] This growing awareness of the problems being created by the inadequate supply of cadavers to teachers of anatomy was, as Ward has recently pointed out, the main initial reason why (only seven months after *The Times* article was published) Wilberforce introduced his bill 'for regulating the disposal of the bodies of criminals ... condemned and executed for certain heinous offences' including rape, arson, burglary and highway robbery with violence.[120] However, that bill, and in particular its active sponsorship by the government, also arose out of a second, and completely different, set of concerns.

In the early to mid-1780s crime rates increased rapidly following the demobilization at the end of the American war. The level of capital convictions rose in parallel and so did the percentage being executed.[121] Transportation to the USA was no longer an option and many voices were demanding increased severity and a reduction in the pardoning of capital offenders.[122] As a result by the mid-1780s more offenders were being hanged than had been the case for nearly 200 years. In 1785 156 people went to the gallows for property offences alone in London and the Home Circuit counties. Twenty of these were hung outside Newgate on one day in early February 1785, prompting *The Times* to launch a highly critical campaign. Fewer executions had occurred in all the cities of Europe during the last year than were to take place in one day in London, it pointed out. 'The long and dreadful list of persons ordered for execution' will astonish 'every country in Europe', who 'will naturally suppose that in England there is no more government than in a horde of wandering tartars'.[123] The unprecedented number of hangings was partly caused by a rise in robbery prosecutions, but an important role was also played by the rapid rise of burglary convictions, which outnumbered robbery prosecutions for the first time in the mid-1780s, and had a particularly heavy impact on the numbers being hanged because a very high and rising proportion of burglars failed to get pardons and therefore ended up on the gallows.[124] Faced by these mass hangings and by the growing criticism they were attracting, some members of Parliament clearly turned their minds towards the use of post-execution punishment. A few days after the publication of this critical article in *The Times*, it was reported that 'a bill will be brought to Parliament directing the bodies of all persons executed for burglaries to be given immediately after their sentence takes place, to the surgeons for public dissection'.[125] In April 1785 the hanging of nineteen more offenders in one day brought a renewed attack in the press. 'The carnage of yesterday is a disgrace' *The Times* announced, while arguing simultaneously that the capital code was 'failing to prevent the commission of crimes' and that 'the frequency of capital punishments has evidently done away with the awe and example of untimely death'.[126] In the same month Commodore Thompson, one of the government's advisors on the establishment of penal colonies, also suggested the introduction of post-execution punishment as a response to this crisis. Building on the proposal made two months earlier in relation to burglars, he suggested expanding the use of post-execution punishment much further. 'The many executions of late and the increase of crimes … leads me to recommend', he wrote in a letter to the Home Secretary, 'ordering every body for dissection that was executed'.[127] Thus when Wilberforce introduced his prospective bill to Parliament a year later he did so in the context of previous discussions about both the surgeons' need for cadavers, and the wider use of dissection as a possible response to the acute penal crisis of the mid-1780s.

7 The 1786 Bill: Attempting to Expand the Remit of the Murder Act

Two excellent recent articles have explored, from slightly different angles, the origins, context and nature of Wilberforce's 1786 bill, and the reasons for its failure.[128] Richard Ward's work, by uncovering the importance of the Yorkshire surgeon William Hey (a close friend of Wilberforce) as a key originator of the Act, has emphasized the role of the growing demand for cadavers.[129] Devereaux's article, by contrast, is particularly strong in its analysis of how the bill may have fitted into the broader response of Pitt's government to the penal crisis of the mid-1780s.[130] Readers wishing to understand in detail the roles of Wilberforce, Hey, Pitt and the bill's main opponent—Lord Loughborough—should consult these works. In this study we will look at the 1786 bill, and at a similar but the less successful bill suggested to Parliament in 1796, which advocated dissection for burglars and robbers—from a rather different perspective. These two bills, and particularly the government-backed 1786 legislative initiative, resulted in a series of relatively well-recorded debates and these will be used here to gain rare insights into how the Murder Act was regarded three or four decades after its introduction.

Although during the first parliamentary debate on the bill in May 1786, Wilberforce made much of 'the extreme difficulty which surgeons experienced in procuring bodies for dissections' [131] and of the problems of preventing the 'stealing of corpses from churchyards',[132] and although some newspaper reports suggested he made no reference to criminal justice matters, this was not the case. He specifically referred to 'the hope of deterring many persons' from committing capital crimes, and this penal context was also highlighted by Dundas's contribution to the same debate.[133] When the bill finally emerged, after being redrafted with the help of the government's law officers, it differed in two important respects from Wilberforce's initial proposal that (as it was reported in the *General Evening Post*) 'the bodies of all persons executed for capital crimes should be delivered … for … dissection'.[134] First, the categories of offenders covered by the bill were more limited. Burglary, violent robbery, arson and rape were the main types of offence that fell under its provisions.[135] However, since these offenders represented the bulk of the convicts sent to the gallows, this would still have increased the use of dissection five or six fold.[136] Secondly, the corpses of these offenders would not all have been 'delivered to the Surgeons' Company' as Wilberforce had proposed.[137] A short clause in the bill stipulated that 'nothing in this act … shall … prevent any judge … from appointing the body of the offenders aforesaid, to be hanged in chains'.[138] The judges already had the right to gibbet these offenders. The bill simply added the dissection option and insisted that one of these two post-execution punishments be stipulated in the sentence. The penal options it wished to impose on this much wider range of offenders were therefore precisely the same as those in the Murder Act.

Devereaux's excellent, if sometimes inferential, reading of the evidence suggests that the government's aim in backing this bill was not as harsh as its wording implies. Faced by the transportation crisis, the failure of the London Police Bill of 1785 and most of all by growing criticism of the huge numbers going to the gallows, Pitt backed Wilberforce's measure because he wanted to steer a middle path between the desire to execute fewer criminals and the desire to punish those that were executed with more exemplary severity.[139] With the Government's backing the bill passed through every stage in the Commons and even got through the committee stage in the Lords before hitting the opposition and invective of one of the leading judges, the future Lord Chancellor, Lord Loughborough.[140] Loughborough's reasons for opposing the bill were complex and have been analysed in detail elsewhere.[141] His opposition may have been motivated mainly by personal or political priorities and he was certainly no friend of Pitt's administration. He also appears to have been angry that the twelve judges had not been properly consulted. In a lengthy and wide-ranging speech he portrayed the bill as cruel, inaccurate, loosely worded and serving to remove the judges' vital right to reprieve offenders. Whether these criticisms were entirely fair or accurate is a matter for debate, as are Loughborough's motives in view of his reputation for changing side politically whenever it suited him.[142] However, his remarks do contain some very interesting reflections on the Murder Act and on the importance of differentiation in the punishment of offenders.

One of Lord Loughborough's most substantial arguments was that the 1786 bill would undermine the very positive impact that the Murder Act had achieved. The 1752 Act's 'taking away the right of burial and destining the body of the criminal to dissection' had 'been found of essential advantage to the community', he argued. When informed that they were going to be dissected he had observed that many criminals 'trembled and exhibited … the extremist horror', which also made a 'forcible impression on the minds of the bystanders and … was attended with the most salutary consequences'. He and his fellow judges had seen 'repeated instances' of the good effects of the Murder Act's additional punishments. Given that the Murder Act had contributed so much to the 'morals of mankind and to the good order of the community', he asked 'was it wise therefore to destroy the salutary effect' by making dissection and the loss of burial rights 'an ordinary consequence of every conviction of almost every capital offence?'[143] The bill, he went on to argue, 'lost sight of all distinction between crimes of very different magnitude'. Were 'the man who deprived a fellow creature of life and he who lifted a latch and stole the most trifling article … equally deep in guilt?' Were 'the man who committed a violence on a common prostitute, and he who robbed a virtuous woman of what she held most dear' to be treated without admitting any distinctions?'[144] To pass the promiscuous sentence of dissection on all of them would, he argued, be to destroy the positive impact of the 1752 Act, the preamble of which he then had read to the House. Loughborough also defended the Murder Act on other grounds. If the new bill was passed and 'the same punishment … attend the convict for burglary as for murder, breaking open a house would generally be attended with murder', he argued. He also praised the Murder Act for its role in reinforcing the superior nature of the English criminal justice system because, by using an extra punishment that involved 'no great degree of personal pain', it ensured that, unlike 'other states', England used no punishments (such as 'breaking on the wheel') that were attended with 'aggravated severity and cruelty'.[145]

Whether all the other judges felt quite as positive about the 1752 Act as Loughborough purported to be, remains unclear. However, the fact that not one of the Lords sitting that day, voted in favour of the bill[146] and that Loughborough confidently claimed during the debate that many of his fellow judges felt as he did, suggests that the Murder Act still had the broad support of those on the bench, despite the criticisms sometimes levelled at it. The debate that was generated in 1796, when Richard Jodrell briefly attempted to get the Commons' permission to introduce a bill that would have sent all burglars and highway robbers for dissection, also produced evidence that key judicial figures had a positive view of the Murder Act. Sergeant Adair, a very experienced Old Bailey judge, argued that 'the law had set up this barrier between murder and all other crimes' and that it would be very unwise to break it, and several others opposed the bill on similar grounds. The Attorney General argued, in addition, that the Murder Act had acted as a major deterrent to violence. 'The experience of those who were employed in administering the criminal law', he suggested, 'frequently have shown them how often the dread of anatomization had arrested the arm uplifted to commit murder',[147] (though how any of the judges would know this had happened remained unexplained). However, although the 1786 and 1796 debates induced several important legal figures to make strong and detailed defences of the use of penal dissection under Murder Act—defences that some of them continued to advance until the early 1830s—it was also in the later 1780s and the 1790s that the tide began very gradually to turn against the use of the other post-execution punishment the Act had relied on—hanging in chains.

8 1786–1808, The End of Burning at the Stake and of Support for Hanging in Chains

Ironically, the first eighteenth-century Act that removed at least one category of offenders from the risk of being subjected to aggravated or post-execution punishment was first mooted in Parliament by Wilberforce during his attempt in 1786 to greatly widen the range of offenders subjected to dissection. On June 23rd 1786, two days after the public burning at the stake of Phoebe Harris for coining, Wilberforce asked Parliament to instruct those involved in drafting his bill 'to insert a clause for … altering the punishment of females convicted of petty treason'.[148] The newspapers had reported in detail the four-hour process by which Harris's body had been reduced to a small pile of ashes and bones in the street outside Newgate and they had been extremely critical. This 'inhuman execution … is a disgrace to our laws' one concluded, while *The Times* described it as 'a scandal upon the law … inhuman …indelicate and shocking'.[149] Wilberforce's request, which was almost certainly a reaction to this event and its coverage, was immediately granted by the Commons,[150] and a clause ending the punishment of burning at the stake was duly inserted into the 1786 bill, was objected to by Lord Loughborough and was then rejected with the rest of the bill.[151] However, almost exactly four years later a new bill, introduced after two further burnings and a furious campaign in *The Times*,[152] passed fairly easily through Parliament and burning at the stake, and the obliteration of the offender's corpse, which it inevitably involved, was abandoned.[153] For the 'high treason' offence of coining females were now, like their male counterparts, simply to be drawn and hanged, thus removing the post-execution element of their punishment. However, the corpses of female murderers found guilty of petty treason did not avoid post-execution punishment under this new act. They were now publicly dissected under the Murder Act rather than being reduced to ashes.[154]

As Devereaux's detailed account of the passing of the 1790 Act has pointed out, the abolition of burning women at the stake was not, as some historians have suggested, simply an inevitable product of the increasing impact of 'enlightened attitudes towards punishment'.[155] The timing of the Act is better explained, he argues, by the conjunction of four more specific changes—an unprecedented rise in the number of female coiners being subjected to burning at the stake[156]; the transfer in 1783 of the place of execution from Tyburn to the street outside Newgate, which meant that the burnings were now performed in a crowded urban thoroughfare where residents could not avoid seeing them; a growing sensitivity to the public punishment of women; and, most importantly, the increasingly overt hostility of London's sheriffs whose role it was to conduct these burnings.[157] However, while this particular conjunction of factors may explain the specific timing of the 1790 Act, broader changes in cultural attitudes to punishment undoubtedly also played a role. As Devereaux points out, 'that only three such executions in the late 1780s could have the decisive impact they did speaks volumes for some kind of basic transformation in … public sensibilities over the long term'.[158] The sheriffs of earlier periods had not agitated for the repeal of the petty treason laws after being forced to put them into practice. By the late 1780s they were publically doing just that, and it was one of their number who introduced the 1790 Bill in the Commons.[159] It is therefore difficult to explain this turnaround in attitudes without some reference to broader long-term changes in attitudes and sensibilities.

The extensive press criticism of burning at the stake between 1786 and 1790 was part of a much broader critique of capital punishment, which forced the government to institute policies that would drastically reduce the huge numbers reaching the gallows. In 1788–1789 the numbers executed fell more than three-fold compared to their peak levels between 1785 and 1787, because Pitt used the backlog of pardoning decisions created by the King's temporary illness as an excuse to drastically cut the percentage of capital convicts that were executed.[160] This new policy then continued for the next decade. Between 1790 and 1799 an average of nineteen property offenders were hung in London each year. Between 1785 and 1787 the average had been seventy-eight.[161] The government had been forced by the mid-1780s crisis, and the negative press coverage it created, both to repeal the laws relating to burning at the stake and to institute a drastic cut in the proportion of London's offenders being hanged, which had a long term impact on the administration of the Bloody Code in the capital. After a brief rise in the famine year of 1800 the number of hangings in London halved again between 1801 and 1810, averaging only nine per year and reaching an all-time low of three in 1808.[162]

The huge reduction in the number of offenders hanged in London, combined with the end of the transportation crisis and the newspapers' obsession with the revolution unfolding in France, meant that criticism of the capital code was more muted in the early to mid-1790s, but important elements of that criticism clearly influenced the parliamentary debate on Jodrell's 1796 proposal that dissection should be introduced for all burglars and robbers. The Attorney General used the occasion to point out that capital punishment for burglary was already thought by many to be too severe, while Sergeant Adair argued strongly against the proposal partly on the grounds that 'the complexion of our criminal laws were already too sanguinary and severe', and that 'it was a painful reflection to think that it [the death penalty] was not entirely reserved for murder and high treason'.[163] The ideas voiced by these speakers were part of what John Beattie has termed 'the mental sea change' that lay behind the late-eighteenth century 'withering of support for a penal system that depended fundamentally on the threat of execution'.[164] A many-stranded critique was emerging. A correspondent of the *Gentlemen's Magazine*, for example, argued in 1790 that

> the laws of England ... are cruel, unjust and useless. The number of our fellow-mortals hung up so frequently like the vilest animals is ... proof of their cruelty; the same punishment inflicted on the parricide and the man who takes three shillings ... is a proof that they are unjust; the frequency of crimes ... is proof that they are useless.[165]

This change in attitude had important implications for the future of post-execution punishment in England. In attacking the underlying assumptions that supported the use of the gallows, the reformers used a range of arguments many of which were not only applicable to post-execution punishments but also had particularly strong critical purchase in relation to burning, gibbeting and, to a much lesser extent, dissection.

In his work on the body and punishment in the later eighteenth century McGowen has argued cogently, for example, that as the treatment of the criminal body gradually ceased to be a metaphor for expunging threats to the health of the social body, the reformers were able to replace this discursive framework with a new focus on the fate and experience of the individual, which in turn 'produced a demand for different punishments in part because the inflictions suffered seemed so disturbing and negative'.[166] 'The spectators seem to contemplate not the punishment of a criminal, but merely the death of an individual', Romilly wrote in 1786. 'They go away impressed' not by 'the justice of the law', but by 'compassion for a fellow creature, to whose suffering they have been witnesses'. This argument that, to quote McGowen, 'the mistreatment of the body prevented observers from seeing the social necessity of punishment' was clearly equally applicable to post-execution punishment. So was another argument frequently used by opponents of capital punishment, that is, that the gallows produced insensitivity and hardened the hearts of both the crowd and the criminals themselves.[167] 'Barbarous spectacles of human agony' and 'cruel or unseemly exhibitions of death' were opposed by Paley in 1785 'as tending to harden or deprave the public's feelings'—and a year later *The Times* echoed this sentiment in its comments on the burning of Phoebe Harris. 'Sanguinary and terrible punishments' it argued, quoting Montesquieu, 'tend to harden the human heart'.[168] Eden not only observed that 'the sensibility of the people, under so extravagant an execution of power, degenerates into despondency, baseness and stupidity' but also suggested that hanging in chains was particularly likely to generate these responses. It could not be doubted, he argued after being relatively positive about dissection, that the inevitable effect of forcing citizens to view 'gibbets … crowded with human carcasses' would be 'to blunt the sentiments and destroy the benevolent prejudices of the people'.[169]

This was not the only argument put forward by the late-eighteenth-century penal reformers that was easily and frequently turned into a critique of post-execution punishments. The growing sense—created by the combination of mass executions and continually growing indictment rates[170]—that the gallows rituals were not conveying any effective messages and that capital punishment was not working as a deterrent (which even the Solicitor General had to accede to during the 1785 London Police Bill debate) was paralleled by a long-running critique of the efficacy and morality of post-execution punishments and more particularly of hanging in chains.[171] Although the dissection of murderers was criticized in 1794 for failing to be 'any preventive to others for the future commission of such crimes', and for providing 'so small a distinction in the punishment' of the murderer and the thief,[172] by the 1790s and early 1800s it was hanging in chains that was the main target of disapproval. 'The exhibition of lifeless carcasses on gibbets … cannot be viewed by the humane and feeling without horror', wrote Beccarius Anglicus in a long diatribe against gibbeting. Echoing Blackstone, he then pointed out that, 'to prevent the brutalizing effect of such spectacles', Jewish law only allowed offenders to be left suspended for one night, whereas in England the country was 'polluted' by leaving them 'suspended on gibbets till their flesh has mouldered away or been devoured by the fouls of heaven'. He then entreated the English judges to discontinue this 'disgusting' practice of allowing the law 'to pursue the offender beyond the portals of mortality and to vent its fury on his senseless form'.[173] In 1799 another writer on capital punishment, having argued that 'dissection, if performed with proper decency and in the presence of persons who are studying anatomy, may tend to the advancement of science', then launched into an equally strong critique of hanging in chains. 'This … is productive of very little or no good' he argued. 'How many times are robberies and murders committed very near and even under a gibbet?'. The practice is, he suggested, 'disgraceful to a civilized nation; and while it fails in the intention, which is that of deterring the atrocious offender, it must shock the tender traveler, whose sensations are awake to the shocking degraded situation of a loathsome carcass'.[174] This critique was echoed in a wide range of London newspapers in the later 1790s, which frequently carried reports of crimes committed around the capital's gibbets. The *St James's Chronicle*, for example, reported in 1796 that 'The Chester Mail was robbed within 100 yards of the gibbet on which Lewin hangs, who suffered for a similar offence two years ago'.[175] Abershaw's gibbet on Wimbledon Common, on which the corpse of another highwayman was displayed, was the scene of a considerable number of widely reported robberies between 1796 and 1800,[176] as well as being the site in 1798 of a duel involving

Prime Minister Pitt—an act which could technically have resulted in Pitt being gibbeted had he killed the radical MP who had challenged him.[177] By this time both the gallows and the gibbet were not felt to be performing their most vital function—deterrence—and the latter in particular was therefore in danger of appearing not only cruel and highly distasteful, but also superfluous.

Broader changes in penal policy and discourse were beginning to move decisively away from punishments such as hanging in chains by the final quarter of the eighteenth century. Physical publically inflicted punishments directed at the body, symbolized by the gallows, the pillory and the gibbet were giving way to private, non-physical and mainly prison-based sanctions directed at the mind and aimed at generating the reform of the offender, as can be seen in the rapid growth in the use of imprisonment to punish property offenders and in the building of new penitentiary-style prisons in several counties.[178] The solitary cell hidden from contact with the world, rather than the solitary corpse gibbetted by the roadside was becoming the new focus of attention in late-eighteenth-century penal debate. Historians are deeply divided about whether we should see this movement from the gallows to the prison as simply a new and deeper strategy of control and social discipline, or as a function of a fundamental change in sensibilities towards violence.[179] However, punishments relying on the public display of rotting, burning or newly dismembered corpses were inevitably going to come under increasing scrutiny as this movement gathered momentum.

By arguing that the later eighteenth century witnessed a turning away from public execution rituals designed to 'bombard the visual senses' of the viewers, to 'increasingly hidden punishment that relied upon the imagination to conjure up frightening images of the unseen', Steven Wilf's work on 'execution aesthetics' has suggested another related way in which changing penal sensibilities may have undermined support for post-execution punishment.[180] His argument is not always convincing. Devereaux has shown, for example, that this was clearly not the reason why the gallows was moved from Tyburn to outside Newgate in 1783, since that change was mainly designed to make public executions more effective.[181] However, Wilf's work has usefully spotlighted the significance of another potentially influential strand of contemporary penal discourse, by pointing out that 'the 1780s witnessed a growing number of proposals for various forms of private executions.'[182] This idea had been floated by Henry Fielding a year before the Murder Act. 'I question whether every object is not lessened by being looked upon', he argued. If executions were private 'they would be much more shocking and terrible to the crowd outdoors ... as well as more dreadful to the criminals themselves'.[183] However, opposition to this idea remained very strong. As one legal writer put it in 1759 'No criminal ought to be executed in the dark'. Not only would there be 'some risk that an innocent person, either by accident or design, might be made to suffer for the guilty' but the whole purpose of public execution—'to strike terror into the spectators'—would be lost.[184]

The idea of private executions was revived in the 1785 when *The Times*, searching for a way to reinvigorate the deterrent effect of the gallows, published two proposals on these lines. After arguing that hanging in secret 'would strike a greater terror' the paper went on two months later to make a more detailed suggestion: 'Let us now try what terrors may arise from the certainty of being cut off in the privacy of an inclosure to which none can be admitted but the necessary officers, and from which all ... who might afford consolation are excluded', it suggested. The effects of such executions would not 'be blunted by frequency', it then argued, 'for as the whole apparatus would remain always invisible to the multitude, every repetition ... would never lose the force of novelty'.[185] William Paley's proposal in 1785 that criminals should be fed to wild beasts also included a proviso that they should 'perish in a manner dreadful to the imagination yet concealed from view',[186] and in 1787 the *Gentlemen's Magazine* went further, demanding 'an act of parliament ... for conducting the punishment privately in the press yard' after which, if required, 'the corps should be exposed on a stage before the prison'. This temporary gibbeting was designed to create terror in the minds of the common people 'by playing on their imaginations' for 'they would suppose cruelties in the executioner which had not been practiced'.[187] Fears that hidden punishments threatened English liberties meant that these ideas were never fully developed in the eighteenth and early-nineteenth centuries and public executions were not abandoned until 1868.[188] However, these proposals indicate both a growing desire (which can also be observed on the continent) to move the offender's body away from centre stage in the rituals of execution[189] and a broader sense that visual spectacles were often highly problematic—both ideas that raised increasing questions about the use of hanging in chains. These changes in the underlying discursive structures that were shaping penal policy, combined with the gradually developing sense from the mid-1780s onwards that exposure to decaying bodies was unhealthy and potentially dangerous,[190] clearly raised big questions about the continued use of hanging in chains, and in this context the eventual collapse of gibbeting just after 1800 (which we saw in Chap. 3) seems almost inevitable. It does not, however, explain the incredibly sudden and complete ending of the gibbeting of property offenders in 1802 (Fig. 3.2) and the almost complete collapse in the proportion of murderers who were hung in chains which is observable from that moment onwards (Fig. 3.1).

To understand why gibbeting collapsed so suddenly as a substantial penal practice in the first two or three years of the nineteenth century we need to see it in the context of the simultaneous changes that occurred in two other aspects of the administration of capital punishment. The first of these involved the related but separate practice of hanging offenders at the scene of their crime. As Steve Poole's recent work has shown crime-scene executions followed a very similar pattern of decline. Having peaked in the 1780s at more than three a year, this type of execution then declined to only one every other year 1806–1810 and one per decade 1821–1830, after which their use completely ceased.[191] The decline was particularly rapid in the metropolis. Thirteen London convicts were hanged at the scene of their crimes 1785–1795. None suffered that fate after 1816.[192] Since a very considerable number of crime-scene executions also involved gibbeting, the long-term correlation between these two changes is hardly surprising, but many crime-scene hangings did not include hanging in chains and the decline of the former therefore indicates another deliberate policy change. Since the judges increasingly ignored this option and the government encouraged them to do so by refusing to reimburse local sheriffs for the very considerable expenses involved (unless the offence involved some form of social unrest),[193] the authorities clearly decided to turn away from the crime-scene execution option in the first decade of the nineteenth century. Moreover this period also witnessed a much more fundamental change in execution policies.

In 1801–1802 those in charge of the administration of the capital punishment system in England and Wales suddenly instituted a more merciful approach to thepardoning of capital offenders. Between Pitt's rethinking of pardoning policies in 1788 and the famine year of 1800 just over 25% of those capitally convicted at the Old Bailey were hanged. This fell in 1801–1804 to less than 10% and although it rose briefly in mid-decade it then fell to an all-time low of around 5% in 1808. This meant that between 1801 and 1810 the average execution rate was half that experienced between 1788 and 1800 and about one-fifth of the rate in 1785–1787, a pattern that continued (apart from a brief period in the late 1810s and early 1820s) until the repeal of most of the capital code in the early 1830s.[194] Moreover, Douglas Hay's recent calculations on pardoning rates across all of England and Wales suggest that an equally sudden change also took place outside London. The percentage of all capital convicts left to hang fell from around 30% in 1800–1801 to about 18% in 1802–1803 and, despite similar fluctuations as those seen in London by the mid-1820s it was only slightly above 5%.[195] The Bank of England's aggressive prosecution policies meant that hanging rates for forgery did not fall overall, but those for robbery and stealing from houses nearly halved across England and Wales between 1800 and 1803.[196] Gatrell has argued that, following the massive increase in prosecutions for capital offences that occurred in late 1810s and 1820s, after the huge post-war demobilization of 1815, the system of capital punishment effectively collapsed under its own weight.[197] However, the judges appear to have made a decisive change between 15 and 20 years before this by largely abandoning gibbeting and crime-scene execution, and by simultaneously reducing more than two-fold the proportion of capital convicts that they left to hang.

The reasons for this change of policy were never explained, and the change itself was never publicly announced, but it is possible that Lord Eldon, who became Lord Chancellor in 1801, may have been at least partly responsible for it. He later claimed that in 1801 he had initiated a new means of restraining the numbers subjected to the death penalty in London, and it is certainly true that execution rates for the group he particularly singled out—those convicted of robbery—halved between Lord Loughborough's chancellorship 1793–1800 and Eldon's first decade in charge (1801–1810).[198] Was the new Lord Chancellor also responsible for persuading both the Old Bailey and the circuit judges to completely abandon the gibbeting of property offenders in 1801 and to confine the gibbeting of murderers to only two occasions 1802–1810?[199] On the surface this seems unlikely since Eldon was a staunch defender of the death penalty, as was Lord Ellenborough who became Chief Justice in 1802,[200] but whether either of these two was the prime mover, or whether the twelve judges between them decided on a new set of policies,[201] there is no doubt that the collapse of gibbeting was part of a much broader rethinking of penal policy in 1801–1802, which also involved a major movement downwards in execution rates and a rapid decline in the use of crime-scene hangings. By 1808, the year in which Romilly launched his parliamentary attack on the Bloody Code, ten months would pass by without a single hanging in London, and crime-scene hangings had reached their lowest levels for nearly 100 years.[202] By that year the Old Bailey judges had not ordered any offender to be hung in chains for nearly a decade and they would never do so again, the only criminals gibbeted in the capital after that date being the four Admiralty Court offenders hung in chains in 1814 and 1816 respectively. Between 1808 and the passing of the Anatomy Act in 1832 only three murderers (less than 1% of those fully convicted) were gibbeted by the provincial assize courts. Given that burning at the stake had been abolished nearly 20 years earlier, and that only a very small number of offenders were punished for high treason in this period, post-execution punishment was now effectively confined to one form only —public dissection.

9 The Modification and Gradual Privatization of Post-execution Punishment, 1808–1828

Romilly's attempts to persuade Parliament to repeal parts of the capital code in the decade after 1808 were not especially successful and his only attack on aggravated/post-execution punishments also had only a limited impact.[203] In 1813 he introduced a bill 'To Alter the Punishment of High Treason', which proposed that the sentence for that crime be changed from drawing, hanging, disemboweling, beheading and quartering to simply drawing and hanging. The parliamentary debates on the 1813 bill (which failed) and on Romilly's second bill in 1814, revolved around a familiar set of issues.[204] Its opponents mainly stressed two arguments: deterrence and the need for differentiation in punishment. Even though these incredibly painful procedures were now inflicted only after the executioner had made sure that the offender was dead, they would still, they argued, induce terror and thus help to prevent high treason.[205] Equally importantly, they suggested, 'by confounding the punishments for high treason and common felonies' the bill would destroy all 'distinctions between crimes' and would make the punishment for murder more stringent than that for treason.[206] Romilly and his supporters, by contrast, stressed that cruel punishments produced cruelty in the people. 'The real effect of such scenes', Romilly argued, 'is to torture the compassionate and to harden the obdurate'.[207] Echoing their broader critique of discretionary justice,[208] the bill's proponents also pointed out that the executioner was given huge discretionary powers, being left totally responsible for the punishment inflicted and for ensuring that it became a post-execution punishment rather than a torture-based execution of the living.[209]

The 'disgusting severities' of the existing law 'ought not … to stain our penal code', they argued. It was important to have 'laws … in unison with the manners of the times', and this dissonance between 'a gentle country and cruel laws' threatened to delegitimize the law.[210] The judges who led the opposition largely won the day, but Romilly did score a minor victory. Disemboweling at least was ended. Although, unlike De Motte and Tyrie in the 1780s, the leaders of the 1817 Pentrich Rising and the 1820 Cato Street conspiracy avoided having their entrails cut out, they were still draw, hanged and beheaded, their dripping bloody heads being then shown to the crowd.[211] These rituals may or may not have cowed their audiences, but as Gatrell has pointed out, the judges and arch Tories who led the opposition to Romilly's initiative clearly believed that they had that effect.[212]

Given the limited concessions Romilly achieved in the 1814 Act and the fact that only 8 of the 241 men subjected to post-execution punishment in England and Wales between 1814 and the passing of the 1832 Anatomy Act were executed for treason, the 1813–1814 debates had relatively little direct impact—especially since the main form of post-execution punishment still in use by the mid-1810s—dissection—was never used against traitors and was not therefore a focus of debate. However, the dominance of dissection, and the core reasons why it was proffered to hanging in chains, was very well summarized by the final speaker in the 1814 Treason Act debate. Only one of the two options created by the Murder Act was now used, or of use, the Whig reformer Samuel Whitbread pointed out:

> A discretionary power given to the judge to order them to be hung in chains … has now been for years abandoned—it was not found to operate in the slightest degree to the prevention of crimes, while it placed before the public eye the most disgusting spectacle. The dissection of bodies has not this effect: for the public are not then shocked by any exhibition beyond the death of the criminal, and this has been found to be as useful as the former spectacle was disgusting.[213]

Whitbread's dismissal of hanging in chains and his observation that 'the judges never avail themselves' of their discretionary power to gibbet murderers proved slightly premature.[214] There was a brief 3-year revival of hanging in chains between 1814 and 1816 when nine murderers were gibbeted, eight of them (including four Malayan sailors) by the Admiralty Court. However, since only one offender was ordered to be gibbeted between 1817 and the Anatomy Act of 1832 his analysis was broadly correct. Overall his brief speech highlighted the three core features that shaped both discussions about, and the practical application of, post-execution punishment in the final two decades before 1832—the marginalization and almost complete dismissal of gibbeting; the continued enthusiasm for (or at least acceptance of) the remaining post-execution sanction, dissection; and the growing belief that dissection should no longer involve any element of 'exhibition' that might shock the public.

Gibbeting continued to attract very negative opinions throughout this period. It did still have a few advocates. Bathurst praised it during the 1813 debate and the aging Bow Street runner, John Townsend, recommended it when giving evidence before the 1816 London Police Committee, claiming that he had recently persuaded the Admiralty Court to hang two men in chains on the Thames.[215] However, gibbeting was increasingly seen, and often described, as 'barbaric' and as a disgusting exhibition, a filthy and odious nuisance which had 'no other end but that of annoying the unoffending inhabitants'.[216] This 'offence against public feeling' was not only useless but also, to quote a 1824 letter to the Home Office, 'revolting, disgusting and pitiable' bringing disgrace to the law and discrediting its administrators.[217] Having seen his female companions scuttle below decks to avoid the sight of the Admiralty Court's Thames-side gibbets, the author of this letter then asked 'surely, sir, the days of Lewisham have passed, Tyburn, Kensington, Hounslow, Wimbledon are all freed from the sad practice, why should it be perpetuated to the disgrace and nuisance of the Port of London?'[218] Three years later in 1827 the inhabitants of Lincolnshire, following the example set by the Cornish nearly a century earlier, prevented Judge Best from gibbeting a murderer on a local high road. The felling of the surviving gibbets also began around this time. In 1826 the Derbyshire magistrates demolished a 10-year-old gibbet[219] and in the following year the destruction of a London gibbet was evocatively recorded in a sketch showing it lying on the ground with the bodies it had exhibited laid beside it.[220] Although, as we will see, the twists and turns of the 1828–1832 debates on the ending of dissection resulted in the momentary reintroduction of hanging in chains, gibbeting was effectively dead as a sentencing option by the mid-1810s.

Whitbread's observation that dissection had a completely different effect to hanging in chains, because 'the public are not shocked by an exhibition',[221] was much less accurate than his dismissal of gibbeting. Given the huge discretion given to the surgeons, dissection practices varied widely between regions and even between individuals. However, as Hurren's work has made clear, the public display of the criminal corpse was frequently part of the dissection process—a process that could last several days.[222] Although there is clear evidence that by the later 1810s and 1820s the dissection of criminal corpses was beginning to be privatized in some places, huge crowds still flocked to see the mutilated bodies of celebrity offenders such as Bellingham, who assassinated the Prime Minister in 1812, and William Corder, the famous Red Barn murderer, executed in 1828.[223] As late as 1818 a parricide and his accomplice were publically anatomized in the kitchen of the house were the murder took place and 'the bodies ... left exposed to the view of thousands'.[224] By that time, however, the tide was beginning to turn. As early as 1802 the Lord Chief Justice had ruled that surgeons were not legally obliged to expose the corpse to public view during the dissection process and by the early 1810s critiques of public dissection had begun to appear in the press.[225] In 1822, for example, the governors of Leicester Infirmary decided that exhibiting the bodies of those given for dissection was 'improper' and should not be permitted. Five years later the Devon and Exeter Hospital made a similar decision and a growing number of surgeons and hospitals in other areas also began to develop nearly identical policies in the 1820s.[226] The gradual privatization of dissection had only just begun as the debates on its future as a post-execution punishment reignited in the late 1820s but there was definitely movement in that direction.

The third element of Whitbread's speech—his very positive attitude to the use of dissection—was still being echoed by a number of writers in the 1820s. Although an increasing number of surgeons were beginning to develop the more hostile attitudes to penal dissection that would be partly responsible for its demise in 1832, dissection was still seen by many as an appropriate response to murder.[227] Moreover, several writers continued to echo the late-eighteenth-century proposals of Wilberforce and others by advocating its use against other types of offenders. In 1826 John Disney included in his 'Outlines of a Penal Code' both a general recommendation of dissection as operating strongly in preventing murder, and specific laws that would have mandated dissection 'in all cases of capital convictions' (including high treason) and for all suicides.[228] In the same year a letter sent to the parliamentary committee on criminal convictions advocated both the repeal of some capital statutes and the use of dissection against all those who were still executed, in part as response to the growing problem of body snatching.[229] That problem had already inspired two articles in the

Gentlemen's Magazine in 1814 and 1821 advocating in the first case that 'the body of every criminal that is executed' be given to the surgeons, and in the second that suicides and those 'killed in a duel' should be sent for dissection along with all those who died 'by the hands of justice' in order to supply the surgeons' needs and 'stop the trade of the resurrection men'.[230] Although, as a public event, dissection was under increasing pressure, it was still widely felt to be an appropriate punishment for murder, as Parliament's refusal to repeal the relevant clause of the Murder Act in 1828 and 1829 indicates.

10 The 1828–1829 Debates and the Reluctance to End Post-execution Punishment

The story of the surgeons' campaign to find alternative sources of cadavers, which gained momentum in the 1820s and finally gave them access to the bodies of the poor through the Anatomy Act of 1832, has already been analysed in detail, as has the long-term impact of the that Act.[231] However, the element within the surgeons' campaign that is most relevant to the history of post-execution punishment—their demand that dissection no longer be used as a penal strategy—has not been fully analysed and this will be the main focus here. Although the surgeons had only played a relatively minor part in the eighteenth-century debates about the use of dissection as a sentencing option, in the early-nineteenth century they became increasingly convinced that their penal role had become highly counter-productive, and that it was therefore time to put pressure on Parliament to repeal the relevant clauses of the Murder Act and thereby put an end to dissection as a post-execution punishment. By the mid-1820s this had become an increasingly fixed element in their campaign. When they petitioned the Home Office in 1825 for permission to use the bodies of those who died in workhouses, infirmaries or prisons, they also requested the repeal of the law 'which gives over certain executed criminals for dissection' because this would remove 'the prejudices now existing against anatomy'.[232] When Bentham, who played a seminal role in the campaign, wrote a draft 'Body Providing Bill' in 1826 he included a section repealing the relevant parts of the Murder Act and in 1827 *The Lancet*, having previously published an article proposing the repeal of 'those barbarous laws … which consign criminals to dissection', reported that it 'had been given to understand, from undoubted authority, that it (the repeal) will be accomplished by Mr. Peel during the next session of Parliament'.[233] It was not accomplished that year, and Peel's attitude at this point appears to have been much less positive than *The Lancet*'s report implied, but Lansdowne, who (due to a temporary change of government) replaced Peel at the Home Office from July 1827 to January 1828, was clearly committed to repeal by 1828.

Richardson did not analyse this aspect of the period leading up to Warburton's request for a Parliamentary Select Committee on 22nd April 1828, but between mid-March 1828 and 22nd April Lansdowne made a concerted attempt to obtain repeal.[234] On 14th March, after presenting a petition sent to Parliament by the surgeons of Worcester asking for a new means of obtaining bodies for dissection, Lansdowne announced that 'he thought the best way to proceed, in the first place, would be to repeal the existing law'[235] and he put that plan into action two weeks later at the end of parliamentary discussions on a different bill that eventually became the 1828 'Offences against the Person Act'. That legislation, thereafter known as Lansdowne's Act, was mainly a consolidating measure covering many forms of violence including murder, although it also introduced new powers enabling the summary courts to punish offenders for assault.[236] However, on 28th March, when the bill was in the committee stage, Lansdowne brought forward a late amendment proposing that the penal dissection clause of the Murder Act be left out when it was consolidated within the new Act.[237] The precise conjunction of events that brought this about is difficult to reconstruct and it is interesting that Peel, who was now back in post as Home Secretary, did not speak in the debate. However, Lansdowne openly declared that he was proposing the amendment because 'he had had some correspondence with medical men' who were concerned about 'the stigma' that 'condemning criminals to dissection' created,[238] and it seems clear that by March 1828 a large group of surgeons and Benthamites, with the help of the ex-Home Secretary, were mounting a concerted parliamentary attack on penal dissection.

This was no easy task. At the third reading of the Offences Against the Person Bill in the Lords on 15th April Lansdowne's amendment ran into concerted opposition from two very different quarters. Both the future Whig Prime Minister, Earl Grey (a long-term supporter of Romilly's campaign to repeal the capital code), and the high Tory Lord Chief Justice, Lord Tenterden (who like most of the judges was an avowed opponent of criminal justice reform), began by expressing doubts about whether penal dissection really did create any stigma against anatomy. Following this,

Tenterden's main argument was that any amendment 'which might tend … to make men feel less terror at the punishment for murder and might lessen their motives for abstaining from … such a crime' should not be considered, even if it only prevented one murder every 20 years.[239] Grey based his much more detailed critique mainly on the two themes we have already identified in the early-nineteenth-century discourse—differentiation and deterrence. 'The punishment of death was unhappily extended to many offences of an inferior nature to …murder', he argued,[240] '[t]hat being so … the distinction now attached to … murder … that the body of the murderer was given up for dissection', should be preserved.[241] He opposed the extension of the punishment of dissection to other crimes and, 'as the converse of that position', rejected Lansdowne's attempt to end the differentiation between murder and 'minor offences'. Grey then went on to discuss the deterrent value of dissection. Although he admitted that 'no effect would be produced on the individual' who had made up his mind to commit murder, Grey still contended that 'the additional punishment of dissection' created 'a salutary terror' in the community and maintained 'a horror of the crime of murder' within it.[242] This argument was not entirely consistent. As the *Morning Chronicle* pointed out, 'he wishes to terrify those who are not likely to commit murder by means which will have no effect in terrifying those likely to commit murder'.[243] Despite these criticisms, and Lansdowne's concluding speech stressing that 'it could not be idle theory' that condemning murderers to dissection prevented people giving their bodies, on 15th April the House of Lords voted down Lansdowne's attempts to repeal this part of the Murder Act.[244]

However, the issue continued to attract the attention of Parliament. Petitions carried on pouring in from the surgeons of major cities such as Glasgow, Leeds and Liverpool, who not only asked for help in obtaining cadavers, but also referred to their fear of being prosecuted for possessing exhumed bodies as a result of a recent judgment at the Lancashire assizes, which had created new case law to that effect.[245] Six days after Lansdowne's amendment was defeated, the current Home Secretary, Peel, after presenting a petition from the Royal College of Surgeons, informed the Commons that since Warburton would 'bring forward a motion for an inquiry into the subject' the following day, he would 'reserve any decisive opinion' on the matter till he had heard Warburton speak.[246] During the ensuing debate that day one high Tory MP suggested expanding the use of dissection to include suicides, an idea quickly refuted by Peel and by the radical MP Joseph Hume, who argued that 'making dissection at any time a penalty' could only increase the aversion of the community to it.[247] The penal reformer, Sir James Mackintosh, having pointed out that 'the bodies of murderers proved a source of supply entirely unworthy of notice', and that no threat 'could add practically to the terror of the punishment of death' then ended the debate with a comment that had important long-term implications. The way to make a 'true distinction … between the crime of murder and less heinous offences', he argued, 'would be to lighten … the punishments inflicted for the latter'[248]—an argument against the underlying logic of post-execution punishments for murder which as we will see, would become increasingly relevant as the reformers succeeded in obtaining the repeal of the capital statutes relating to most property offences in the early 1830s. Thus when, on the following day, Warburton asked the House to appoint a Select Committee on Anatomy, he did so in the context of an ongoing battle for the repeal of penal dissection, and of Lansdowne's failure, just one week earlier, to win that battle. Although the Committee focused most of its attention on creating alternative sources of supply to meet the surgeons' need for cadavers, it was also designed to be a major intervention in the debate on penal dissection.

Most of the witnesses appearing before the 1828 Parliamentary Select Committee on Anatomy, many of whom were handpicked 'first degree Benthamites', overwhelmingly endorsed the view that the dissection clauses of the Murder Act should be immediately repealed.[249] With monotonous regularity more than fifteen witnesses responded to leading questions such as 'do you concur in the opinion, that the giving up the bodies of murderers for dissection tends to aggravate … public feeling against dissection' by talking about its injurious effects and recommending repeal. For example, the President of the Royal College of Surgeons, Sir Astley Cooper, argued that 'the dissection of murderers' was 'the greatest stigma on anatomy … and extremely injurious to science', while another witness pointed out that 'to make an anatomist the executioner of the laws, must … create an odium against us'.[250] Although one or two mildly dissenting voices were allowed,[251] those who guided the membership and terms of reference of the 1828 Committee, and the questions it asked, were highly successful in marshalling evidence recommending that dissection needed to be immediately abandoned as a penal option. The committee's report, offered to Parliament in 1829, clearly reflected this. It recommended repealing the clauses of the Murder Act directing 'that the bodies of murderers be … anatomized' because, 'by attaching to dissection the mark of ignominy', it increased 'the dislike of the public to anatomy'.[252] Those who orchestrated the committee were well aware that they had to tread carefully on this issue and in the report's conclusion they professed themselves 'very unwilling to interfere with any penal enactment which might ... prevent the commission of atrocious crimes'. However, they argued strongly that 'as it can be reasonably doubted whether the dread of dissection can be reckoned amongst the obstacles to the perpetration of such crimes and as ...the clause in question must create a strong and mischievous prejudice against the practice of anatomy' it should therefore be repealed.[253]

Given that the Benthamites behind the 1829 Anatomy bill were clearly committed to ending penal dissection, and had organized a chorus of witnesses to advocate the repeal of the Murder Act's key clauses, it is extremely surprising that the Bill introduced into Parliament by Warburton in March 1829 did not included any attempt to repeal those clauses. Richardson has suggested that the repeal clause was mysteriously dropped from the bill for tactical reasons. 'The Royal College, of which Cooper was president, wanted to preserve its privileged right to corpses', she suggested, but Warburton and his supporters 'were opposed to ceding this power to the Royal College and probably thought that the omission of Bentham's clause repealing the dissection of murderers a small price to pay to pacify the College'.[254] However, there are a number of problems with this explanation, not the least being Cooper's direct advocacy of repeal before the 1828 committee. While Richardson may conceivably be correct that internal politics between different surgical interest groups played a role in the dropping of the repeal clause, a closer analysis suggests that it was the potential opposition of key parliamentary figures, who wanted to preserve dissection because of its value as a post-execution punishment, which played a central role in Warburton's 1829 decision.

Not all members of Parliament wanted to continue with the use of dissection as a punishment for murder. Lansdowne could still be relied on to advocate repeal in the Lords and when the 1829 Bill was debated in the Commons in May the Tory MP Sir Robert Inglis also made a long speech demanding the end of penal dissection. It was vital, he argued, to make a distinction between 'the man who dies on the scaffold' and the poor man dying in a workhouse. 'For my own part', he observed, 'I have no wish to alter the law relative to the bodies of murderers; but if this bill is to pass, I think that law ought to continue no longer'. You therefore need, he told the advocates of the bill, to 'take your choice between criminals and the friendless', and since only eleven murderers' bodies were available in the year 1827 (and only seventy were executed for any offence) choosing the criminal option would 'not furnish one-tenth of the subjects necessary for science'.[255] This argument made very little headway. Even before Inglis proposed it in open debate, it 'had been already discussed in the committee on the bill, and there rejected', and Inglis's attempt to revive it was voted down by a huge majority of forty votes to eight.[256] However, Warburton's immediate response to Inglis's reintroduction of the repeal issue into the 1829 debate offers important clues about why he chose not to include a repeal clause in the original 1829 Bill.

When he had first introduced the Bill, Warburton reminded the House, he felt 'the evidence was in favour of the repeal of this clause' but 'after conferring with … those Honourable Gentlemen on whom the fate of the bill depended' he was convinced that for the bill to be successful 'in this and another place (i.e. the House of Lords), it must contain no such provision'.[257] The resounding vote against Inglis's proposed amendment in the Commons (which then passed the bill without it) and the fact that the bill was then rejected by the Lords, where it failed to get support from key figures such as the Chief Justice, Earl Grey and the Archbishop of Canterbury, suggests that those Warburton conferred with were absolutely right.[258] Moreover, although Peel deliberately kept a low profile on the issue, he was also against repeal. In the May 1829 one of the MPs who responded to Inglis's proposal expressed his regret that Peel had not bothered to attend the debate 'to state the reasons which induced him, as well as the committee', to reject it, and as current Home Secretary Peel he was almost certainly one of the 'Honourable Gentlemen' who advised Warburton to drop the repeal clause. Thus even at this point, after more than three-quarters of a century as a penal sanction, and after the almost complete disappearance of hanging in chains, the use of dissection as a post-execution punishment still had widespread support in Parliament and in government circles. However, those wishing to repeal the relevant clause of the Murder Act were not about to give up. Nor were the supporters of the much broader Anatomy Bill. Even though he could see that the 1829 Lords debate was going against him, Lansdowne still used that debate as an opportunity to suggest that 'when another measure should be brought forward, he would certainly propose that the law directing that the bodies of malefactors should be given over for dissection … be repealed'.[259] At the close of the parliamentary session three weeks later, Warburton duly gave notice that he intended to bring in another bill in the next session[260] and although the political turmoil of the following year caused a temporary delay, the bill that became the 1832 Anatomy Act was eventually introduced to parliament at the end of 1831.[261]

11 The Final Repeal of the Dissection Clause of the Murder Act, 1829–1832

Richardson has already provided a good overall analysis of the complex and multi-stranded debate that developed between the failure of the 1829 bill and the passing of the 1832 Anatomy Act. Warburton and his Benthamite colleagues had always intended 'to single out the very poor for dissection' and by a variety of linguistic dishonesties and parliamentary malpractices, and by using the growing outcry against the resurrection men and the sense of urgency created by the prosecution of 'the London Burkers', they achieved this aim in 1832.[262] In the process they put an end to penal dissection, Warburton's second anatomy bill specifically enacting that 'so much of the Murder Act as directs that the bodies of murderers may be dissected', be repealed.[263] Between 1829 and the introduction of the second bill to Parliament in December 1831 the surgeons' concern to separate the dissection process from any association with executions and punishment grew ever stronger. In 1829 a pamphlet on obtaining bodies for anatomy, having pointed out that the dissection of murderers was a major cause of 'public prejudice', argued that the legislature's first step should be the repeal of the Murder Act.[264] In the following year *The Lancet* not only pointed out that penal dissection lowered the social standing of the surgeons' profession, but also questioned, along with other contributors to the debate, the surgeons' role as 'finishers of the law'—a role in ensuring medical death that Hurren has shown was much more frequently exercised than most contemporaries realized.[265] Other writers pointed out more pragmatically that patients dying in hospital expressed strong feelings against being dissected because it would be treating them like murderers, and that 'brutal and disgusting exhibitions of the murderer's body' were 'inculcating a horror of anatomy'.[266] In 1830 a writer in the *Quarterly Review* went further. Angry at the 'unfortunate association produced by penal dissection', and worried that 'several of those who have spoken in Parliament on the subject have declared that they will never consent to its abolition', he suggested a strike. After pointing out that the law could not legally compel a surgeon to perform a penal dissection (as the case law we have already discussed had long established), he suggested that the surgeons simply 'decline a task that requires them to become post-mortem executioners' and 'let Jack Ketch … take to himself the office of anatomical executioner'.[267]

Although this view that penal dissection was a major source of 'public repugnance'[268] was powerfully advocated by Warburton and his colleagues between 1829 and 1831 (as it had already been before the 1828 Select Committee), there remained significant dissenting voices who not only opposed the curbing of penal dissection but also advocated that its use be extended to cover other types of offender. In 1829 Professor Guthrie, a prominent member of the Royal College of Surgeons, argued that the operation of the Murder Act did not, in itself, create any adverse feelings about dissection, and went on to suggest that the bodies of all executed offenders and of all those who died whilst imprisoned for criminal offences should be given to the surgeons.[269] In 1831, an article in the monthly magazine, *The Moral Reformer*, also suggested that the bodies of those found guilty of 'other crimes as well as murder' and those who might be given a life sentence as 'a substitute for the punishment of death' should be sent for dissection.[270] In February 1832 a petition from the inhabitants of Blackburn suggested giving over, for dissection, the bodies of murderers, suicides and 'all persons who die by the scandalous practice of dueling', and the petition sent in by the Mechanics of Lambeth was even more radical, suggesting that—as well as suicides, duelists and convicted felons—all those 'in receipt of unmerited pensions', all surgical practitioners and all the MPs who 'voted for Mr. Warburton's Bill' should also have their bodies sent for dissection.[271] Whilst this suggestion was clearly regarded as too extreme, the expansion of penal dissection to include a broader range of offenders continued to be put forward during the debate on the Second Anatomy Bill, which began in December 1831. The Bill's main opponent in the Commons, the radical reformer Henry Hunt, having criticized 'the insufferable doctrine' that the poor were to be dissected because of their poverty while murderers and thieves would 'escape this process', suggested on two separate occasions that all capital convicts, suicides and 'persons dying after a conviction for felony' should be given to the surgeons.[272] In the Lords a very similar position was taken up by a recently retired judge, Lord Wynford, an opponent of parliamentary reform, who not only demanded that 'the law which gave the bodies of murderers up for dissection should not be altered', but also argued that 'those convicted of felony, whether executed or dying in prison' and 'those who destroyed themselves' should be ordered for dissection.[273]

This continued advocacy of the large-scale expansion of penal dissection on the very eve of the passing of the Anatomy Act, which would end its use even for murder, indicates how deeply attached judges like Wynford still were to the use of post-execution punishment, but it may also be partly explained (in Hunt's case at least) by the difficult strategic situation these opponents of the Act found themselves in. Both would have been well aware by this point that they had little chance of success. Every time Hunt brought an amendment, and at every stage of the bill's journey through the Commons, Warburton's supporters defeated him by massive majorities. Things were a little better in the Lords, but Wynford also sounded resigned, observing at one point that 'he should divide the House, even if he had to go to the bar alone'.[274] To prevent the poor becoming the main targets of the anatomists the bill's opponents had to come up with a viable alternative, and to do so they drew on a long tradition that stretched back to Wilberforce's 1786 bill and beyond, and involved massively expanding the types of offenders to be sentenced to dissection. This Wynford pointed out, would provide 'a sufficient supply of subjects for the study of anatomy', without 'the necessity of passing the present invidious measure which … left the poor and miserable unprotected'. Wynford could, and did, also claim that his experience as a judge had proved to him that dissection was 'a useful and effective punishment' and although Hunt had no such experience, and came from the opposite end of the political spectrum, he seems to have thought it expedient to take the same view.

However, the idea of expanding penal dissection in this way received very little support in the parliamentary debates of 1831–1832. One MP spoke briefly in favour of giving the 'dead bodies of all criminals' to the surgeons[275] and another highly eccentric Tory MP, Colonel Sibthorpe, requested that 'those most rascally of all criminals, horse-stealers', should be dissected along with murderers.[276] On the other hand a chorus of voices demanded that the House go the other way and end penal dissection completely. Sir Robert Inglis, who had already attempted to get a repealing amendment through in 1829, made several speeches to that effect.[277] The Cornish MP Sir Richard Vyvyan argued that repealing the Murder Act was 'absolutely necessary' and other MPs made similar speeches.[278] When Hunt tried a new tactic and proposed an amendment designed simply to 'leave the Judges the power of ordering murderers … for dissection' he got nowhere. He was the only MP out of fifty who voted in favour.[279] In the Lords, where the judges and particularly the leading judge—the Lord Chancellor—traditionally had a major say when any changes in penal policy were proposed, the argument followed a rather different path. During the debate on the second reading in June 1832, just after Wynford had suggested greatly expanding the types of offender subjected to dissection, the Lord Chancellor quietly refuted his argument by reasserting the need for differentiation between different offences. 'As to giving up the bodies of all persons dying under sentence of felony', he observed, 'that might enhance the penalty on some felonies, but would lower it in the case of murder' and changing the current situation in which 'dissection was … only attached to the highest species of crime' would in his view be 'extremely prejudicial'.[280] He did not, however, commit himself on the more limited question that the debate now focused on—should the relevant clause of the Murder Act be repealed? While observing that 'some doubted' that 'dissection ought to be made the sentence for murder', the Lord Chancellor very pointedly avoided stating that he agreed with that view, while at the same time making it clear that he was not happy with 'every provision of the bill'.[281]

This may well have encouraged Wynford to follow Hunt's example and focus on preserving the penal dissection of murderers alone. During the bill's third reading in the Lords, Wynford proposed that the clause repealing the Murder Act be deleted because 'it was well known that the fear of dissection' was a powerful deterrent, and his proposal may well have had significant support. Lord Kenyon, son of the famous Lord Chancellor who had preceded Lord Eldon, was recorded as concurring in 'the learned Lord's view of the subject' and the Lord Chancellor, having made some vague, but probably supportive, remarks a month earlier, certainly did not speak against it.[282] Wynford might also have expected support from Earl Grey, who had opposed repeal in 1828, and in his speech in the debate Grey did indeed admit 'the justice of the learned Lord's remarks' before observing that 'he should be sorry to do away with any portion of the effective punishment of murder, without providing an adequate substitute'.[283] However, it soon became clear that Grey was looking for a compromise. He was prepared to end penal dissection but did not think it was possible to do so without keeping some form of post-execution punishment as a means of preserving differences in sentencing between murder and lesser offences. 'Unfortunately', Grey observed, since penal dissection created so many prejudices against anatomy 'it was thought advantageous to do away with the dissection of murderers'. He therefore proposed, 'in order to distinguish murder from other crimes', and avoid 'lessening the moral horror of the offence' a new clause which (after some honing down in discussion with other members) was designed to enact that 'the bodies of all prisoners convicted of murder should either be hung in chains, or buried under the gallows on which they had been executed, or within the precincts of the prison' where they had been confined.[284] Although it remains unclear whether Wynford was entirely happy with this, Grey was Prime Minister by this point and therefore in an ideal position to broker a compromise, and at the end of the debate *Hansard* simply records 'clause agreed to, and the bill read a third time and passed'.[285]

The ending of dissection as a post-execution punishment had not gone uncontested, and, even at the death, the idea that the use of penal dissection should be expanded to all criminal offenders, and also to suicides, was still being seriously debated. The House of Lords, unable, it seems, to give up the idea that murder should be punished more severely than other capital offences, had compromised by introducing a new, if very private, form of post-execution punishment—burial in the prison grounds. (The less practical option of burying the corpse under the gallows was left largely unused.) At the same time they had reasserted the judges' right to sentence murderers to hanging in chains—an option that the Anatomy Act had not in any case aimed to remove. The judges who were now deprived of the ability to use their preferred post-execution option—dissection under the Murder Act—could still order that an offender's corpse be hung in chains. However, when two of them did just that almost immediately after the passing of the Anatomy Act, a massive reaction against the use of gibbeting quickly extinguished this final vestige of the era of public post-execution punishments in England.

12 Brief Revival and Rapid Repeal: The Abolition of Hanging in Chains

Hanging in chains was rarely mentioned during the 1828–1832 debates. During the second reading of the 1832 Anatomy Bill Hunt briefly referred to the fact that it would 'restore the old brutal system of hanging in chains', and in opposing the third reading another MP announced 'he should never consent' to the barbarous idea of reviving 'the custom of hanging in chains'.[286] Although Earl Grey eventually agreed to its inclusion in his compromise amendment, he does not appear to have been particularly positive about it either. Two months after the 1832 debate the *Morning Herald* reported that, in his desire to appease Lord Wynford, Grey had only initially proposed 'a clause providing that the bodies of murderers should be buried beneath the gallows ... or within the precincts of the prison'. This does not seem to have been enough, however, and subsequently, the paper reported, he 'was weak enough to be induced' to include hanging in chains as an option.[287] The pressures Grey was under at this point remain unclear, but when he was a circuit judge Lord Wynford had been the last member of the assizes bench to sentence an offender to hanging in chains only 5 years before 1832, and it is quite likely therefore that Wynford persuaded Grey to include this punishment in his amendment.[288]

Since 'in the two first instances of conviction for murder which followed the passing of the Act' two of the current circuit judges immediately resorted to the use of hanging in chains, it is possible that Wynford was not alone in his advocacy of gibbeting.[289] However, Judge Parke, who passed the first of these sentences on the remote Northern Circuit only seven days after the Act received the royal assent, may have done so mainly because he was unsure how to proceed. Since dissection was now abolished, he observed when addressing the convict, William Jobling, 'in order that he should not have an erroneous sentence, by directing the body of the prisoner to be dissected, he should direct that it should be hung in chains'.[290] However, by the time the second gibbeting sentence was passed two weeks after the 1832 Act had received the royal assent, the new law had been fully communicated to all the circuit judges and was being formally announced by them at the commencement of each assizes.[291] The second assize judge's decision to gibbet the Leicestershire murderer James Cook was not therefore a simple matter of avoiding error. Instead it was clearly a deliberately punitive response, since the judge referred in passing sentence, to 'the atrocious circumstances' of the case.[292] However, the judges would never again be allowed to respond to particularly 'atrocious' cases such as this (Cook had cut up and burnt the body of his victim) by punishing the criminal's corpse in any way apart from burial in the prison grounds.[293]

These two gibbetings in early August 1832 attracted huge crowds and in Leicester a fairground atmosphere quickly developed around Cook's suspended body. However, neither corpse stayed long on its gibbet. Jobling's body was quickly rescued by his fellow colliers and buried in a local churchyard.[294] Cook's carcass was taken down after three days by order of the Home Secretary—a decision much praised in the press, which had been highly critical of 'the disgraceful revival' of this 'brutal antiquated custom'.[295] The *Royal Cornwall Gazette*, for example, rejoiced at the remitting of this part of the sentence after three days. 'Even this tardy repeal', it reported, 'is creditable to the feeling of the King'.[296] In the months that followed this 'practice of barbarous origin, which the progress of civilization had exploded' was widely criticized on a number of grounds.[297] It tended 'to brutalize the populace, not to improve or instruct them', the *English Chronicle* observed.[298] The *Morning Herald* agreed. 'The gibbet', it observed in August 1832, 'never reforms, but always brutalizes—just as breaking on the wheel and exposing the body afterwards, under the old regime of France, only tended, by hardening the feelings of the spectators' to increase murder rates.[299] Hanging in chains was also regarded as inefficient, since 'the exhibition of the body shocked those only on whom it was never meant to exercise as a warning, and became nothing but an object of idle curiosity to those to whom it was meant to be an awful example'.[300] Even more important, perhaps, it delegitimized the law. 'We would have the laws reasonable, temperate, and decent, that they may not be despised or insulted' the *Morning Herald* commented a few days after Cook's gibbeting. 'The revival of the odious practice of gibbeting which had been banished by the progress of civilized habits', it later added, 'was a great disgrace to the legislature of England in the nineteenth century'.[301] More pragmatic considerations were also important. When speculating about why the government had taken down Cook's corpse after only three days, the local paper pointed out that should murders be as frequent during the next 12 years as they had been in the last 12 years 'the county would be frightfully studded with such exhibitions'.[302]

It is difficult to find any contemporary commentators who responded to these criticisms by arguing in favour of hanging in chains, and it is not therefore surprising that when the penal reformer William Ewart introduced a bill into Parliament 'To Abolish the Practice of Hanging the Bodies of Criminals in Chains' it went through the Commons unopposed.[303] Ewart did not even bother to make a case for abolition. It was unnecessary, he argued, since the government had indicated it was 'willing to abolish this odious practice'.[304] The bill had an equally easy passage through the House of Lords, where the liberal reformer, Lord Suffield said 'he was at a loss to find any reason for continuing such a practice'. Burying the offenders' bodies within prison precincts was, he argued, carrying 'vengeance' far enough.[305] After the committee stage in the Lords, the Earl of Shaftesbury reported that no amendments had been thought necessary, and a day later the bill passed its third reading without further debate.[306]

Given that only 2 years earlier the Lords had presented enough opposition to the ending of penal dissection to force Grey into producing a compromise amendment involving the continuance of hanging in chains, the 1834 bill's easy passage through the upper house may seem surprising. However, between 1832 and the passing of Ewart's bill in July 1834 a vital change had taken place. Under Earl Grey's leadership the reforming Whig government had not only passed the First Reform Act and abolished slavery, but had also begun to repeal many of the statutes that had made a wide variety of property crimes into capital offences. Coinage offences and nearly all forms of forgery were made non-capital in 1832, and in the same year Ewart's bill making horse, sheep and cattle stealing, and larceny in the dwelling house non-capital had also passed, despite strong opposition from Peel in the Commons and from the Lord Chief Justice and Lord Wynford in the Lords, where Wynford managed to force through another short-lived but harsh amendment.[307] The repeal of the Bloody Code was still going on in 1834, with a leading role being played by the same two men who were pushing for the end of hanging in chains. Two weeks after introducing his anti-gibbeting bill, Ewart asked the Commons for leave to bring in another 'Capital Punishment Bill' abolishing the death sentence for letter-stealing, burglary and returning from transportation, and two weeks after Suffield introduced the anti-gibbeting bill in the Lords he was supporting the passage of the same 'Capital Punishment Bill' through the upper house.[308]

As it became clear that almost all property offences would soon be non-capital but that murderers would still be sent to the gallows, the core argument of those who opposed the ending of penal dissection (and the few who still advocated hanging in chains)—that it was necessary to impose a more severe form of capital punishment on murderers than on mere property thieves—was completely undermined. In 1834 an MP arguing that robbery should no longer be a capital crime adapted the familiar eighteenth-century argument—'that, by putting the punishment of robbery on a rank with that for murder, murder was brought down to the rank of robbery'[309]—to this new context. Differentiation could now be achieved, he and others argued, not by adding extra post-execution dimensions to the punishment of murder but by removing the death penalty from other lesser crimes. This idea had already been floated before the large-scale repeal of the Bloody Code had begun. In 1829, for example, one commentator argued that the dissection of murderers should only be discontinued once the punishment of death was attached to murder alone, and by 1832 the Whig Lord Chancellor, Henry Brougham, was arguing along similar lines.[310] Only 6 years before the 1834 Act Mackintosh's rejection of penal dissection on the grounds that the best way to distinguish 'between murder and less heinous offences would be to lighten the punishments inflicted on the latter' had seemed extremely idealistic.[311] However, as the Whigs reversed the Tory policy of consolidation and very limited actual reform, and began the wholesale repeal of almost every capital statute that could result in the sentencing of a significant number of property offenders to the gallows, the death sentence itself had indeed become the key method of creating differentiation in penal policy. The complete lack of opposition to the ending of public post-execution punishment in 1834 and the obvious willingness of the House of Commons to end penal dissection in 1832 needs to be seen in this context, as does Grey's change of heart over penal dissection. In 1828 and 1829 he had been one of the main advocates of retaining penal dissection. However, by July 1832, when he brokered the compromise in the Lords that put an end to penal dissection, many key property offences had already been, or were about to be, made non-capital.[312] Given that even those who opposed the repeal of the Murder Act were, by this point, admitting that penal dissection did not usually deter offenders from committing murder, the only effective rationale for that Act was the need to differentiate the punishment of murder from that for other capital offences. As it became clear in the new political situation of the early 1830s that differentiation could now be achieved by leaving murder, and one or two other particularly heinous offences, as the only crimes that would be punished by death, the main argument in favour of retaining any major form of post-execution punishment was decisively undermined.

The surgeons' very urgent need to find new sources of supply, the growing public opposition to the activities of the resurrection men, and the panic created in the late 1820s and early 1830s by 'Burkophobia' undoubtedly provided the short-term catalyst for the ending of penal dissection. However, by the early 1830s the surgeons were pushing at an open door. The formal post-execution regime created by the Murder Act lasted for as long as it was thought to be necessary and useful by the judges and their parliamentary supporters. When, in the early 1830s, it was clearly becoming redundant because the repeal of the Bloody Code had created a new means of achieving penal differentiation, public post-execution punishment was abandoned. The passing of the 1832 Anatomy Act may well have reflected the increasing power of the anatomists as a parliamentary lobby, and the discretion thesurgeons had been given by the Murder Act meant that a surgeons' strike was a real possibility, or at least a useful bargaining tool. However, ending the use of dissection as a penal strategy proved beyond the powers of Warburton and his supporters in 1829, just as their attempt to add it to the 1828 Act had done. They received no visible support from Peel, and although they got temporary backing from Lansdowne they failed to persuade the key Whig leader Earl Grey to back them. In 1829 they were told quite categorically that any Anatomy Bill with such a clause in it would fail, and they didn't even try to get the penal dissection clause past the judges in the Lords. Nor was this a new situation. At various intervals throughout the Murder Act period between 1752 and 1832, and especially in 1786 and 1796, they tried to get the principle of penal dissection extended to a range of other offences, with the aim of turning the almost insignificant trickle of cadavers made available by the Murder Act into an important supply stream. In 1786 they even got limited government backing, which enabled them to get the bill through the Commons. However, the House of Lords (and the judges that formed such a powerful pressure group within it) consistently rejected those attempts for the same reason that they later rejected the repeal of penal dissection—that it would undermine the principle of differentiation in punishment. Although the extension of penal dissection to other types of offender, and even to all felons dying in prison, continued to be advocated in the 1828–1832 debates, this argument was no more successful than it had been in 1786 and 1796. By this point the surgeon's had, in any case, focused on a much more convenient and easy target—the destitute and friendless poor—but when it came to expanding the categories of offenders covered by the Murder Act the Lords remained as intractable as ever.

Seen in this light, it seems clear that from 1752 until the radical penal reforms of the 1830s the ways post-execution punishment was used in England were almost entirely determined by criminal justice priorities. The Murder Act never gave the surgeons a significant supply of cadavers. Indeed, if Devereaux is correct, the number of criminal corpses given to the London surgeons may even have declined as a result of the Act.[313] When the provincial surgeons pressed for extension in 1786 they were vetoed by the Law Lords, and the surgeons' victory in 1832 was also more apparent than real. Even after producing a large array of witnesses demanding repeal before a carefully selected parliamentary committee in 1828, they faced implacable opposition to the repeal of penal dissection and did not even attempt to include it in the first anatomy bill. Only in 1832, after the repeal of the Bloody Code had begun and the underlying logic of post-execution punishment was being fundamentally undermined, did the surgeons finally achieve repeal of the dissection clauses of the Murder Act, which could only come once the penal foundations that held those clauses in place had begun to crumble.

Notes

1. S. Devereaux, 'England's "Bloody Code" in Crisis and Transition: Executions at the Old Bailey, 1760–1837' *Journal of the Canadian Historical Association*, 24 (2013) p. 77.
2. *The Times*, 31 January 1800; Almost every eighteenth-century legal commentator blamed the uncertainty of English law on the confusions produced by poorly expressed statute law. D. Lieberman, *The Province of Legislation Determined. Legal Theory in Eighteenth-Century Britain* (Cambridge, 1989) p. 237.
3. P. King, *Crime and Law in England 1750-1840: Remaking Justice from the Margins* (Cambridge, 2006) pp. 22–25.
4. These issues are recorded in the Judges 'Resolution on the Manner of Sentencing under the Murder Act', 7 May 1752 in the National Army Museum Archives, (hitherto NAMA) ref 6510-146(2) -24.
5. Ibid. and W. Hawkins, *A Treatise of the Pleas of the Crown* (London, sixth edition, 1787) pp. 659–661; M. Foster, *A Report of Some Proceeding for the Trial of the Rebels … and of other Crown Cases* (Dublin 1791) p. 107. The Murder Act had stipulated that the convicted murderer be hanged within two or three days of sentencing and this was the part deemed to apply also to women.
6. 'Judges' Resolution on the Applicability of the Murder Act to the Case of Earl Ferrers', 23 April 1760 in the NAMA, ref 6510-146(2) -30.
7. 25 Geo II. c. 37—An Act for Better Preventing the Horrid Crime of Murder.
8. Ibid. In any other county the body was to be delivered to 'such surgeon as such judge … shall direct'.
9. Ibid.
10. R. Richardson, *Death, Dissection and the Destitute* (London, 1989) p. 37.
11. J. Sawday, *The Body Emblazoned; Dissection and the Human Body in Renaissance Culture* (London, 1995) p. 54.
12. E. Hurren, *Dissecting the Criminal Corpse; Post-execution Punishment in Early Modern England, from the Murder Act (1752) to the Anatomy Act (1832)* (Basingstoke, 2016) pp. 7–8.
13. Ibid., p. 7.
14. Ibid., pp. 6–9.

15. Ibid., p. 10.
16. Ibid., p. 23.
17. Ibid., pp. 22–23, 38–39.
18. Ibid., pp. 22–23.
19. Ibid., p. 155 and 191.
20. Ibid., p. 39.
21. *Public Ledger*, 6 May 1760.
22. Hurren, *Dissecting*, pp. 157–158.
23. Described in C. Wall, *The History of the Surgeons' Company 1745-1800* (London, 1937) p. 103.
24. Ibid.
25. Hurren, *Dissecting*, pp. 157–160. Publicly displaying the corpse was criticised severely in the *London Evening Post*, 28 March 1760 for debasing his rank and for making a spectacle 'for gratifying the insolence of the Mob'.
26. D. Gray and P. King 'The Killing of Constable Linnell: The Impact of Xenophobia and of Elite Connections on Eighteenth-Century Justice' *Family and Community History*, 16 (2013).
27. Anon, *An Account of the Trial and Conduct of John Webborn* (Place of publication unknown, 1799).
28. *Bath Herald*, 15 August 1795.
29. *St James Chronicle and British Evening Post*, 18 March 1762.
30. TNA, E389/250/79, 245/186, 242/380 and 383.
31. Hurren, *Dissecting*, pp. 125–126; R. Ward, 'The Criminal Corpse, Anatomists, and the Criminal Law: Parliamentary Attempts to Extend the Dissection of Offenders in Late Eighteenth-Century England' *Journal of British Studies*, 54 (2015) pp. 76–79.
32. Ward, 'The Criminal Corpse', p. 77.
33. Hurren, *Dissecting*, pp. 155–156.
34. *Ordinary's Account*, 3rd October 1759, (OA17591003 www.oldbaileyonline.org version 6.0., 14 September 2012).
35. Ibid.
36. Royal College of Surgeons, cos/1/1 min book of the Court of Assistants Vol. 1 1745-1800 108/4032-3 indicates the skeletons in the theatre were ordered to be cleaned and repaired. 108/4095-4113 Triennial Report, vol. 1 indicates the disposal of bodies of dissected murderers was left to the discretion of the master and wardens.
37. In the famous Burke case the Scottish judge observed in giving sentence. 'I trust that if it is ever customary to preserve skeletons, yours will be preserved'. W. Roughead, *Burke and Hare* (London, 1921).
38. *Public Advertiser*, 16 September 1767. For a contemporary drawing of the corpse in its niche—D. Rumbelow, *The Triple Tree*, (London, 1982) p. 181.

39. The newspapers gave considerable publicity to Weil being hung up in Surgeons' Hall, *London Evening Post*, 10 December 1771.
40. *Annual Register*, 1771, pp. 161 and 210–215.
41. *Public Advertiser*, 14 December 1771.
42. *London Daily Advertiser*, 3 July 1752; Hurren, *Dissecting*, pp. 136–138.
43. P. Beirne, *Hogarth's Art of Animal Cruelty. Satire, Suffering and Pictorial Propaganda* (Basingstoke, 2015) pp. 71–72; R. Ward, *Print Culture, Crime and Justice in Eighteenth-Century London* (London, 2014) p. 196; T. Hitchcock and R. Shoemaker, *Tales from the Hanging Court* (London, 2006), pp. 255–269. Attitudes to highwaymen were changing, see A. McKenzie, *Tyburn's Martyrs; Execution in England 1675-1775* (London, 2007), pp. 115–117: *The Ordinary of Newgate's Account … Of the 10 Malefactors Who were executed at Tyburn On Monday the 11th of February, 1751*.The practice went back at least to the 1630s: Sawday, *The Body*, pp. 60–61.
44. *Morning Post and Daily Advertiser*, 17 January 1786. Hogan was described as 'black' or as 'a mulatto from the Madieras', P. King and J. Carter Wood 'Black People and the Criminal Justice System: Prejudice and Practice in Later Eighteenth- and Early Nineteenth-Century London' *Historical Research*, 88 (2015), pp. 116–117. The *Public Advertiser* did report on 20 January 1786 that 'a skeleton will be made of the Mulatto and placed in a niche in the hall by that of Mrs. Brownrig and other notorious offenders'.
45. *Morning Post and Daily Advertiser*, 18 December 1787.
46. They might also create skeletons from those deemed to have deformities e.g. the four-foot high murderer John Pycraft, *Bury and Norwich Post*, 25 August 1819 quoted in S. Tarlow, *Hung in Chains: The Golden Ghoulish Age of the Gibbet in Britain* (London, Palgrave, Forthcoming) p. 22.
47. For provincial convicts hung as skeletons see T. Lambley, *Nottingham a Place of Execution from 1201 to 1928* (Wilford, 1981) p. 33, and two Suffolk examples, *Bury and Norwich Post*, 25 August 1819 and *Lancaster Gazette and General Advertiser*, 23 August 1828.
48. For a more general discussion of this process see King, *Crime and Law*, pp. 1–72.
49. Ward, *Print Culture*, pp. 200–201.
50. *Ordinary's Account*, 2 July 1752, (OA17520702 www.oldbaileyonline.org version 6.0., 16 July 2013).
51. *Old England or the National Gazette*, 27 June 1752.
52. *Ordinary's Account*, 22 September 1752, (OA17520922 www.oldbaileyonline.org version 6.0., 16 July 2013).
53. Anon, *A Warning Piece Against the Crime of Murder* (London, 1752) p. iii.

54. *Gentleman's Magazine*, 24 (1754) p. 506; W. Romaine, *A Method for Preventing the Frequency of Robberies and Murders* (London, 1754) p. 21.
55. Romaine, *A Method,* p. 3.
56. *Gentleman's Magazine*, 25 (1755) p. 295; *London Magazine*, (1755) pp. 159 and 211–212.
57. *Ordinary's Account*, 3rd October 1759, (OA17591003 www.oldbailey-online.org version 6.0., 14 September 2012).
58. *Harrop's Manchester Mercury*, 3 April 1759.
59. W. Blackstone, *Commentaries on the Laws of England* (4 volumes, Oxford, 1765–1769) 4; W. Eden, *Principles of Penal Law* (London, 1771); H. Dagge, *Considerations on Criminal Law* (London, 1772); M. Dawes, *An Essay on Crime and Punishments with a View of a Commentary Upon Beccaria, Rousseau, Voltaire, Montesquieu, Fielding and Blackstone* (London, 1782); J. Howard, *The State of the Prisons in England and Wales* (Warrington, 1777); J. Hanway, *The Defects of the Police ... with ... Proposals for Preventing Hanging and Transportation* (London, 1775); R. McGowen, 'The Body and Punishment in Eighteenth-Century England' *Journal of Modern History*, 59 (1987) p. 667.
60. L. Radzinowicz, *A History of English Criminal Law and its Administration from 1750*, 1 (London, 1948) pp. 269–286, 301.
61. C. Beccaria, *An Essay on Crimes and Punishments* (translation Dublin, 1767) pp. 74, 79; Radzinowicz, *A History,* 1, pp. 270–271.
62. Beccaria, *An Essay,* p. 82.
63. Ibid., p. 75.
64. Ibid., p. 76.
65. Ibid., p. 84.
66. Dawes, *An Essay on Crime,* pp. 54–55.
67. *Bingley's Journal*, 13 June 1772.
68. Ibid.
69. Ibid.
70. R. Shoemaker, 'Male Honour and the Decline of Public Violence in Eighteenth-Century London' *Social History*, 26 (2001), p. 193. However, murder rates declined most rapidly before the Murder Act.
71. *Bingley's Journal*, 13 June 1772.
72. *Gentleman's Magazine*, 41, (1771), p. 147; Radzinowicz, *A History,* 1, pp. 427–431.
73. *London Magazine*, 39, (1770) p. 448.
74. *Gentleman's Magazine*, 41, (1771), p. 147.
75. *London Magazine*, 39, (1770) p. 448.
76. Ibid., p. 447–448.
77. *Gentleman's Magazine*, 41, (1771), p. 147.

78. Dawes, *An Essay*, pp. 54–55; D. Hay, 'The Laws of God and the Laws of Man: Lord Gordon and the Death Penalty' in J. Rule and R. Malcolmson (eds.), *Protest and Survival: The Historical Experience* (London, 1993) p. 65–66; W. Turner, 'Extract from an Essay on Crimes and Punishments' *Memoirs of the Literary and Philosophical Society of Manchester*, 2 March 1785 not only criticised the fact that 'crimes of different degrees of enormity' were 'punished equally' but also argued that even 'the punishment of murder by death' was 'a barbarous expedient'.
79. *The Times*, 21 November 1786, 5 May 1785, 20 October 1785, 5 November 1786.
80. Eden, *Principles*, p. 80.
81. *St James Chronicle or British Evening Post*, 24 May 1777.
82. *General Evening Post*, 9 April 1785.
83. *The Times*, 16 July 1786.
84. *The Times*, 20 January 1786; *General Evening Post*, 19 January 1786.
85. *Lady's Magazine*, May 1782.
86. Blackstone, *Commentaries*, 4, (12th edition, London, 1795) p. 201.
87. *London Magazine*, 38, (1769) p. 384.
88. *Gazetteer and New Daily Advertiser*, 26 July 1766.
89. *York Chronicle*, 26 March 1773.
90. S. Devereaux, 'Recasting the Theatre of Execution: The Abolition of the Tyburn Ritual' *Past and Present*, 202 (2009) p. 150.
91. *Public Advertiser*, 20 July 1770; *Westminster Journal and London Political Miscellany*, 21 July 1770. 1768–1771 did witness above average numbers of London murder prosecutions.
92. Blackstone, *Commentaries*, 4, (12th edition, London, 1795) p. 202.
93. P. Smith, *Punishment and Culture* (Chicago, 2008) p. 50.
94. *Public Advertiser*, 20 July 1762.
95. Hanway, *The Defects*, pp. 245–246.
96. *The Times*, 7 December 1785.
97. *Gentleman's Magazine*, 46, (1776), p. 449. The author's confidence that the half-hanged offender could be revived may have partly arisen from contemporary reports that this happened. *Public Advertiser*, 5 November 1774; Hurren, *Dissecting*, pp. 36–62.
98. *Gentleman's Magazine*, 25, (1755), p. 295.
99. TNA, SP.44/88/81.
100. Ibid.
101. TNA, SP.44/89/190.
102. *St James Chronicle or British Evening Post*, 6 and 16 June 1767; *Gazetteer and New Daily Advertiser*, 10 and 17 June 1767; *London Chronicle*, 6 June 1767; *London Evening Post*, 9 June 1767.

103. *London Chronicle*, 20 and 23 June 1767; *London Evening Post*, 25 June 1767; *Gazetteer and New Daily Advertiser*, 29 June 1767, which reported that the King changed his mind after being told 'there were opportunities enough by the frequent accidents' to try out the styptic.
104. D. Barrington, *Observations on the More Ancient Statutes* (London, 1769) p. 401.
105. Eden, *Principles*, p. 81.
106. *Gentleman's Magazine*, 24, (1754), pp. 506–507; *Gazetteer*, 20 July 1764.
107. *Middlesex Journal*, 16 May 1769.
108. *London Magazine*, 24, (1755) p. 23.
109. *General Evening Post*, 24 August 1790.
110. Radzinowicz, *A History*, 1, p. 217 and R. Houston, *Punishing the Dead? Suicide, Lordship and Community in Britain 1750-1830* (Oxford, 2010) p. 257.
111. On profane burial for suicides -Tarlow, *Hung*, pp. 16–17.
112. *Read's Weekly Journal or British Gazetteer*, 18 April 1761.
113. *St James Chronicle or British Evening Post,* 28 May 1768.
114. *London Magazine*, 35, (1766) p. 406.
115. *Gazetteer and New Daily Advertiser*, 26 July 1766.
116. *Middlesex Journal*, 15 June 1776.
117. *Morning Post*, 16 December 1777.
118. Ward, 'The Criminal Corpse', p. 77; S. Devereaux, 'Inexperienced Humanitarians? William Wilberforce, William Pitt and the Execution Crisis of the 1780s' *Law and History Review*, 33 (2015) p. 858.
119. *The Times*, 21 October 1785.
120. Parliamentary Archives, HL/PO/JO/10/2/61.
121. This was true both in London and in the rest of England and Wales, Devereaux, 'England's', p. 82; D. Hay, 'Hanging and the English Judges' in D. Garland, R. McGowen and M. Meranze (eds.), *America's Death Penalty: Between Past and Present* (New York, 2011) p. 135.
122. The rising percentage hanged was partly caused by a government crack-down but in 1785 it was also linked to the judges' response to Madan's pamphlet demanding that all pardoning be ended. P. King, *Crime, Justice and Discretion in England 1740-1820* (Oxford, 2000) pp. 276–277.
123. *The Times*, 31 January 1785.
124. Devereaux, 'Inexperienced Humanitarians', pp. 863–865.
125. *The Times*, 7 February 1785.
126. *The Times*, 25 and 29 April 1785.
127. Devereaux, 'Inexperienced Humanitarians', p. 867.
128. Ward, 'The Criminal Corpse'; Devereaux, 'Inexperienced Humanitarians'.
129. Ward, 'The Criminal Corpse', pp. 70–79.
130. Devereaux, 'Inexperienced Humanitarians', pp. 842–856.

131. House of Commons Parliamentary Papers, http://parlpapers.chadwyck.co.uk accessed 8 November 2013, Parliamentary Register (henceforth HOC Papers PR) 20, p. 227.
132. *Morning Herald*, 17 May 1786; *Gentleman's Magazine*, 56 (1786) p. 766.
133. *General Evening Post*, 18 May 1786; *Public Advertiser*, 17 May 1786; Different reports contain different aspects of the speeches of Wilberforce and Lord Loughborough. I have assumed that if either was recorded anywhere as saying something he actually did so. For Wilberforce's earlier announcement about introducing a bill *London Chronicle*, 13 May 1786.
134. *General Evening Post*, 18 May 1786. Other reports say he was less ambitious referring to 'certain heinous crimes', *Gentleman's Magazine*, 56 (1786) p. 766. Hey's original scheme certainly envisaged the release of all capital convicts' corpses. Ward, 'The Criminal Corpse', p. 71.
135. Parliamentary Archives, HL/PO/JO/10/2/61. The inclusion of high treason cases 'except where the body ought to be quartered' appears to have been designed to include coining.
136. Ward calculates that the Bill would have produced another seventy cadavers a year nationwide 1776–1785. On average the Murder Act produced just 11.3 cadavers a year in that period. Ward, 'The Criminal Corpse', p. 66.
137. *General Evening Post*, 18 May 1786.
138. Parliamentary Archives, HL/PO/JO/10/2/61.
139. Devereaux, 'Inexperienced Humanitarians', pp. 842–856.
140. On Loughborough taking the lead in the Lords and as an opponent of Pitt, B. Montagu, *The Opinions of Different Authors on the Punishment of Death* (London, 1813), p. 180 and M. McCahill, *The House of Lords in the Age of George III* (Chichester, 2009) p. 115.
141. Ward, 'The Criminal Corpse', pp. 80–83.
142. 'Of public principle he was wholly destitute, repeatedly going over from the Whigs to the Tories', J. Campbell, *The Lives of the Lord Chancellors*, 6 (London, 1847) p. 336.
143. HOC Papers, PR, 20, p. 163.
144. *London Chronicle*, 6 July 1786; *Whitehall Evening Post*, 6 July 1786.
145. *Morning Chronicle*, 6 July 1786.
146. Radzinowicz, *A History*, 1, p. 479.
147. *Oracle and Public Advertiser*, 12 March 1796.
148. *London Chronicle*, 24 June 1786.
149. *General Evening News*, 22 June 1786; S. Devereaux, 'The Abolition of the Burning of Women in England Reconsidered' *Crime, History and Societies*, 9, (2005) p. 79. For other coverage see *Whitehall Evening Post*, 22 June 1786, *Morning Chronicle and London Advertiser*, 22 June 1786.
150. *London Chronicle*, 24 June 1786.

151. Devereaux, 'The Abolition', p. 77.
152. Radzinowicz, *A History*, 1, p. 213; Devereaux, 'The Abolition' p. 75. For the early campaign—*The Times*, 27 June 1786.
153. R. Campbell, 'Sentence of Death for Burning by Women' *Journal of Legal History*, 5 (1984) p. 55 suggests that the lack of opposition to the bill was partly due to the backing of many of the judges.
154. Blackstone, *Commentaries* (12th edition, London, 1795) 4, pp. 203–204; Radzinowicz, *A History*, 1, pp. 212–213.
155. Devereaux, 'The Abolition', p. 76.
156. Ibid., pp. 73–87 and 94; One in 1786, 1788 and 1789. Only two women were burnt at the stake in London 1759–1785 one for coining, one for the murder of her husband. In 1790 another coiner Sophia Girton was awaiting burning but was saved by the 1790 Act, www.oldbaileyonline.org version 6.0., 10 July 2013 t17900424-6.
157. Devereaux, 'The Abolition' pp. 82–93.
158. Ibid., p. 89; Bentham joined the critics suggesting that 'so horrible a punishment as burning alive' should not be used against coiners, J. Bentham, *An Introduction to the Principles of Morals and Legislation* (London, 1789) p. 177.
159. Ibid., p. 86.
160. Devereaux, 'England's', pp. 82–90. Similar, if less drastic reductions, occurred on various assize circuits, King, *Crime, Justice*, p. 276; Hay, 'Hanging and the English Judges' pp. 133–134.
161. Devereaux, 'England's', p. 85.
162. Ibid.
163. *Oracle and Public Advertiser*, 12 March 1796.
164. J. Beattie, *Crime and the Courts in England 1660-1800* (Oxford, 1986) p. 631.
165. Ibid., p. 630.
166. McGowen, 'The Body', p. 655.
167. Ibid., pp. 670–671.
168. *The Times*, 27 June 1786.
169. Eden, *Principles*, p. 57; McGowen, 'The Body', p. 670.
170. Ward, 'The Criminal Corpse', p. 67.
171. Devereaux, 'England's', p. 89.
172. *The Pocket Magazine*, 1 (Issue 4), p. 253.
173. "Beccaria Anglicus", *Letters on Capital Punishments* (London, 1807) p. 11.
174. J. Bransby, *The Ipswich Magazine for the Year 1799* (Ipswich 1800) pp. 108–109.
175. *St James's Chronicle or British Evening Post*, 23 January 1796.

176. *Evening Mail*, 7 March 1796; *Lloyd's Evening Post*, 19 December 1796; *London Chronicle*, 3 January 1797; *General Evening Post*, 20 November 1800.
177. *Mirror of the Times*, 26 May 1798.
178. Beattie, *Crime*, p. 620; M. Ignatieff, *A Just Measure of Pain; The Penitentiary in the Industrial Revolution 1750-1850* (London, 1978) pp. 53–54, 96–100.
179. M. Foucault, *Discipline and Punish; The Birth of the Prison* (Harmondsworth, 1979); P. Spierenburg, *The Spectacle of Suffering* (Cambridge, 1984); Ignatieff, *A Just Measure;* R. Ward 'Introduction' in R. Ward (ed.), *A Global History of Execution and the Criminal Corpse* (Basingstoke, 2015) pp. 18–20.
180. S. Wilf, 'Imagining Justice: Aesthetics and Public Executions in Late Eighteenth-Century England' *Yale Journal of Law and the Humanities*, 5 (1993) pp. 53–54.
181. Devereaux, 'Recasting the Theatre of Execution'.
182. Wilf, 'Imagining Justice', p. 75
183. H. Fielding, *An Enquiry into the Causes of the Late Increase of Robbers* (London, 1751) pp. 123–124; Smith, *Punishment*, p. 50.
184. Anon, *Observations on Some Points of law with a System of the Judicial Law of Moses* (Edinburgh, 1759) p. 163.
185. *The Times*, 7 December 1785 and 16 February 1786.
186. Smith, *Punishment*, p. 51.
187. *Gentlemen's Magazine*, 56 (1787) p. 1050.
188. V. Gatrell, *The Hanging Tree;* (Oxford, 1994) pp. 589–591.
189. J. Delaney, 'Bourgeois Bodies—Dead Criminals; England 1750–1850' *Diogenes*, 36 (1988) p. 80. Ward 'Introduction', pp. 17–18.
190. Ibid., p. 74.
191. S. Poole, '"For the Benefit of Example": Crime-Scene Executions in England, 1720-1830' in Ward (ed.), *A Global History*, p. 76.
192. Ibid., pp. 76–83.
193. Ibid., p. 96.
194. Devereaux, 'England's', pp. 82–91.
195. Hay, 'Hanging and the English Judges' p. 134; There were slight differences between circuits, King, *Crime, Justice*, p. 275.
196. R. McGowen, 'Managing the Gallows: The Bank of England and the Death Penalty 1797-1821' *Law and History Review*, 25 (2007) pp. 241–282; Hay, 'Hanging and the English Judges', p. 135.
197. Gatrell, *The Hanging Tree*, p. 9.
198. Devereaux, 'England's', pp. 90–91.
199. 23 murderers were gibbeted 1792–1801.

200. Radzinowicz, *A History*, 1, pp. 506–509, 517, 522, 539. Eldon certainly believed that it was not 'the severity of the law being put into execution to the fullest extent' that mattered 'so much as the imaginary terror of it', and he may therefore have decided that the best way to preserve the capital code was to keep almost all of it on the statute books but make more limited use of it in practice. As Radzinowicz noted, both Eldon and Ellenborough agreed that crime was best prevented by appointing capital punishment for many offences, but then executing it in a few cases only (p. 506). Since Hay has shown that Ellenborough was much less punitive than most other judges his influence cannot be ruled out, despite his harsh approach to political trials and penal reform, 'Hanging and the English Judges' pp. 139–150.
201. On the judges high level of general agreement see Radzinowicz, *A History*, 1, pp. 508–509.
202. Ibid., pp. 497–503; Devereaux, 'England's', p. 91; Poole, 'For the Benefit', p. 76.
203. Radzinowicz, *A History*, 1, pp. 497–525.
204. This was passed after much amendment as 54 Geo.3, c.145 (1814). J. Chitty, *A Practical Treatise on the Criminal Law* (London, 1816) p. 702.
205. B. Montagu, *The Debate upon Sir Samuel Romilly's Bill on the Punishment for High Treason* (London, 1813) pp. 16 and 25. On the mitigation of aggravated treason execution rituals in practice see Blackstone, *Commentaries*, 4 (a new edition with analysis by J. Archibald, London, 1811) p. 376.
206. Ibid., p. 3 and 15.
207. Ibid., p. 41.
208. R. McGowen, 'The Image of Justice and Reform of the Criminal Law in Early Nineteenth-Century England' *Buffalo Law Review*, 37 (1983) pp. 99–100.
209. Montagu, *The Debate*, p. 38.
210. Ibid., p. vii and 7.
211. Gatrell, *The Hanging Tree*, pp. 298–321; For more detail on these treason executions see Tarlow, *Hung*, pp. 13–16.
212. Gatrell, *The Hanging Tree*, p. 321.
213. Hansard, *The Parliamentary Debates*, 28 col. 187.
214. Ibid.
215. Montagu, *The Debate*, p. 25; *Clement's Official Edition of the Police Report* (London, 1816), pp. 212–213.
216. H. Woolrych, *The History and Results of the Present Capital Punishments in England* (London, 1832) p. 104; Gatrell, *The Hanging Tree*, p. 268;

217. TNA, HO 44/14/87 letter from Mr Dykes to Robert Peel; Gatrell, *The Hanging Tree*, p. 268.
218. TNA, HO 44/14/87.
219. Gatrell, *The Hanging Tree*, p. 268.
220. Radzinowicz, *A History*, 1, p. 219; London Metropolitan Archive, Print Collection, Pr.P2/BLA.
221. Hansard, *The Parliamentary Debates*, 28 col. 187.
222. Hurren, *Dissecting*.
223. *Lancashire Gazette and General Advertiser*, 23 August 1828; *Jackson's Oxford Journal*, 23 May 1828.
224. Poole, 'For the Benefit', p. 72.
225. *Bury and Norwich Post*, 3 February 1802; G. Durston, *Fields, Fens and Felonies; Crime and Justice in an Eighteenth-Century English Region* (forthcoming) p. 278–279 quoting *Ipswich Journal*, 3 April 1813.
226. E. Frizelle, *The Life and Times of the Royal Infirmary at Leicester* (Leicester, 1988) pp. 261–264; Hurren, *Dissecting*, pp. 219–239.
227. *Ipswich Journal*, 22 November 1817.
228. J. Disney, *Outlines of a Penal Code on the Basis of the Laws of England* (London, 1826) pp. 2–12, 23, 61.
229. *PP.*, 1826-7, (534) vi, p. 61.
230. *Gentlemen's Magazine*, 84 (1814) p. 620; 91 (1821) p. 482.
231. Richardson, *Death*. For the growth of a massive trade in pauper cadavers E. Hurren, *Dying for Victorian Medicine: English Anatomy and its Trade in the Dead Poor 1832*-1929 (Basingstoke, 2011).
232. TNA HO44/15/83-83a.
233. *Lancet*, 11, p. 324–325.
234. Richardson, *Death*.
235. Hansard, *The Parliamentary Debates*, 2nd Series, 18 col. 1137.
236. 9 Geo.4, c.15; Radzinowicz, *A History*, 1, p. 586.
237. Hansard, *The Parliamentary Debates*, 2nd Series, 18 col. 1358.
238. Ibid.
239. *Morning Chronicle*, 16 April 1828.
240. Hansard, *The Parliamentary Debates*, 2nd Series, 18 col. 1443–45.
241. *Morning Chronicle*, 16 April 1828.
242. Hansard, *The Parliamentary Debates*, 2nd Series, 18 col. 1443–44.
243. *Morning Chronicle*, 16 April 1828.
244. Hansard, *The Parliamentary Debates*, 2nd Series, 18 col. 1444.
245. Richardson, *Death*, p. 107; *Manchester Courier and Lancashire General Advertiser*, 15 March 1828.
246. Hansard, *The Parliamentary Debates*, 2nd Series, 18 col. 1611–23.
247. Hansard, *The Parliamentary Debates*, 2nd Series, 18 col. 1613–14.
248. Ibid.

249. Richardson, *Death,* pp. 108–110.
250. *PP.* 1829 (568) vii, p. 19 and 38. Witnesses—pp. 19, 33–34, 41, 42, 43, 47, 55, 74, 76, 81, 83, 86, 105, 115 and for slightly more guarded endorsements pp. 24, 31, 77, 100
251. Ibid., p. 95.
252. Ibid., p. 11.
253. Ibid., p. 11–12.
254. Richardson, *Death,* pp. 113–114.
255. *Mirror of Parliament* (1829), pp, 1672–1673.
256. Ibid., p. 1675.
257. Ibid., p. 1673.
258. Hansard, *The Parliamentary Debates*, 2nd Series, 21, col. 1747–9, and 3rd series, 9 col. 300–301.
259. Ibid., pp. 1748–1749.
260. Ibid., pp. 1831–1835.
261. Hansard, *The Parliamentary Debates*, 3rd Series, 9, col 252–316.
262. Richardson, *Death,* pp. 143, 199–215; B. Bailey, *The Resurrection Men; A History of the Trade in Corpses* (London, 1991), pp. 142–149.
263. HOC, *PP*, 1831–1832 (35)2 Will.IV.—Sess 1831-2 A Bill for Regulating Schools of Anatomy.
264. Medicus, *An Exposure of the Present System for Obtaining Bodies for Dissection and a More Consistent Plan Suggested* (London, 1829) p. 11.
265. Richardson, *Death,* p. 144; Hurren, *Dissecting,* pp. 43–60 argues that (p. 55) 'the surgeons were duty bound by the legislation to keep secret the conundrum of medical death'. By 1832 surgeons were beginning to go public on the fact that bodies were given over to them for 'the completion of the penalty' (p. 38).
266. J. Somerville, *A Letter Addressed to the Lord Chancellor on the Study of Anatomy* (London, 1832) p. 8; *Proceedings of the National Political Union Respecting the Legislative Interference in the Study of Anatomy* (London, 1832) p. 18.
267. *Quarterly Review*, 42 (1830) p. 15.
268. J. Riadore, *Suggestions on the Best Means of Supplying Anatomical Schools* (London, 1831) pp. 3–4.
269. G. Guthrie, *A Letter to the … Home Department, Containing Remarks on the Report of the Select Committee on Anatomy* (London, 1829) pp. 11–12. He also suggested other categories including the unclaimed poor.
270. *The Moral Reformer*, 1 (1831) p. 13.
271. HC/CL/JO/6/167 pp. 152 and 66.
272. Hansard, *The Parliamentary Debates*, 3rd Series, 9, col. 701-3, 838–842.
273. Ibid., 13, col. 824-8 and *Times*, 20 June 1832.
274. Ibid., 13, col. 825–8.

275. Ibid., 10, col. 838–9.
276. Ibid., 10, col. 836–8.
277. Ibid., 9, col. 558–585 and 10, col. 833–5.
278. Ibid., 9, col. 304–7; see also Cresset Pelham M.P.—9, col. 558–585, Rigby Wason M.P.- 10, col. 834–6.
279. Ibid., 12, col 667–9.
280. *The Times*, 20 June 1832.
281. Hansard, *The Parliamentary Debates*, 3rd Series, 13, col. 827–9; *Morning Chronicle*, 20 June 1832.
282. *Morning Chronicle*, July 20 1832.
283. Hansard, *The Parliamentary Debates*, 3rd Series, 14, col. 531–6.
284. Ibid.
285. Ibid.
286. *Freeman's Journal*, 24 January 1832; Hansard, *The Parliamentary Debates*, 3rd Series, 9, col. 827–8.
287. Anon, *The Punishment of Death: A Selection of Articles from the Morning Herald* (London, 1837) p. 11.
288. On Wynford in 1827 (as Judge Best) Gatrell, *The Hanging Tree*, p. 268.
289. Anon, *The Punishment of Death*, p. 12.
290. *Morning Chronicle*, 4 August 1832; *Hull Packet and Humber Mercury*, 7 August 1832; *Belfast New-Letter*, 10 August 1832 best conveys the judges tentative understanding of the new law.
291. *Morning Chronicle*, 10 August 1832.
292. Ibid., and *Newcastle Currant*, 4 August 1832.
293. *Morning Chronicle*, 10 August 1832.
294. Gatrell, *The Hanging Tree*, p. 269; Radzinowicz, *A History, 1,* p. 220. Jobling's corpse hung on the banks of the Tyne attracted great crowds especially at high tide—Anon, *The Punishment of Death,* p. 9.
295. *Bristol Mercury*, 25 August 1832.
296. *Royal Cornwall Gazette*, 25 August 1832.
297. Anon, *The Punishment of Death,* p. 144.
298. Quoted in Ibid., pp. 144–145.
299. Anon, *The Punishment of Death,* p. 7.
300. *Bristol Mercury*, 25 August 1832.
301. Anon, *The Punishment of Death,* pp. 8–11.
302. *Leicester and Nottingham Journal*, 18 August 1832.
303. *GIJHC,* 89, pp. 195, 291, 355, 367, 394, 414. The bill was 1834(221) 4 Will.IV –Sess1834;
304. Hansard, *The Parliamentary Debates*, 3rd Series, 22, col. 126–190. Radzinowicz, *A History,1*, p. 601.
305. *GIJHL,* 66, pp. 650, 780,793; Hansard, *The Parliamentary Debates*, 3rd Series, 22, col. 1213–1222.

306. *GIJHL*, 66, pp. 800, and 805.
307. Radzinowicz, *A History*, 1, pp. 601–605.
308. Hansard, *The Parliamentary Debates*, 3rd Series, 22, col. 674–733; and 25, col. 91–126.
309. Ibid., 23, 894–950.
310. Alexipharmacus, *A General Exposition of the State of the Medical Profession* (London, 1829) p. 13; In the *Examiner*, 1 July 1832 Brougham argued that while 'the taking away of human life was justly punishable by death', he did not approve of crowding under one head a number of offences that ought not to be so punished.
311. Hansard, *The Parliamentary Debates*, 2nd Series, 18 col. 1613–14.
312. Radzinowicz, *A History*, 1, pp. 601–605.
313. Devereaux, 'Inexperienced Humanitarians', pp. 857–858 argues cogently that the Murder Act actually reduced the number of cadavers the London surgeons received.

5

Reflections and Concluding Remarks

Historians have found it difficult to locate the Murder Act, and the regime of post-execution punishments that it consolidated and preserved for eight decades, within the broader history of penal change, and have therefore tended to leave its role largely unexplored (Chap. 1). Even Cockburn's article on 'Punishment and Brutalisation in the English Enlightenment', which did at least briefly attempt to examine the Act's role, mainly used it as an illustration of the government's failure to develop 'a coherent and consistently applied penal philosophy' during this period, and concluded that that it illustrates the problems contemporaries had in reconciling 'traditional' and 'enlightened' strands of thinking about the death penalty.[1] However, the detailed study presented here suggests that we need to see it not as an aberration or as the product of inherent contradictions in penal thinking, but rather as an important and functional part of the core penal policies that dominated the long eighteenth century. As we saw in Chap. 2, it certainly cannot be regarded as simply the result of one brief intense wave of demands for greater severity in the infliction of capital punishment. At intervals throughout the period from the 1690s to the early 1750s Parliament debated introducing various forms of aggravated death penalty procedures. Many contemporaries clearly believed that 'hanging was not punishment enough' and some advocated solutions that would have increased the torment experienced by the condemned during the execution process, such as breaking on the wheel or burning alive. These views did not in the end prevail, and two post-execution punishments were introduced instead, but in England and Wales, as in countries like Holland,

Germany and Ireland, the first half of the eighteenth century was certainly not a period when aggravated forms of execution were being increasingly shunned.[2] Indeed a significant minority of penal writers were vociferously advocating their introduction. When the early 1750s moral panic about violent robbery and murder made it expedient to increase the depth of sanctions imposed on those fully convicted of homicide, the authorities very deliberately chose two post-execution punishments as their means of doing so. They could have ridden the storm or used temporary expedients that would have avoided introducing any form of aggravated or post-execution punishments for the long-term. Why did they choose the combination of hanging in chains and dissection that became enshrined in the Murder Act?

1 The Logic of the Murder Act and Its Role in the Capital Punishment System

In 1752, under pressure from the press and the London public, but wishing to maintain the English law's reputation as much less barbarous and torment/torture based than its continental counterparts, the authorities may well have seen post-execution punishment as a useful compromise. The superior quality of the English law was an important plank in contemporary rhetoric about the rights of every 'Free-born Englishman'. Making either dissection or hanging in chains into the standard penalty for murder not only built on already existing British penal traditions, but also avoided the introduction of what were regarded as continental extremes. These short-term factors do not, however, explain the longevity of the post-execution punishment regime introduced by the Murder Act. If the Act had been only a temporary compromise it would surely not have lasted for 80 years. Its longevity can certainly not be ascribed to its usefulness to Britain's surgeons and anatomists. Although, until the 1820s, they generally welcomed the trickle of murderers' cadavers they received, the Murder Act supplied only a tiny and ever decreasing proportion of their needs. Indeed in London, which remained a very important centre for the teaching of anatomy throughout this period, the Act probably resulted in a reduction in the number of bodies available to the surgeons. Although historians have assumed that the Act increased the number of criminal corpses that were given to anatomy teachers in the metropolis, in fact it appears to have encouraged the development of procedures that meant that the opposite would be the case. While the Act did not specifically lay down that from 1752 onwards only the bodies of murderers were to be made available to the surgeons, it appears that from that date onwards they were, in reality, almost completely restricted to this category alone. Before 1752 the surgeons had been entitled to a certain number of executed bodies regardless of the nature of the crimes for which they had been sentenced to death. In the 1730s, for example, they received an average of five or six a year on this basis. After 1752 the supply of non-murderers bodies quickly disappeared and, given that an average of only two offenders a year were executed for murder in London between 1752 and 1832, the surgeons of the metropolis were clearly not major beneficiaries of the 1752 Act.[3] It was the judicial authorities rather than the surgeons that made sure that the Murder Act passed in the form it did. Given the power of the Law Lords in the Upper House, it could not have gone through so quickly without their approval and their leader—the powerful Lord Chancellor, Lord Hardwicke, who had great influence in both Houses of Parliament[4] —appears to have been quite intimately involved in shaping, or at the very least amending, the Act (Chap. 2). Moreover, once it was passed the judges stoutly defended it and made sure it stayed in place as an important part of the penal landscape for over three-quarters of a century. What functions did they see it as performing?

Some of the Murder Act's supporters may well have thought, at least initially, that it would act as a deterrent, and as late as 1796 the Attorney General was still suggesting that those about to commit murder might be prevented by their fear of dissection from going through with their intentions.[5] 'From what little evidence we have,' Richard Ward has suggested, 'it seems that the crowd and those capitally convicted did indeed consider the exposure and desecration of the dead body to be a terrifying and shameful fate (although such a view was by no means universal).'[6] However, while it was probably the case that, as Rawlings has argued, 'the threat of being dissected was presumed to be a great aggravation to the penalty',[7] and while it was almost certainly true that many of the poor cared deeply about the respectful burial of their remains,[8] we cannot assume (as Ward has rightly pointed out) that 'the message that the authorities intended offenders … to take from the punishment of the criminal corpse was inevitably internalised'.[9] In Holland there is no evidence that post-execution dissection caused any concern,[10] and many contemporaries were well aware that the belief that post-execution punishment had a real role in preventing a significant number of murders was based on very shaky foundations. Several writers recognized, for example, that many of those who chose to commit murder clearly believed that they would never be detected or prosecuted. As one 1750s commentator on the Murder Act observed 'it is to be feared that this law will not produce the desired effect, for it is beyond all doubt that those who commit this crime always flatter themselves that they shall perpetrate it so secretly that it will never be discovered'.[11] Other writers quite evidently appreciated that many murderers acted without even considering the future consequences. 'I am convinced', a correspondent wrote in the *Gentlemen's Magazine* in 1786, 'that, at the time of committing the offence, the offender reflects not upon the punishment annexed to his crime'.[12] Equally, as contemporaries often pointed out, if any did consider the consequences of committing homicide, it would have been their fear of death—rather than of their corpse's post-execution treatment—that would have been crucial. 'Surely', as one nineteenth-century commentator observed, 'if the risk of suffering the extreme penalty of the law would not keep a man from crime, the extra chance of being dissected after death could hardly be expected to do so.'[13] By the early-nineteenth century even the most ardent supporters of post-execution punishment were admitting that the notion that it acted as a deterrent was almost completely irrelevant. Although both Tenterden and Grey continued, rather illogically, to suggest that penal dissection would help to 'keep up that horror of committing murder' for which the English had always been praised, by this point the idea that either penal dissection or hanging in chains would actually deter potential murderers had very little purchase, if indeed it had ever had any.[14]

When arguing in favour of penal dissection a number of the judges found it convenient to suggest that, since some convicted murderers broke down in court only after this part of the sentence had been read to them, the prospect of dissection must surely have acted, at least occasionally, as a deterrent.[15] However, a convict's post-sentencing behaviour was no guide to his or her pre-crime thinking, and the only murderers that the judges were able to observe were, of course, precisely those whom the prospect of dissection had failed to deter. The very real distress shown by a small number of convicts after sentencing cannot therefore be taken to indicate that fear of such a distant prospect had any general deterrent effect on those about to commit murder. 'It is vain to plead, as an apology for such treatment, the influence of dissecting the murderer's body upon the spread of crime. If the terrors of a violent death cannot deter the murderer, will the dread of having a few incisions drawn upon his lifeless and unfeeling corpse wield a greater influence?' the *Leicester Chronicle* asked in 1832. 'Can it be supposed that it is the surgeon's knife after death, and not the hangman's halter before it, that binds the check upon his sanguinary purpose', it continued, 'never was there yet one life preserved by that part of the judge's sentence which consigns the body to the table of the surgeon.'[16] As Foucault has argued in relation to the use of imprisonment, it is possible for a punishment to be an almost complete failure as a means of preventing or reducing crime, but for it still to successfully achieve other social or penal effects that ensure that it remains an important part of the criminal justice system, and the Murder Act may well have survived for such a long time for very similar reasons.[17] The continued support that penal dissection received well into the nineteenth century from the judges and from influential figures of various political persuasions, such as Peel and Grey, primarily arose not from its power as a preventive measure, but from its vital role in creating a significant degree of differentiation in the punishments inflicted on murderers, compared to those imposed on the many minor non-violent offenders who were also being sentenced to death throughout the long eighteenth century.

As the Bloody Code expanded rapidly in the seventeenth and early-eighteenth centuries, and as the range of small-scale thefts, coinage offences, forgeries and Black Act-related offences that were subject to the death penalty constantly increased, the criminal law became very vulnerable to the criticism that it lacked sufficient differentiation. By the 1740s, when several other frequently committed felonies such as sheep-stealing were added to the penal code, these criticisms were becoming ever more strident. The post-execution punishments imposed by the Murder Act gave the authorities a means of responding to these criticisms without having to remove the capital sanction from any of the relatively minor property offences they had recently added to the Bloody Code. Although some later eighteenth- and early-nineteenth-century commentators still criticized these post-execution punishments for not creating a sufficiently large differentiation in the sanctions imposed on murderers, the representatives of the judicial establishment continued to regularly argue in Parliament in 1786, 1796, 1813–1814, 1828, 1829 and even in 1831–1832 that this was precisely what these extra punishments achieved. Even if, as seems likely, hanging in chains and dissection were not usually effective as deterrents, some form of post-execution punishment was clearly regarded by the judicial authorities as a necessary component of the capital punishment system and as an important part of its rationale, and their belief in it as such was the main reason it remained largely intact until the early 1830s.

When the Bloody Code was criticized for punishing a starving sheep stealer or an impoverished young pickpocket with the same sentence as that given to someone who had murdered his or her master, marital partner or robbery victim, the Murder Act enabled the authorities to argue (and perhaps to believe) that this was not the case. For this reason, even as late as 1829, when they warned Warburton not to even attempt repeal, they were prepared to stoutly defend penal dissection. Only when the Whigs finally began to sweep away the Bloody Code in the early-to-mid 1830s could the differentiating role of penal dissection in particular be allowed to disappear and/or be replaced by the relatively minor post-execution sanction of burial in the prison grounds, which was to last for more than a century.[18] In order to understand why the administrators of the criminal justice system used the criminal corpse in the way they did, and why post-execution punishment survived for so long in the face of both complex changes in society's attitudes to death,[19] and growing sensibilities about violent punishments, we need to take this contemporary legal rhetoric about the need for differentiation more seriously than historians have hitherto done. Few contemporaries believed in penal dissection as a deterrent, but successive judges, Lord Chancellors, Attorney Generals and Home Secretaries (with the very brief exception of Lord Lansdowne) were well aware of its important role within the broader rationale of the capital punishment system and stoutly defended it principally for that reason.

2 The Broader Questions Raised by the History of Post-Execution Punishment and the Murder Act

This analysis of the inner logic of the Murder Act, and of the reasons why it inaugurated such a lengthy period of mandatory post-execution punishment, has also highlighted the role played by both the twelve judges, and by specific Lord Chancellors and Lord Chief Justices, in making and shaping the English criminal law in this period. The formative roles played by men like Hardwicke, Loughborough, Eldon and Ellenborough in debates and legislative initiatives about post-execution punishment clearly support Hay's suggestion that though 'few in number', the judges 'had great legislative influence.'[20] In defending the use of post-execution punishment as a means of creating penal differentiation during the 1786 debate the future Lord Chancellor, Lord Loughborough, made it clear he believed that, by custom and precedent, the judges should have almost complete control over any major piece of criminal justice legislation. 'In all preceding times,' he suggested, 'every bill relative to the criminal justice of the country, and its mode of execution, was submitted to the opinion of the Judges in the first instance', the judges being the group 'most likely to discover any defects.'[21] In this he clearly had the support of both the Prime Minister and the Home Secretary who in the 1786 debate announced that 'he concurred entirely with the noble Lord (Loughborough) that all bills affecting the criminal justice of the country, ought to receive the approbation of the judges previous to their being proposed to Parliament.'[22]

Judges like Eldon and Ellenborough, who played a vital role in delaying the repeal of the Bloody Code in the early-nineteenth century also appealed to what Hay has described as the 'quasi-constitutional doctrine that criminal law bills had to originate with the judges or at least be endorsed by them'.[23] The great opponent of capital punishment in this period, Samuel Romilly, regarded this as a 'most unconstitutional doctrine', and after being informed by Lord Ellenborough that any bill 'commenced in the Lords' would always be 'referred to the judges in the first instance'[24] he made his disagreement clear. The judges, he argued, were like 'a fourth member of the Legislature who are to have … a power of preventing any proposed measure not only from passing into law, but even from being debated and brought under the view of Parliament'.[25] Romilly's failure to get significant elements of the capital code repealed before his death in 1818, which was in no small part due to the concerted opposition of the judges, suggests that his constitutional arguments made little headway. As we have seen in this study, the judges remained very powerful right up to the early 1830s. In 1813–1814 Ellenborough and Eldon undermined Romilly's attempts to completely abolish the use of aggravated execution methods against those found guilty of high treason,[26] and right through to 1831 the judges continued to successfully defend the use of penal dissection because they believed that some form of differentiation should be preserved in cases involving murder. The longevity of both the Bloody Code and the Murder Act was in no small measure a function of the powerful voice the judges continued to have throughout the Georgian period.[27] Further research is needed on private and governmental sources in relation to other types of penal legislation before we can fully understand how deep the judges' stranglehold was, and how long it lasted. However, the debates studied here suggest that in the eighteenth and early-nineteenth centuries the balance of constitutional arrangements between the legislature, the executive and the judicial authorities gave the judges very substantial power.[28]

We also need more research on the relationship between English policies in relation to both aggravated forms of execution and post-execution punishments, and the rituals used in colonial and semi-colonial contexts—for example in the West Indies, in America and in Ireland. The oft-repeated rhetoric about the mildness of English punishments and their lack of any elements of torture had relatively little purchase in many colonial contexts. The rulers of British colonies such as Jamaica, for example, made considerable use of aggravated forms of execution such as burning without previous strangulation and gibbeting whilst still alive. They also resorted to spiking (decapitation followed by the display of the offenders head on a pole), a punishment that was still being used quite extensively in Ireland during the crisis years of the 1790s.[29] As Clare Anderson has pointed out, 'in the colonies, gruesome forms of mutilation constituted an element of capital sentences for much longer than in Great Britain',[30] and further research is clearly needed to analyse when and why this pattern changed.

It is also clear from both the work presented here and from Rachel Bennett's research on Scotland (which was also undertaken as part of the Wellcome-funded 'Power of the Criminal Corpse' project) that the use of post-execution punishment and of aggravated execution rituals was by no means uniform across the United Kingdom. Although it was not in use during the period considered here, breaking on the wheel was still being used in Scotland in the seventeenth century despite the fact that no such usage can be traced in England. Moreover, individual Scottish criminals were still having their hands cut off prior to execution in 1750, 1752, 1754 and 1765—despite the fact that this punishment had long been abandoned in England and Wales by the eighteenth century. Conversely, the use of gibbeting in a significant number of cases was effectively over in Scotland by 1780—two decades before the same change happened in England—although the final occasion on which a Scottish offender was hung in chains was in 1810, which was not dissimilar to the timing of the ending of gibbeting in England if the two very short-lived attempts to revive it in 1832 are set aside.[31] In Ireland, by contrast, although gibbeting seems to have been less widely used after the Act of Union in 1800, it could still be resorted to quite extensively—as it was in the punishment of those found guilty of the Wild Goose Lodge outrages in 1816.[32]

There were also, as we saw in Chap. 3, very significant differences within England and Wales in the use of post-execution punishments. The geography of gibbeting polices analysed in Chap. 3 indicates clearly that the main areas on the western periphery—Cornwall, Cumbria and almost all of Wales were much more reluctant to hang offenders in chains than the rest of the country, and almost completely refused to gibbet those only accused of property crime. This new research therefore confirms Peter King and Richard Ward's recent work on the very different penal regimes to be found on the western periphery. Not only, as they have shown, were these regions very reluctant to execute offenders for anything but murder but there was also concerted and often vocal opposition in many of these areas to the use of gibbeting.[33] The complex reasons behind these patterns require further research, but the limited colonial and Irish evidence available suggests that there may well have been a relationship between the level of post-execution or aggravated execution methods resorted to and the degree of threat that the authorities perceived themselves to be under in any particular area.[34]

The intensive study of contemporary discourse and practice in relation to post-execution punishment presented in Chaps. 3 and 4, when combined with recent work by Devereaux and Poole and others on various aspects of the capital punishment system, raises important questions not only about the geography but also about the chronology of penal change. Why did the period from the late 1780s to the early-nineteenth century witness such important changes in execution policies, and in attitudes to both gibbeting and scene of crime hangings? The mid-1780s, it seems, marked the high watermark of the Bloody Code regime. In the midst of yet another post-war panic about rising crime rates, Madan's pamphlet demanding the execution of all capitally convicted offenders coincided in 1785 with a brief experiment in which certain assize judges did just that.[35] However, this policy quickly proved unsustainable, provoking a very negative reaction in the press, and within a few years it began to be very gradually reversed. By 1788 Pitt was quietly but systematically upping pardoning rates, and within three years the aggravated punishment of burning at the stake was ended by Parliament.[36] During the first decade of the nineteenth century gibbeting was almost completely abandoned, scene of the crime hangings nearly ceased and another very distinct policy change by the judges further reduced the proportion of capital convicts that were actually hanged.[37] Historians have yet to fully explore some of the paradoxes of this period. Precisely why Pitt's so called 'Reign of Terror' was a period of relatively low hanging rates still needs to be fully researched,[38] and some historians have struggled to explain why Eldon and Ellenborough, both of whom were staunch supporters of the Bloody Code, decided to drastically cut the proportion of capital convicts that were hanged in the first few years of the new century. On reflection, however, the policies pursued by these leading judges, which also included ending the use of hanging in chains against property offenders (Chap. 3), were entirely logical. These men set about quietly modifying the use of post-execution punishment and expanding the pardoning system not for reasons of humanity but as a defensive strategy. The policies they pursued were designed to achieve a broader goal—the preservation of the Bloody Code. In the face of increasing opposition to the hanging of property offenders, higher pardoning rates were the price that had to be paid in order to maintain the judges' ability to use capital punishment against a wide variety of offences. In the 1820s Peel followed the same broad logic, making relatively minor legislative concessions in Parliament in order to delay the large-scale repeal of the capital code.[39] Indeed Peel and Eldon, as Home Secretary and Lord Chancellor, combined in that decade to deliberately keep the numbers going to the London scaffold down. Eldon had clearly learnt important lessons from the wave of anti-hanging publicity produced when as many as twenty metropolitan offenders were hanged at one time in the mid-1780s.[40] 'Times are gone by when so many persons can be executed at once' he told Peel in 1822,[41] and the significance of Eldon's remark was clearly not lost on the Home Secretary. Peel was aware of 'the increasingly obvious moral and practical limits of England's bloody code,' and it is no coincidence that he worked hard throughout his tenure at the Home Office to insure that no more than three or four offenders usually went to the London gallows at any one time.[42] Both the positive changes in pardoning policies adopted by Pitt, Eldon and Peel, and the changes made during the same period in post-execution punishment policies—seen in the abandonment of burning at the stake, the virtual ending of gibbeting and the partial repeal in 1814 of the aggravated penalties imposed on the bodies of traitors—can best be seen as gradual but cumulative retreats in the face of a growing groundswell of opinion that was increasingly critical of both the Bloody Code and of the public post-execution punishments that remained part of the same penal package.

From this perspective Gatrell's model of criminal justice reform, which argues for a sudden and unprecedented change in the early 1830s and against any notion of an effective medium- to long-term erosion in support for the death penalty before that date, appears highly problematic.[43]

By highlighting key changes in post-execution policy, such as the fundamental collapse in the use of hanging in chains in 1802, this study has added further weight to those who have put forward a very different view.[44] This suggests very strongly that public attitudes were changing well before the end of the eighteenth century, forcing the judicial authorities to increase pardoning rates at fairly regular intervals and to abandon or heavily curtail those execution processes that the public were finding increasingly unacceptable or barbarous. The capital punishment system did not therefore, as Gatrell has argued, suddenly fall off a cliff around 1830. Nor is it possible to agree with his suggestion that sensibilities only changed at this point because the Bloody Code was already collapsing.[45] As Devereaux has pointed out as part of an excellent and much broader critique of Gatrell's position, the latter's own analysis acknowledges a growing public sensibility compared to earlier periods, but then ignores the implications of his assertion that the people 'would not put up with' mass executions by the early-nineteenth century.[46] There are many other problems with Gatrell's analysis.[47] He wrongly minimalizes the significance of the mass petitions against capital punishment that were received by Parliament in the 1820s, by comparing them with other campaigns, such that against slavery, which would inevitably have attracted greater attention because they invoked the sympathy of large sections of the population, rather than being simply concerned with the treatment of a group towards whom most people would inevitably have felt ambivalent (if not downright hostile).[48] Gatrell also failed to understand the chronology of what was happening outside the metropolis and its immediate environs. My own recent work with Richard Ward, for example, has shown that on the periphery of England and Wales the inhabitants began to oppose and largely end capital punishment for property crimes more than three-quarters of a century before 1830.[49] Moreover, the history of post-execution punishment presented here casts further doubt on Gatrell's view. The collapse of hanging in chains in 1802–1803, for example, which clearly coincided with an increasing sense that this practice was now seen as barbarous, indicates that sensibilities were already changing well before 1830 and that the authorities recognized that fact.

The fundamental problems that undermine Gatrell's insistence on discontinuity—on the primacy of the 1830s as a moment of sudden and unprecedented change—can, however, lead us into putting too much emphasis on continuity. The changing policies towards post-execution punishment (or towards capital punishment more generally) we have observed here cannot be explained by any simple unidirectional model based on the assumption that the main driver of change throughout this period was the gradual growth of humanitarian ideas and sensibilities about the use of violent punishments. Rather than a pattern of general long-term decline in support for the use of post-execution punishments throughout the period from the early-seventeenth century to 1832, this detailed study has suggested a very different chronology. As Ward has pointed out the Murder Act 'cuts across the growing humanitarianism, civility and urbanity which several historians have posited as defining features of penal reform.'[50] Rather than a picture of continuous decline in both execution levels and in the degree to which execution processes contained extra and aggravating procedures, the eighteenth century stands out as a separate and very distinct era in the history of capital punishment, and this is further confirmed when the patterns found in England are compared to those on the continent.

As Ward has pointed out in his recent comparative overview, the growing use of post-execution punishments in England—both informally in the first half of the eighteenth century and then formally from 1752 to the early nineteenth–was part of a much more general eighteenth-century European resurgence in execution levels and in the severity of the capital sanctions meted out to offenders.[51] Citing evidence from Holland, Germany and Ireland he argues that in many parts of eighteenth-century Europe (and indeed of North America), aggravated forms of the death penalty became more frequent, especially in the first half of the century.[52] However, since by 1700 most of these aggravated execution procedures had been quietly transformed by the authorities from pre- to post-execution punishments, (by, for example, discretely strangling the victim before breaking on the wheel or burning at the stake) in many parts of Europe the net effect was to make the eighteenth century into the prime century of post-execution punishment.[53] However, although there was a brief but large surge in the numbers executed in England during the crime wave that followed the end of the Napoleonic wars, this eighteenth-century European resurgence did not continue into the nineteenth century. Spierenburg has argued that increased sensitivity moved the authorities to discontinue the display of the bodies of executed offenders in Western Europe around 1800, and there is considerable evidence suggesting that he is correct.[54] The exposure of criminal corpses in the Netherlands was ended in 1795, in Bavaria in 1805, in Prussia in 1811 and in Wurttemberg—where many of the bodies where then given to the anatomy schools—in the same year. Most of the rest of Germany soon followed, while the final gibbeting in Scotland took place in 1810.[55] Since the collapse of gibbeting in England also took place at the beginning of the nineteenth century, those who ran the English criminal justice system were very much in step with their continental counterparts. Formal repeal in relation to hanging in chains may not have come until 1834, but practice on the ground in England was changing at a very similar pace to that found in Europe.

Given that at various times in the half century before 1752, (1694–1701, the mid 1730s and the early 1750s) the English Parliament came much closer than historians have previously realized to adopting some of the aggravated execution methods used on the continent (Chap. 2), much of this study has indicated that English and European capital punishment debates and practices may not have been as divergent as contemporaries often suggested. The mixture of post-execution punishments used in England was more centred on penal dissection than that found on the continent. However, although the history of penal dissection in Europe has still to be properly researched, some continental countries did make considerable formal and informal use of dissection.[56] England's mixture of post-execution punishments was not necessarily always the same as that found on the continent, but when we study the chronology of change the similarities clearly outweigh the differences.

3 Rethinking Garland's Model of Changing 'Modes of Capital Punishment'

Finally it is important to review the implications of the history of post-execution punishment in England for David Garland's interesting and much-used model of changing 'modes of capital punishment.'[57] Garland's model is based on three categories and periods—'early modern', 'modern' and 'late modern', the last of which will be ignored here since it deals with the period after 1945. In the early modern mode newly emergent states gave the death penalty a central role in the task of state building, rather than seeing it simply as a means of responding to or preventing crime. By ensuring that the death penalty involved elaborate public ceremonies and horrifying and painful aggravated execution techniques, usually followed by the long-term public display of the criminal's corpse, early modern states turned the infliction of capital punishment into a key instrument of rule and an elaborate display of their power. The death penalty was also used against a large number of offenders and a very considerable range of offences in the early modern period and the diverse forms it took—from simple hanging to elaborately choreographed breakings on the wheel—enabled the precise level of torment involved to be adjusted in individual cases according to the status of the accused or the heinousness of the offence.[58]

By contrast, in Garland's 'modern' mode the death penalty was no longer a central plank of penal policy but merely its ultimate sanction. It was used against very few offenders and confined to a very small range of offences—primarily murder and treason. The key purpose was penal not political—to control and deter crime. In the 'modern' era executions became private rather than public events, and followed a single format with no variations according to status or offence. Executions were not designed as spectacles of suffering but were meant to be both efficient and humane, with no elements of pre- or post-mortem torment, nor of any other form of aggravated execution procedure. The aim was speed not ceremony. Executions were now intended to be simple silent backstage events rather than noisy public performances in which elaborate rituals were followed.[59] It will be clear by now, however, that—in England at least—the capital punishment regime of the long eighteenth century, and the growing role of post-execution punishment within that regime, fits very uneasily into either Garland's 'early modern' mode or into his 'modern' one.

By the early-eighteenth century at the latest the English were moving rapidly away from many of the key characteristics of Garland's early modern stage in which 'the order of the world depended on these slaughters' and the state used 'shock and awe' tactics (i.e. intensely choreographed public and often cruel execution rituals) to assert its claims to authority, to impress the populace and to strike fear into its enemies.[60] English penal debate and the punishment policies it generated had moved decisively towards the 'modern' stage in which the death penalty was no longer an unquestionable expression of sovereign power but a tool of penal policy like any other.[61] The British fiscal-military state was well established by the second third of the eighteenth century and no longer needed elaborate and painful execution rituals to make claims about its right to rule, although such rituals could still be useful at moments of crisis such as the Jacobite Rebellions.[62] Instead the gallows was now a subtle and selective policy instrument, adapted to the needs of the criminal justice system and therefore increasing subject to debates about its utility and efficiency in comparison to other emerging modes of punishment such as transportation or imprisonment.

On the other hand, however, several features of the capital punishment system that developed in England between the early eighteenth century and the capital punishment reforms of the early nineteenth do *not* match in any way the characteristics of a 'modern' capital punishment regime put forward by Garland. Although executions were less frequent in the eighteenth century than they had been in sixteenth, the death penalty was still used very extensively against a wide range of offences, many of which were minor property crimes. Capital punishment therefore remained a central plank of penal policy rather than being the punishment of last resort used only in particularly heinous cases. Methods were also far from uniform. Indeed the growing use of hanging in chains and of penal dissection well before 1752 and their formal adoption under the Murder Act, along with the proliferation of crime scene hangings, suggests that modes of execution were becoming more diverse rather than moving towards the 'modern' more uniform mode. Moreover, far from being privatized speedy backstage events, executions remained very public and, since newly gibbeted corpses and public dissections attracted huge and often unruly crowds, the introduction of post-execution punishments made the execution process even more public, prolonged and difficult to control than it already was. Dissections could last several days. Gibbeting deliberately created a long-lasting and very public presence, which was designed to be highly visible and shocking. The choice of punishment—simple hanging, burning at the stake, dissection, skeletonization, hanging in chains, crime-scene hanging (or sometimes a combination of these) was often related to the nature of the crime and sometimes to the status or gender of the offender. Several features of eighteenth-century practice therefore stood in stark contrast to the 'modern' model put forward by Garland.

The mode of capital punishment that was used in England for most of the eighteenth century and for the first third of the nineteenth was therefore neither 'early modern' nor 'modern'. Nor can this 'long eighteenth century' be seen as a period of gradual transition from early modern to modern modes. Eighteenth-century historians have rightly emphasized that the number of capital statutes grew from 50 to around 200 between 1680 and 1820,[63] but those parts of the Bloody Code that resulted in significant numbers of death sentences were largely, though not entirely, in place by the early 1740s if not before. Most of the key characteristics of the Bloody Code and of the capital punishment and post-execution punishment regime that we have analysed here stayed in place for nearly a century. Thus, what we might call 'the long eighteenth-century mode' of capital punishment had its own character and logic very different from either of Garland's two ideal types/periods.

The intermediate and yet distinct nature of this separate period in the history of English capital punishment comes out clearly when we study both its quantitative and its qualitative dimensions. In the century before the 1830s the English courts did not execute the huge numbers seen in the sixteenth and early-seventeenth centuries, especially on the periphery in Wales and western England where very few property offenders were actually hanged,[64] but across the rest of England many non-violent property offenders were still sent to the gallows. Moreover, the distinct character of the capital punishment regime of this period is even more evident when we look at its qualitative dimension. Faced with the need to punish certain particularly heinous offences with a greater scale and depth of sanctions than simple hanging, the British Parliament considered, but ultimately rejected, the torment-based punishments that in their new post-execution forms were undergoing something of a renaissance in early-eighteenth-century Europe. Instead they chose to adopt two already rapidly developing post-execution punishments—hanging in chains and dissection (as well as turning burning for petty treason and almost all high treason sanctions into post-execution punishments by ensuring the offender was killed before being subjected to them). In order to create at least some element of differentiation, they moved even further away from uniformity and deliberately introduced a greater diversity of execution forms, while at the same time developing an increasing number of sentencing options in non-capital cases by the use of transportation, imprisonment, hard labour on the Thames and solitary confinement.[65] In this period, when a much wider range of minor property crimes could potentially be punished by death than had even been the case in the classic 'early modern' period, post-execution punishment provided a coherent response to those who pointed to the unfairness of giving the same sentence to both minor thieves and those who had committed premeditated murders. This long eighteenth-century capital punishment regime had its own logic within which post-execution punishment undoubtedly played an important part. The century before the reforms of 1830s was not only the period during which the Bloody Code was both well established and almost completely unrepealed, it was also the age of capital punishment diversity and penal differentiation. For at least 70 years from the rise of hanging in chains in the 1720s and 1730s to around 1802–1803, and then in its modified dissection-centred form until the repeal of the Murder Act in the early 1830s, post-execution punishment played a significant role. It is no coincidence that that the Murder Act was repealed just as most of the Bloody Code was also being expunged from the statute books. There was an intimate relationship between changes in the breadth and quantity of capital punishment (i.e. in number of offences deemed worthy of the death sentence and in the frequency of executions) and changing policies in relation to the quality of that punishment (i.e. in the level of post-execution punishments inflicted on the corpse of the condemned). This study therefore suggests two broader conclusions that may help us to think in fresh ways about the history of capital punishment in this period. First, that the long eighteenth century was a very separate and specific era in the history of the death penalty in England and Wales. And secondly, that post-execution punishment played a significant role within the framework of ideas, policies and rationales that shaped that era.

Notes

1. J. Cockburn, 'Punishment and Brutalisation in the English Enlightenment' *Law and History Review*, 12 (1994) pp. 171–172.
2. P. Spierenburg, *The Spectacle of Suffering* (Cambridge, 1984) p. 74; R. Ward 'Introduction' pp. 4–8 and J. Kelly, 'Punishing the Dead: Execution and the Executed Body in Eighteenth-Century Ireland' pp. 46–49, both in R. Ward (ed.), *A Global History of Execution and the Criminal Corpse* (Basingstoke, 2015).
3. S. Devereaux, 'Inexperienced Humanitarians? William Wilberforce, William Pitt, and the Execution Crisis of the 1780s' *Law and History Review*, 33 (2015) pp. 857–858 for a fuller analysis.
4. E. Foss, *The Judges of England* (London, 1864) 8, p. 195.
5. *Oracle and Public Advertiser*, 12 March 1796.
6. Ward, 'Introduction', p. 15.
7. P. Rawlings, *Crime and Power: A History of Criminal Justice 1688–1998* (Harlow, 1999) p. 49; on similar attitudes to the impact of gibbeting see J. Beattie, *Crime and the Courts in England 1660–1800* (Oxford, 1986) p. 528–529.
8. For a detailed discussion about the customary beliefs concerning the afterlife which fuelled the desire to have intact burial see R. Richardson, *Death, Dissection and the Destitute* (London, 1989) pp. 12–20.
9. Ward, 'Introduction', p. 16
10. Spierenburg, *The Spectacle of Suffering*, p. 89.

11. Anon, *A Warning Piece Against the Crime of Murder* (London, 1752) p. iii.
12. *Gentlemen's Magazine*, 56 (1786) p. 102.
13. J. Bailey, *The Diary of a Resurrectionist 1811-1812* (London, 1896) p. 100.
14. *Morning Chronicle*, 16 April 1828.
15. Lord Loughborough, for instance, seems to have implied, though he did not explicitly state that he made this assumption when he talked in 1786 about the 'salutary effect' of the Murder Act as reflected in the fact that 'criminals hardened in vice ... when the judge informed them that their bodies were to ... undergo public dissection ... exhibited ... the extremest horror,' thus making 'a forcible impression on the bystanders ... attended with the most salutary consequences.' HOC, PR20, p. 162.
16. *Leicester Chronicle*, 28 July 1832.
17. M. Foucault, *Discipline and Punish: The Birth of the Prison* (London, 1979); D. Garland, *Punishment and Modern Society; A Study in Social Theory* (Oxford, 1990) p. 149.
18. This was still the fate of the corpses of executed criminals in the early 1950s —*Royal Commission Report on Capital Punishment 1949–53* (London, 1953) p. 270.
19. During this period complex changes occurred in attitudes to death and to the dead body and the impact of those changes on approaches to the treatment of executed criminals requires further research. The effects are difficult to identify clearly and the substitution, in 1832, of pauper's corpses for those of criminals as the key source for anatomists, suggests their impact up to that point may have been small. The broad changes that could potentially have had an impact include the 'privatization' of death (Spierenburg, *The Spectacle of Suffering*, pp. 191–192) and a broader movement towards individualization, secularization and elaborate memorialization, C. Bryant, *Handbook of Death and Dying* (California, 2003) pp. 17–19 and P. Aries, *The Hour of Our Death* (London, 1981). Richardson argues that the long eighteenth century witnessed significant underlying changes in imaginative perceptions of the dead body, R. Richardson 'Popular Belief about the Dead Body' in C. Reeves (ed.), *A Cultural History of the Dead Body, Volume 4, In the Age of the Enlightenment* (Oxford, 2010) p. 93.
20. D. Hay, 'Hanging and the English Judges: The Judicial Politics of Retention and Abolition' in D. Garland, R. McGowen and M. Meranze (eds.), *America's Death Penalty; Between Past and Present* (New York, 2011), p. 129.
21. HOC, PR20, p.161 and *Morning Chronicle*, 6 July 1786.
22. HOC, PR20, p. 166; L. Radzinowicz, *A History of English Criminal Law and its Administration from 1750,* (London, 5 Vols., 1948-86) 1, pp. 509–510.

23. Hay, 'Hanging', p. 149; Radzinowicz, *A History,* 1, p. 510. The judges had, of course, always had the right, even before the Murder Act to choose to use hanging in chains as an extra punishment. Here they were in control without even needing to have formal legislative backing. For further discussion see Tarlow, *Hung in Chains: The Golden and Ghoulish Age of the Gibbet in Britain* (London, Palgrave, Forthcoming) p. 10.
24. Radzinowicz, *A History,* 1, pp. 510–511.
25. Ibid., p. 511.
26. V. Gatrell, *The Hanging Tree* (Oxford, 1994) p. 320.
27. Hay, 'Hanging', p. 146.
28. Ibid., p. 129.
29. D. Paton, 'Crime and the Bodies of Slaves in Eighteenth-Century Jamaica' *Journal of Social History,* 34 (2001) pp. 923–954; Kelly, 'Punishing the Dead' p. 60. In pre-independence Maryland quartering was also used against slaves who had committed murder, S. Banner, *The Death Penalty: An American History* (Cambridge, Mass, 2003) p. 75.
30. C. Anderson, 'Execution and its Aftermath in the Nineteenth-Century British Empire' in Ward (ed.), *A Global History,* p. 171. On the complex ways post-execution punishment played into North American capital punishment policies both before and after independence see for example Banner, *The Death Penalty,* pp. 70–86 and S. Wilf, 'Anatomy and Punishment in Late Eighteenth-Century New York' *Journal of Social History,* 22 (1989) pp. 507–530.
31. R. Bennett, 'Capital Punishment and the Criminal Corpse in Scotland 1740–1834' Leicester University Ph.D. 2014, see also her forthcoming book in the Palgrave series.
32. Kelly, 'Punishing the Dead', pp. 61–62.
33. P. King and R. Ward, 'Rethinking the Bloody Code in Eighteenth-Century Britain: Capital Punishment at the Centre and on the Periphery' *Past and Present* 228 (2015) pp. 159–205.
34. Thus offering support for Gatrell's observation that 'culturally dominant groups most deplore brutality when the state's authority or their own is strong enough to obviate the need for its outward display', Gatrell, *The Hanging Tree,* p. 12.
35. P. King, *Crime, Justice and Discretion in England 1740–1820* (Oxford, 2000) pp. 276–277.
36. Devereaux, 'Inexperienced Humanitarians?' pp. 877–878; S. Devereaux, 'England's "Bloody Code" in Crisis and Transition: Executions at the Old Bailey 1760–1837' *Journal of the Canadian Historical Association,* 24 (2013) p. 90.
37. Devereaux, 'England's', pp. 90–92, see Chapter 4 for detail.

38. C. Emsley, 'Repression, 'Terror' and the Rule of Law in England during the Decade of the French Revolution' *English Historical Review*, 397 (1985) pp. 801–825. The 1795 Treasonable Practices Act, which extended the law of treason was never used. C. Emsley, 'An Aspect of Pitt's 'Terror': Prosecutions for Sedition during the 1790s' *Social History*, 6 (1981) pp. 156–157.
39. Hay, 'Hanging', pp. 150–151.
40. Devereaux, 'England's', pp. 85–86 and 93.
41. Hay, 'Hanging', p. 150.
42. S. Devereaux, 'Peel, Pardon and Punishment: The Recorder's Report Revisited' in S. Devereaux and P. Griffiths (eds.), *Penal Practice and Culture 1500–1900: Punishing the English* (Basingstoke, 2004) pp. 259–263.
43. Gatrell, *The Hanging Tree*, pp. 9–10.
44. Devereaux, 'England's'; R. McGowen, 'Revisiting the Hanging Tree; Gatrell on Emotion and History' *British Journal of Criminology*, 40 (2000) pp. 10–11.
45. Gatrell, *The Hanging Tree*, pp. viii–ix.
46. Devereaux, 'England's', p. 94.
47. On the emotionally loaded assumptions he makes about the squeamishness, cowardice and ineffectiveness of the middle-class reformers see McGowen, 'Revisiting the Hanging Tree', p. 7. Gatrell's view that the actions of the 'humanitarian' reformers were ineffective, which is largely predicated on his highly questionable and unsubstantiated assumptions about the suddenness of the reform process, clearly need to be treated with extreme caution.
48. Devereaux, 'England's', p. 96.
49. King and Ward, 'Rethinking the Bloody Code'.
50. R. Ward, *Print Culture, Crime and Justice in Eighteenth-Century London* (London, 2014) p. 159.
51. Ward, 'Introduction', p. 4.
52. Ibid., pp. 4–9
53. Ibid., p. 7
54. Spierenburg, *The Spectacle of Suffering*, p. 190.
55. Ibid., p. 191; R. Evans, *Rituals of Retribution; Capital Punishment in Germany 1600–1987* (Oxford, 1996) pp. 226–227; Ward, 'Introduction', pp. 17–18; Bennett, 'Capital Punishment and the Criminal Corpse.
56. Ward, 'Introduction', p. 9.
57. D. Garland, 'Modes of Capital Punishment: The Death Penalty in Historical Perspective' in Garland, McGowen and Meranze (eds.), *America's Death Penalty;* pp. 30–71.
58. Ibid., pp. 30–48.
59. Ibid., pp. 48–58.
60. Ibid., pp. 38–45.

61. Ibid., pp. 31–45.
62. Gatrell, *The Hanging Tree*, p. 15.
63. D. Hay, 'Property, Authority and the Criminal law' in D. Hay, P. Linebaugh, E.P. Thompson and C. Winslow (eds.), *Albion's Fatal Tree* (London, 1975) p. 18.
64. King and Ward, 'Rethinking the Bloody Code'.
65. Beattie, *Crime*, pp. 520–620.

Permissions

All chapters in this book were first published in PCCAFDPE, by Springer by Peter King; hereby published with permission under the Creative Commons Attribution License or equivalent. Every chapter published in this book has been scrutinized by our experts. Their significance has been extensively debated. The topics covered herein carry significant information for a comprehensive understanding. They may even be implemented as practical applications or may be referred to as a beginning point for further studies.

We would like to thank the editorial team for lending their expertise to make the book truly unique. They have played a crucial role in the development of this book. Without their invaluable contributions this book wouldn't have been possible. They have made vital efforts to compile up to date information on the varied aspects of this subject to make this book a valuable addition to the collection of many professionals and students.

This book was conceptualized with the vision of imparting up-to-date and integrated information in this field. To ensure the same, a matchless editorial board was set up. Every individual on the board went through rigorous rounds of assessment to prove their worth. After which they invested a large part of their time researching and compiling the most relevant data for our readers.

The editorial board has been involved in producing this book since its inception. They have spent rigorous hours researching and exploring the diverse topics which have resulted in the successful publishing of this book. They have passed on their knowledge of decades through this book. To expedite this challenging task, the publisher supported the team at every step. A small team of assistant editors was also appointed to further simplify the editing procedure and attain best results for the readers.

Apart from the editorial board, the designing team has also invested a significant amount of their time in understanding the subject and creating the most relevant covers. They scrutinized every image to scout for the most suitable representation of the subject and create an appropriate cover for the book.

The publishing team has been an ardent support to the editorial, designing and production team. Their endless efforts to recruit the best for this project, has resulted in the accomplishment of this book. They are a veteran in the field of academics and their pool of knowledge is as vast as their experience in printing. Their expertise and guidance has proved useful at every step.

Their uncompromising quality standards have made this book an exceptional effort. Their encouragement from time to time has been an inspiration for everyone.

The publisher and the editorial board hope that this book will prove to be a valuable piece of knowledge for students, practitioners and scholars across the globe.

Index

Printed in the USA
CPSIA information can be obtained
at www.ICGtesting.com
LVHW010813221023
761596LV00005B/488